WITHDRAWN
UTSA LIBRARIES

Supply Chain Security

Supply Chain Security

International Practices and Innovations in Moving Goods Safely and Efficiently

VOLUME 1

THE CONTEXT OF GLOBAL SUPPLY CHAIN SECURITY

Andrew R. Thomas, Editor

Praeger Security International

AN IMPRINT OF ABC-CLIO, LLC
Santa Barbara, California • Denver, Colorado • Oxford, England

Copyright © 2010 by Andrew R. Thomas

All rights reserved. No part of this publication may be reproduced, stored in a retrieval system, or transmitted, in any form or by any means, electronic, mechanical, photocopying, recording, or otherwise, except for the inclusion of brief quotations in a review, without prior permission in writing from the publisher.

Library of Congress Cataloging-in-Publication Data is available at www.loc.gov

ISBN: 978-0-313-36420-4
EISBN: 978-0-313-36421-1

14 13 12 11 10   1 2 3 4 5

This book is also available on the World Wide Web as an eBook.
Visit www.abc-clio.com for details.

Praeger
An Imprint of ABC-CLIO, LLC

ABC-CLIO, LLC
130 Cremona Drive, P.O. Box 1911
Santa Barbara, California 93116-1911

This book is printed on acid-free paper ∞
Manufactured in the United States of America

Contents

Preface			vii
Acknowledgments			xi
Chapter	1	The Mechanics of Supply Chain Theft Erik Hoffer	1
Chapter	2	Supply Chain Security and International Terrorism John Harrison	52
Chapter	3	Legal Environment of Supply Chain Security Mary F. Schiavo	75
Chapter	4	The Complexity of Assessing Supply Chain Risk James R. Bradley	89
Chapter	5	Managing the Twenty-First-Century Piracy Threat: The Somali Example Ruwantissa Abeyratne	121
Chapter	6	The Global Environment and Supply Chain Security Sean S. Costigan	135
Chapter	7	Barbary Coast Revisited: International Maritime Law and Modern Piracy Charles Bumstead	144
Chapter	8	Supply Chain Security in a Developing Economy: India Dr. Mohd. Nishat Faisal	159

Chapter 9	The Human Element of Supply Chain Security: Mobilizing a Workforce After an Emergency *Frank T. Mongioi Jr., Lisa Moraiya McNally, and Ryan Elizabeth Thompson*	176
Chapter 10	International Aviation Security Practices Relating to the Global Supply Chain *Moses A. Alemán*	189
Chapter 11	Customs-Trade Partnership Against Terrorism: A Step Toward Supply Chain Security *John O'Connell*	198
Index		215
About the Editor and Contributors		225

Preface

The "supply chain" encompasses all the links connecting a manufacturer to end users of its products. Links may take the form of plants, supplier warehouses, vendor facilities, ports or hubs, retail warehouses or facilities, and outbound shipping centers. Links also involve all the ways goods are moved—by truck, ship, airplane, and rail car.

A lot can go wrong in the supply chain due to company or systemic mismanagement and inefficiency, criminal activity, employee or technology errors, or terrorism, to name just a few threats. Then there's government regulation, industry or association oversight, and security agencies—both public and private—keeping track. That's why the security of the supply chain has become such an important issue for business people—there's just too much at stake to let problems proliferate or stagnate. It's been estimated, for example, that thieves now steal $50 billion in goods each year from various points along the supply chain.

What's more, problems grow in magnitude when goods cross national borders—as they do with increasing frequency in our global economy. Meanwhile, governments continue to extend security mandates deeper into global supply chains, requiring companies to meet multidimensional security needs to keep goods in motion.

Globalization, stricter security regimes, the threat of terrorism, and increasingly sophisticated criminal activity have made cross-border cargo movements more complex, putting the integrity of end-to-end supply chains at much greater risk. As an executive from a global electronics manufacturer that operates in more than 150 countries put it recently: "We can have the most incredible manufacturing, and the supply chain dies as soon as it hits the border."

So where do students, scholars, and practitioners from around the world go to learn about supply chain security management? The recently founded peer-reviewed *Journal of Transportation Security* is one place. However, there still does not exist a globally centric scholarly reference for those interested in learning more about this vital commercial component. This two-volume set is designed to fill the gap. It is my sincere hope that this work, written from a truly global point of view, will be one of many on this most important topic.

The fact that half of the contributors to this set come from outside of the United States is no coincidence. Although the United States is the world's dominant economic power, the long-term trend is that of a dramatic expansion of the supply chain in high-growth emerging markets across Latin America, South and Southeastern Asia, and Eastern Europe. Although the United States will remain the single largest player, the surge in supply chain usage will come from emerging markets. The chapters in this volume explore the context of global supply chain security and serve as a basis for understanding the unique aspects of the innovative practices that are discussed in the second volume.

To kick off this volume, Erik Hoffer, one of the foremost experts on criminal behavior as it relates to the supply chain, explores in great detail the mechanics of supply chain theft. In addition to criminals, the omnipresent threat of terrorism is also at the forefront of supply chain security. Next, John Harrison of the S. Rajarantam School of International Studies presents a detailed description of international terrorists and how they interface with the global supply chain.

The legal aspects of supply chain security are fully opened up by distinguished attorney and former inspector general of the U.S. Department of Transportation Mary Schiavo. James Bradley of the College of William and Mary details the complexities of assessing supply chain risk. An explanation of the rise of twenty-first century pirates is undertaken by noted author and researcher Ruwantissa Abertyne, and later, Charles Bumstead, USN retired, revisits the Barbary Coast and surveys international maritime law and its relationship to modern piracy.

Sean Costigan, Director of the Lower Manhattan Project, takes a fascinating, in-depth look at how global climate change and supply chain security are interrelated. Mohammed Nishat Faisal of the Institute of Management Technology Dubai provides a substantial contribution in the area of supply chain security in a developing economy when he delves into the environment in India.

Frank Mongioi, Lisa McNally, and Ryan Elizabeth Thompson of ICF International bring forward the human element of supply chain security to provide insight into how to mobilize a workforce after an emergency. Moses A. Alemán, who worked with the FAA in the U.S. and with ICAO (International Civil Aviation Organization) for years, enlightens us on aviation security practices as they relate to the global supply chain.

Finally, John O'Connell of Thunderbird School of Global Management outlines the Customs-Trade Partnership Against Terrorism, a rational step toward operationalizing supply chain security.

Each of these contributors and their work here are intended to provide readers with a broader understanding of the context of supply chain security.

Andrew R. Thomas, University of Akron
Editor
art@uakron.edu

Acknowledgments

A project of this scope and magnitude is the effort of many people whose confidence and hard work must be mentioned here. First and foremost, I wish to thank my editor, Jeff Olson. He believed in this project from the beginning. Jeff is a tough and fair critic of my work, something I am always grateful for. Each of the contributors to this volume set worked on faith to deliver the world-class chapters you are reading here. Their dedication to advancing the global knowledge of supply chain security is to be highly commended.

At the University of Akron, I have been blessed to work with some great colleagues who have supported my desire to explore this research stream. Doug Hausknecht, Deborah Owens, Todd Finkle, Karen Nelsen, Jim Barnett, and Jim Emore were always willing to listen and offer a constructive opinion when needed. In addition, it has been my distinct pleasure to work with the team at the world-class Taylor Institute for Direct Marketing at UA: Dale Lewison, Bill Hauser, Mike Kormushoff, and Steve Brubaker. Thanks to each of you—and Go Zips!

My wife, Jacqueline, and my children, Paul Bryan and Alana, always believe in me. Their unconditional love carries me though.

CHAPTER 1

The Mechanics of Supply Chain Theft

Erik Hoffer

Given an opportunity, most people will steal something at some point in their lives. It could be from their employer, a business, or even a friend or neighbor. As abhorrent and cynical as it may sound, theft is a condition of life to which we have seemingly adapted. We have grown up in a culture of theft and theft-related events our entire lives. From television to movies and from music to media, property theft is truly woven into the fabric of our lives.

Children tend to adopt certain behaviors from what they see in the media and what they learn on the street. At times, they act out criminal behavior as part of their learning and growing experience. Unfortunately these behaviors tend to remain with some individuals throughout adulthood and can manifest themselves at any time and place. It is only through personal morality or fears that these inclinations are suppressed on the individual level.

Although many view stealing from an individual or a business as unconscionable, little thought is given to purchasing goods previously taken by others. Purchasing a stolen item is not a victimless act. Although the purchaser of stolen goods may not realize it, this act drives an underground criminal network. The scope of this network encompasses everything from the single theft of a retail item through the funding of terrorist organizations via cargo theft.

Engaging in this activity is commonplace for many people, primarily due to the prevailing lax prosecutorial remedies for property crime in the United States.

This chapter will deal with the issues surrounding theft and the distribution of stolen property. It will discuss who steals, buys, sells, distributes, and transports stolen goods, and what their unique individual motivation is to be party to this type of illicit activity. Nowhere in the narrative do I discuss any particular person or event; rather, the discussion is a culmination of years of supply chain theft experience and accumulated statistical data from sources such as insurance companies, investigators, law enforcement agencies, and documentary studies by industry-specific trade organizations and consultants.

There are less visible forms of theft that go beyond commonly stolen tangible goods such as computers, cell phones, and jewelry. The theft of energy, transportation services, or intellectual property account for additional billions of dollars lost to property owners. Another form of invisible theft is the replication of branded goods, more commonly referred to as counterfeiting. All of these criminal acts are defined as theft, for they erode corporate profitability, put users at risk, and dramatically affect the economy.

Because of their inherent invisibility, many types of theft become lost in an attempt to quantify them. There is no actual reporting mechanism to calculate theft-based losses, nor is there a repository for such data. Theft can have numerous categories and collaterally affect many more individuals than the brand owner, insurance company, and victim. Collateral losses due to theft cannot be assessed with any degree of accuracy. Even your neighbor who steals cable, water, or electricity commits a blatant act of invisible theft that goes undiscovered, unreported, and unaccounted for in theft calculations.

Who doesn't know someone who got a great deal on something that *fell off a truck*? Who doesn't know someone who has not gotten an equally great buy on branded merchandise online or at a flea market? If these scenarios are familiar, you probably have been touched by a theft-related event. The hidden economic impact of this condition is devastating. Its scope affects nearly every product brand, manufacturer, and retailer. The volume of financial loss and the negative economic impact it has on consumers is tremendous, but it is generally invisible. Few people know the level that theft recuperation plays in the retail price of goods. Product theft can impact jobs, employers, our economy, our way of life, and even our country's wellbeing. The nexus between terrorists being funded by product thieves is a risk to us all.

THE UNDERGROUND SUPPLY CHAIN

Our transportation industry serves as the pulse of commerce and the heart of our economy. Collectively, we move food, clothing, and most other essential goods by truck, rail, and air. The invisible nature of logistics makes for an invisible, or dark, side of an otherwise innocuous industry. The black side that no one sees is the illicit movement of stolen goods through a normal, legitimate transit process, all happening right under our very noses! Besides stolen commodities of every description, contraband drugs and illegal weapons are also commonly transported using commercial trucks and courier services.

The sheer volume of stolen goods handled by thieves, buyers, and fences requires a network of people far too encumbered for an illegal organization.

Because of this dynamic, most movement of goods, even those stolen in trailers and on the highway, wind up moving by a legitimate carrier to their final destination. Of course, this is unbeknownst to the receivers. There are billions in counterfeits filling our stores and pharmacies that have been delivered seamlessly along side of legitimate cargo. Untold billions in illegal drugs and laundered currency take the same distribution channels to market as do normal, legitimate products.

How is this done? Who is responsible? Who makes it happen? Who profits and who loses? How long has this been going on?

Because of the need for speed in illicit logistics, impulse planning is almost never a consideration. Thieves plan and execute these moves as well as any logistic provider ever could. There are many truckers who inadvertently provide this service without knowing they carry stolen merchandise. Many hands touch the cargo, but most eyes look the other way. Transportation providers, eager to satisfy a client or attract new ones, will take on freight moves without ever recognizing or analyzing the facts surrounding the cargo. Even the FBI has a diminished interest in the interdiction of stolen cargo, for its resources are now focused on more conventional counterterrorism. No one in our industry is immune, and no one can be vigilant enough to always see through such clever plans.

Regardless of origin or ownership, freight moves through our normal logistic system and is delivered to markets throughout the country on a daily basis. Goods destined for export move in the same way. The underground supply chain is truly invisible to us all. It will continue to increase costs for shippers and put many innocent drivers at risk until controls are developed to reduce these incidents.

At one point after 9/11, the Department of Transportation began a program known as Highway Watch. This now terminated program was designed to make drivers and carriers aware of potential threats and terroristic activities. It helped create a security standard for drivers and became the eyes and ears of law enforcement. The program was just getting momentum when it was terminated for budgetary reasons. Had the program continued, many illicit cargo moves and suspect loads would have been discovered and the risk posed to thieves and terrorists would have multiplied manyfold. Having a million savvy drivers on the street looking for transit anomalies would have been a tremendous benefit to us all.

Perception of value is the driving factor for most purchases. Little regard is given to the intrinsic value of a high-quality, authentic product over the low price of these knock-off products. There is a major market for aircraft, car, and truck parts throughout the world. In cases in which such parts are just unavailable, sales are easily generated. However, in areas where legitimate parts are plentiful, the substandard, stolen, or remanufactured parts businesses still thrive. Besides the significant level of lost opportunities for the sales of these goods by their rightful owners or resellers, the commercial supply chain is flooded with suspect products causing unjustified claims against the original manufacturer. These claims have to be vigorously defended in courts, causing further economic harm to the original product owner. Discovery of most counterfeit goods in the field, whether stolen, diverted, or substandard, is next to impossible. This is due to the sheer volume of products and the lack of track and trace capabilities of governing authorities.

Factors that affect risk are (1) the timing of the shipment of certain goods from the manufacturer, (2) their availability in the market place or in transit, (3) the level of protection given to the products when unattended, (4) the level of market demand, and (5) the profit associated with the sale of that commodity. These components round out the characteristics of what I call the *product risk factor*. The greater the product risk factor, the greater the need to address protection of that product while in transit and at the retail level. Rarely do organized thieves play in the speculative theft arena, because their marketing and supply chain just do not support this platform. The smaller the organization, the more random the theft and product base; but the larger the organization, the more item-specific its targets are.

THE CRIMINAL ENTERPRISE AND ITS UNDERGROUND ECONOMY

The term *underground economy* defines the entire scope of illicit operations that involve the theft of physical and intangible products and some types of product-associated fraud. The term *criminal enterprise* describes organized groups who engage in stealing and distributing stolen goods and whose efforts perpetuate the problem internationally.

Looking at theft from the monetary rewards prospective is generally easy to comprehend. You steal goods, you sell them, and you make money. The risk is low, the opportunity is pretty consistent, and the demand is high. But what about other motivations that drive industrial, personal, and supply chain theft? How do these areas of concern go far beyond the simple theft, sale, and subsequent purchase of stolen goods? Is the criminal thief on a par with the buyer of stolen merchandise?

Criminal motivation seems to inherently stem from greed, but based on current events, one can make the argument that theft is a direct result of our tenuous economic times. The thief, who claims to steal for survival, appears to be a basis for the problem at the lowest (street) level, where supply chain theft is a totally different condition. Most psychologists say that theft is a subculture—a way of life, even a turn-on to some. It provides a rush through the need for risk in certain personality types. While other more liberal interpretations of lower-level industrial theft motives rationalize theft based on grudges with employers, personal debt, or dissatisfaction with socioeconomic level or salary, many investigations show that greed was the driving force. Some people seem to get a primal satisfaction from beating the system, but at bottom line, they are still turning the product into cash. The ease with which goods are available to take and the lack of risk in taking them remain underlying factors in most industrial thefts. Some other theft motivational factors can include excessive gambling, high personal debts, financial losses, living far beyond one's means, extramarital involvement, blackmail, excessive use of alcohol or drugs, resentment of management, job frustration, threat of job loss, greed, and peer-group pressures. Any of a variety of circumstances can impact a person's life to a serious-enough degree that a person's long-standing attitudes, morality, and values may change. This change does not necessarily mean that a person will steal, but certainly opens the door to that possibility. Therefore, companies need to defend their assets at all times. In many companies, theft in small volumes has been ongoing for years. This type of theft is at an almost unrecognizable level and is dismissed or written off and rarely investigated. It is not until the level escalates that the company realizes the impact of what has been going on and takes action. Embezzlement is just as common an act of theft as stealing tangible products. In many cases, the most trusted employee of a company is found culpable for these behaviors. No one is above theft, and no one should be overlooked in any investigation. Cargo, cash, and data do not disappear on their own.

Criminal behavior at an industrial level is a learned skill that is nevertheless somewhat latent in everyone. It applies to both the thief and the buyer at different levels, although unsuspecting buyers hardly ever see the inherent risks. Both morality and rationalization seem to be easier on the part of the buyer, who feels he has done nothing wrong.

The lack of corporate risk awareness and the use of security processes and controls within an organization can bring out this behavior or create it. When people begin to steal successfully, they invite others to emulate the behavior, which subsequently exacerbates the condition until it becomes a part of the landscape. The snowball effect costs victim companies millions of dollars in losses before they can react. A report prepared by Donald Cressey in 1998 on industrial and supply chain theft identified three conditions that must be met in order to allow theft to grow within a business: motivation, opportunity, and rationalization.

Motivation speaks to the issue of simple greed, which supersedes any rational thinking in new criminals and sets the stage for rationalization of the theft. People are very complex. The ease with which one can extract goods from a business provides ample opportunity for everyone to get in on the action. Since people are uniquely motivated by different conditions in different environments, opportunity driven by motivation yields costly results to victim companies. Being able to steal easily, without risk, and to self-rationalize actions can tempt even a generally honest person to steal. Some exit interviews with common industrial thieves imply that they were just simply emulating what others did, and that they felt justified, thinking that the business "could afford the loss."

Larger product thefts are typically attached to a criminal enterprise. These criminal groups can be large or small, simple or sophisticated, organized or randomly formed. Most groups use trusted personnel with certain skills that are germane to the particular targeted product, supply chain, region, location, modality, and theft category. Regardless of the scale of the enterprise, the focus is consistent and the goals clearly defined. Its focus is stealing targeted products of all types and descriptions—and not getting caught. As with any business, its motivation is the creation of profit. Its individual skill and success is commensurate with its rewards. The broader the base of operations and the more dynamic the enterprise, the greater its profits become. The size of the operation and the targeted category of goods does not correlate directly to profitability.

Many lower-level thefts, which include home invasions, break-ins, some types of shoplifting, and smash-and-grab street thefts, are typically committed by drug users or unsophisticated criminals and do not account for any significant percentage of the billions lost to property thefts. These thieves tend to be more brazen, and the thefts random and rarely organized. These potentially violent criminals basically steal and fence items in order to generate cash or to support their habits. When these criminals escalate their scope of targets beyond petty theft, they become a public risk. Law enforcement is more apt to focus on these crimes rather than on simple product disappearance.

Petty thieves can find immediate buyers for almost any commodity. Recently, carjackings and theft of copper wire, metals, manhole covers, fire hydrants, guardrails, and construction trucks have become more common and visible. As these targeted products become more in demand, the public becomes an active participant in the commission of crime and tends to become collateral victims.

The risks in property crime theft cannot be minimized. Stolen trucks can be driven into crowds, circuitry and wire theft can cause critical infrastructure electronic systems to malfunction (such as in the case of traffic lights and rail signals), stolen valves can open pipes and create costly or dangerous spills, and when manhole covers are removed from streets, drivers and passengers are unnecessarily at risk. Most of these types of criminal acts encumber law enforcement's time and erode its limited resources.

The so called nontraceable events of industrial pilferage include items such as meat and liquor that are distributed to restaurants and barrio stores, where the evidence is quickly consumed. The duplication of movies and their distribution here and abroad is a common untraceable practice. Software and toy replication and resale using inferior components—even book reproductions—are just some of the other notable, nontraceable product events that occur each day.

Because the volume of these losses is totally conjecture, industry estimates are the only way to get a theoretic dollar loss volume. Organizations such as The National Retail Federation (NRF), various insurance groups, the music and recording industry, and even consumer protection groups maintain theories on the financial impact of these events but cannot quantify them using any tangible data.

These losses have a cumulative effect and cannot be attributed to any single event, entity, market, or product. Even manufacturers who are being targeted cannot precisely quantify the impact that supply chain theft has on their bottom line. In some cases, brand owners research certain international and domestic markets only to find that more of their goods seem to have been sold than what they feel were actually manufactured. This discrepancy is due to the blending of stolen goods with replications and diverted goods and the reintroduction of previously stolen goods into the market over time.

The resources needed by law enforcement and local governments to combat, investigate, and prosecute these offenders is also a cost of loss that is most often ignored or overlooked when considering the general impact of inconsequential property theft.

OPERATIONAL FACTORS

The *black market* that operates to resell stolen products is arguably its own free-market economy. The world of distribution of stolen goods is made up of a number of "businesses," all of which have the key elements of any "for-profit company," but without any manufacturing, administrative, or marketing costs. They have no liability or tax responsibility. They do not positively contribute to any local or national economy, and they employ few workers, pay no benefits, and typically have no permanent facilities. These criminal enterprises have no appreciable overhead, although they do have some inherent storage, transportation, and distribution expenses. The companies offer nothing to bolster commerce or create national wealth, but rather drain local resources and erode commercial brand integrity and confidence.

In certain areas of the country, many of these criminal enterprises employ and harbor illegal immigrants and gang members. Their identities are invisible to law enforcement, and their backgrounds unknown. Factors such as this can lead to unpredictable and uncharacteristic violent behavior in the commission of thefts. Most property-oriented crime is nonviolent and occurs while goods are unattended. Some larger, more organized groups are made up of active criminals and operate on a national scale.

We do know that theft-based transportation is frequently masked by clever thieves who move these goods using reputable carriers in normal distribution channels. For example, a truck might be followed from its distribution center and then stolen at a truck stop. The goods are rushed to a public warehouse, where they are quickly offloaded. A fictitious company account is set up in advance for the arrival and short-term storage of these goods at a public warehouse or distribution center. That location is now used as the transship point, and the new shipper (the thief) becomes the carrier client. In this loosely termed cross-dock operation, goods are never repackaged, but rather are quickly reshipped as a full truckload to a port of debarkation, or to another break bulk facility on a clean bill of lading, but under another shipper's name. Carriers, who have no reliable way to vet new clients, accept the goods, move the freight, and are paid by the phantom new shipper—sometimes in advance. In the case of counterfeits, or in more sophisticated criminal enterprises, goods may be further broken down and possibly blended with legitimate goods to mask any chance at traceability prior to reshipping. In either instance, goods may be trucked to any where in the United States, Canada, or even Mexico. Some export goods are either taken through Miami on the East Coast or Long Beach on the west coast and then loaded on containers destined for South America, Russia, India, or other foreign ports in the world for further distribution.

By now, the picture should be coming pretty clear. Stolen goods have suddenly assumed another identity and appear to belong to someone else. This makes those goods the newest members of the underground economy. At the same time, counterfeit goods, posing as legitimate products, are moving to U.S. markets from foreign ports to be blended with prime product. This new dimension further complicates any chance of unmasking the stolen shipments. Upon arrival, the counterfeit goods are distributed by otherwise authorized resellers to retailers or manufacturers just as if they were legitimate, thus becoming a second element of the underground economy.

The speed with which stolen meats, produce, fish, and other temperature-sensitive commodities are repacked for quick sale is remarkable. Unless they are sped off to market, they will be worthless. These time- or temperature-sensitive goods give a new meaning to "custom critical" deliveries. Few cases are made by law enforcement after the evidence is consumed! If you cannot catch thieves in the act or dissuade them from taking the loads in the first place, these goods are long gone. Many of the products are ethically purchased drugs that may have been removed from proper storage conditions for a period of time and potentially cause great public harm when resold. Additionally, many of these drugs have lost their efficacy over time; when used in hospitals or by patients, they may offer no relief or benefit or may even harm users significantly.

Distribution channels for some goods, such as designer clothes, over-the-counter pharmaceuticals (OTC), prescription drugs, fragrances, beer, cigarettes, shoes, sneakers, jewelry, and electronics of all types, have very specific brand-sensitive outlets. These are painstakingly chosen by the brand owner and monitored by regularly. Investigators on the staffs of most brand holders consistently research the market, Web, and trade associations for unknown and unauthorized distributors. In certain cases, the same companies distributing stolen, diverted, or even counterfeit goods can be authorized resellers. This makes flushing out a bad apple from a trusted source a difficult process. Because access to private records is impossible, investigators find it hard to determine anomalies such as volumes of certain goods sold versus those legitimate goods purchased by the vendor for resale.

OUTLETS

The National Retail Federation is quoted as saying that "[p]eople have quickly learned that the Internet presents a low-risk way to sell stolen goods . . . . More disturbing, however, is that the [I]nternet seems to be contributing to the creation of a brand-new retail thief. These are people who have never stolen before but are lured by the convenience and anonymity of the [I]nternet." eBay currently has about 2,000 paid employees whose only job is to investigate reports of stolen goods, fraud, and other illicit activities that may be using eBay's good name and brand as a sales vehicle. Interestingly enough, many retailers and few buyers seek this information out. A good deal is simply a good deal—investigating the lineage of a product is unnecessary.

In many cases, recovery after a loss may not be desirable to the affected party. This is due to a number of factors in addition to the possible compensation received from insurance. In cases in which manufacturers have dated items such as current fashion styles in clothing and shoes, or in which the item has an expiration date, the recovery of such goods months after the theft puts the owner and retailer in a tough spot. The goods have either gone out of season or out of style or have missed the advertising window. Hence, the goods are more valuable if they remain stolen, rather than recovered. In the case of electronics, the rapid change in technology advancements in any one area such as cell phones or cameras can literally make a device undesirable. Software can be outdated months after its initial release, and competitor copies can make such recovery unwelcome for those already compensated for the theft. Because of these factors, some stolen property is best left unrecovered.

Efforts by law enforcement and some corporate investigations meet with resistance when and if the goods are found. In many cases, the retailer, who may have owned the goods in transit rejects the recovery and defers it back to the original manufacturer. The ability of law enforcement to sort out the rightful owner, or, at minimum, the party willing to take the goods, can be costly. These products, once recovered as evidence, must be stored; such expenses revert back to the product owner, if found. Because of issues with ownership, many such goods are sold at police auctions on eBay. Law enforcement has the right to sell for a profit any articles recovered in the course of an investigation that have not been identified as the property of a specific person or entity. The municipality recovering the goods is also obliged to store these products and make an effort (in accordance with specific applicable ordinances on stolen goods) to find the rightful owner. If the rightful owner cannot be located in that period of time, the goods are sold.

The proceeds of stolen and recovered items benefit the law enforcement agency selling them. The dichotomy is that the original theft, now sold twice and paid for twice, has both positively and negatively affected all parties who have come in contact with the cargo. Most recovered property is discovered during routine investigations and is not typically tied to any one crime, so finding the owner becomes complex.

ASSESSMENT

Theft is arguably one of the oldest crimes. When the risk is low enough and the reward great enough, theft will always take place. Whether in the workplace, at school, or at home in your neighborhood, some form of theft is consistently present. Theft has been a human condition since the beginning of time, but it affects us all now more than ever—and not just victims. Supply chain theft is no longer the stepchild of corporate losses, but a prime factor in reducing business profits at every level. This otherwise invisible condition goes far beyond tangible monetary losses. The relationship of many types of theft to drug smuggling, terrorism, and money laundering will become clear.

Most attempts to statistically quantify the volume of property theft in terms of dollars lost, types of products stolen, or resulting costs to industry are conjecture. The enormity of the negative effect of supply chain theft on our economy is catastrophic. Yet industry studies are inconclusive, and specific loss data is both hard to come by and difficult to validate. Collected data from insurance losses, law enforcement recoveries, and public information sources is suspect, because it is impossible to interpret or verify. Since most industrial and supply chain theft is unreported, specific data does not exist.

Industry associations such as the National Retail Federation (NRF), American Trucking Association (ATA), pawnshop associations, and jewelry and electronic vendor groups, as well as governmental agencies such as the Drug Enforcement Agency (DEA), Customs, and the Federal Bureau of Investigation (FBI) do try to maintain theft data when it is reported to them. Most law enforcement data is not available to the public, but even that data is only a small portion of actual theft losses, and its impact is theoretical and unsubstantiated. Since the vast majority of supply chain theft is not reported, the collected data cannot be audited. Because of these factors, the impetus of lawmakers to enact more severe remedies to property crime fails to gain the support it needs to be passed. Most states are considering supply chain theft laws, but few have enacted them with the teeth needed to truly affect criminals. Lack of remedy creates a positive and virtually risk-free environment for thieves.

There are accurate data resources to quantify shoplifting losses, including basic retail frauds such as credit card and other white-collar retail crimes, because this data is consistently reported and meticulously maintained by retailers and their credit card processors. Supply chain theft, the larger problem, remains obscure. Because retail theft data is well known, industry and government do more to address these conditions. Retailers spend millions to create in-store risk of loss but little to protect their supply chain.

In the transportation industry, data on cargo theft loss is extremely hard to come by, for it adversely affects the logistics company's reputation as well as that of the brand owner. No one wants to air dirty laundry. Industry associations such as the Eastern and Western States Cargo theft task forces, as well as the ATA, try to quantify loss data to help member companies understand the risks and advise them on suitable best practices for cargo protection. Most of that data is client-specific and unavailable for sharing. But still, few carriers actually do much to protect cargo in their care.

The Government Accounting Office (GAO), the Inland Marine Underwriters Association (IMUA), and law enforcement at both state and federal levels also track and document reported losses in the supply chain. These organizations only collect data on about 10 percent of the reported losses, and they do not interface with one another. Collectively, all these groups are privy to different data—both reported and secret—and in their own ways all try to couch the problem in a manner that sugarcoats their respective risk. No one wants to ship with a carrier who has been a target for thieves, and no carrier wants to accept loads of potentially targeted goods in certain high-risk shipping lanes.

The collected data is rarely made public, for that could seriously affect any national brand or transportation provider. Revealing general facts to the public about certain product theft can cause panic, and therefore unnecessary risk, to the general public. In certain instances in which stolen ingestibles such as foods and pharmaceuticals are immediate risks, brand owners can initiate a product recall rather than identify the root cause of the problem. Additionally, reporting theft data associated with a public company could adversely affect stock price and, ultimately, investors.

Although you might think law enforcement would be more focused on this problem, it is not, either. Federal law enforcement has all it can do to address terrorist and border issues. Most states' limited resources are primarily focused on local violent crimes. Property crime, as was said to me by a prosecutor, is "just not sexy." The question most prosecutors ask is, "Where would you better use resources—on a rape or murder case, or a pallet of stolen cell phones?" Because most states, especially municipalities, have limited funds to prosecute and incarcerate offenders, many of these property criminals fail to serve any appreciable jail time.

THEFT HAS A COST TO ALL OF US

Let there be no confusion over the magnitude and devastating economic effect property crime has on our gross national product. The numbers rival the largest economic downturn possible, but on a consistent annual basis. No bailout can address the unknown factor of the loss of jobs, profits, and taxes that are the direct result of theft. The federal focus today is on antiterrorism and protecting infrastructure such as water supplies, ports, bridges, tunnels, rail, highway, and inner cities from acts of terrorism. We have lost focus on the bigger picture of how these terrorists are funded. The Federal Bureau of Investigation (FBI) dissolved all its cargo theft task forces shortly after 9/11. No one there seemed to understand the overall problem! We must realize just how the activities of cargo thieves facilitate their terrorist activities both here and abroad.

Ideologically, terrorists look to harm their enemy either physically or economically. Economic terrorists can impact the fiscal wellbeing of a country by eroding business and negatively impacting a tax base. Although most of the annualized dollar volume data of product theft is conjecture and "guesstimates," its significance is no less compelling. This consistent growth of product theft losses for the past fifteen years is the basis for evaluating this threat as the largest single economic risk to legitimate business that exists today. In short, the perceived sanctity of the commercial supply chain is all but nonexistent and has been replaced by a level of risk that must be accounted for and paid for in any logistical, retail, or manufacturing operation. You and I pay for theft losses with each item we buy and each service we use, from manufacturing to insurance to transportation to retail goods. Each costs a bit more because of theft.

Theft Architecture

In many cases, those who hijack trucks and cargo watch these vehicles from where they originate and throughout their routes in order to better study the practices of drivers and to ensure that the trucks are not being escorted. Many warehouses are unmarked, and thieves must survey these buildings in order to assess the cargo coming and going from these centers before deciding on a target.

Most truck drivers are creatures of habit and stop to eat and sleep in the same places. Because of gas contracts, they often get fuel from the same vendors and stay at the same predictable truck stops, thereby making surveillance easy. Given that information, taking a vehicle at a fuel island or when the driver is eating or showering becomes far easier than you might otherwise think. Almost all hijacked trucks and trailers are taken when the rigs are unattended. Most thieves avoid contact to avoid identification and resistance by the driver.

A driver moving a load may purposely discuss the nature of the goods with someone who offers him cash for leaving his vehicle unattended. Many warehouse workers offer up information on their jobs and products at bars or restaurants, where this information is overheard and gathered by thieves.

A driver giving up his load en route may agree to be tied up or in some way delayed by the thief who takes his truck and load. At times even these trucks are stripped and broken down for parts or shipped outside the country, but it is usually the cargo in the trailer that is the ultimate target. Most often, the cargo is removed, and the truck and trailer are returned to the street to be discovered by law enforcement in another state or county and returned to the owner.

This theft category does elicit both an internal investigation by the owners of the cargo and the trucking company and also triggers a law enforcement property case. Many times the driver is identified as the conduit to the theft ring and becomes legally culpable for the crime. Because of the *employee infidelity clause* in most carrier insurance contracts, insurance will not cover such product losses for the owner of the freight, the trucking company, or pay for the stolen equipment and downtime. Furthermore, the limits of liability on stolen goods may, absent specific coverages, revert to the Carmack amendment, by which freight is rated at $0.50 per pound, making stolen computer chips and diamonds equal in value, by weight, to wood or steel. This inequity provides little remedy for victims of cargo theft.

Most cargo theft is litigated. Much of this litigation turns into subrogation, because few carriers were alone in handling the goods. Many interline with other carriers, break bulk in warehouses, drop ship to multiple locations, and, as in the case of less than a truckload (LTL) of freight, have multiple loads on board, each of which is owned by a separate party.

The Carmack Amendment governs the manner in which interstate cargo claims are handled by law, in 49 U.S.C. §14706. Carmack controls and limits the liability of common carriers for in-transit cargo losses and, absent specific peril insurance, preempts state law remedies that increase the carrier's liability beyond the actual loss or injury to the property. In many cases, cargo theft and liability issues are settled using the standards of this law, which relate to weight rather than commodity value and are always detrimental to the owner of the cargo.

LOGISTICS

Stolen goods have to be moved after they are taken. In the past, when goods were distributed locally, the supply chain requirements of thieves and fences were manageable at the street level. Today, things are radically different. Even at the lowest levels of theft, items are distributed anywhere they are needed. In many cases, a fence or middleman facilitates the movement of goods from party to party until they reach a market, whether it is regional or international. Buyers or end-use clients can be anywhere in the world. A fence's response time in reaching the market must rival that of his legitimate "competitors" so that the products can be turned back into cash.

During their travels, stolen goods must be appropriately stored and, in some cases, repackaged before they can be reshipped. Certain goods are large and must be concealed or reduced to avoid detection. Items such as trucks themselves are stripped and sold for parts. Pharmaceuticals are broken into smaller packages for distribution and shipped to multiple locations. The network for the resale of stolen goods is as extensive as the legitimate supply chain in that it involves shippers, carriers, warehousemen, jobbers, and sales representatives—commonly referred to as fences, media, Internet, bulk buyers, and direct clients, respectively. It must work under the radar of law enforcement and private investigative services by the intellectual property holder and insurance providers. None of this could happen without the inherent sophistication of skilled and educated thieves. The point is that most people engaging in the distribution and resale of stolen goods are highly intelligent and capable. The "on-the-ground" thieves who actually effectuate the theft are street-smart and are capable adversaries for business and law enforcement.

At lower theft levels, like simple shoplifting and other nonorganized petty crimes, the use of simple techniques to move goods is common. These include returning stolen goods to stores for cash credits or selling them on the Internet or the street. These direct individual product sales are barely visible on the law enforcement radar screen. If apprehended, the thief rarely serves jail time. The problem is that the actual volumes of goods moved back into circulation becomes staggering when multiplied by the amount of these "street" vendors.

Many cities have large areas where "black market" goods are sold freely on the streets and in flea markets—always in plain view of law enforcement. In most cases, resources for the apprehension and prosecution of this type of criminal is miniscule and most plea out, pay a fine or serve minimal jail time, and are back at their craft in days. The volume of goods and the revenue generated amounts to millions in lost sales and taxes but happens in small enough quantities to be inconsequential in the larger scheme of theft.

Thieves move items quickly through the system. Fencing or reselling stolen goods is a quick, cash-based process. There is almost no track and trace of the goods once taken. It is only after the redistribution of these goods that the possibility of discovery exists. In some cases, warehouses are raided and massive amounts of stolen goods are seized, but this is the exception rather than the rule. Thieves and fences earmark stolen items for sale prior to the theft, so long-term storage becomes unnecessary. Even when theft is random and the product taken is not already promised, the fence network quickly responds to find appropriate buyers.

Empirical product marketing theory can be tested in both the legitimate and illegitimate markets. The notions of supply and demand, profit, unit price, distribution costs and outlets, supplier consistency, and delivery all play a role in the sale of goods, even ones with no base cost. If we are able to understand which factors drive the markets for stolen goods—beyond price alone—we can quickly determine theft trends and risk to some products. Using this data, we can more easily predict both the level of protection needed for some commodities and the likelihood that they will be targeted in the supply chain.

Once stolen, goods have to be offloaded into a temporary warehouse until they need to be relocated to a buyer. Stolen goods cannot remain in the trailer unless the trailer itself is concealed in a building. The infrastructure for the movement of stolen goods is sophisticated and dynamic. The efficiency and speed with which these goods are moved defies even the best logisticians and distribution enterprises. In many cases, the goods are then moved by legitimate carriers, who are paid for their services in cash, or, in some cases, even on account through shell businesses.

Most transshipping becomes quickly untraceable. For the most part, domestic carriers have little interest in who provides their next load. To keep their equipment on the road, carriers accept loads from many sources, including Internet dispatchers and consolidators. The fact that much of this freight is nondescript, palletized, and destined for major cities makes contracting a carrier easy. This further complicates the tracking process, even if law enforcement has intelligence as to where the load is ultimately going or who the buyer may be.

WHAT'S BEING DONE LEGISLATIVELY?

Legislatively, we do little to protect businesses and individuals from this known peril. Even if appropriate laws were followed, the impact to reduce the condition would be negligible. Our jails are overflowing with violent criminals. With limited state resources to house offenders, many property criminals are merely fined and never actually serve time in prison. That condition is frustrating to law enforcement officers, who risk their lives in apprehending these criminals only to subsequently see them back in operation.

Because cargo theft is becoming a recognized issue, three bills are now under consideration by the House Judiciary Committee's Subcommittee on Crime, Terrorism, and Homeland Security. The legislative subcommittee hearing testimony in October 2008 heard from many retailers, e-tailers, and manufacturers exhausted in their collective efforts to stop the selling of stolen property in online auctions as well as in normal retail establishments. The bills HR6713, also known as the "e-Fencing Enforcement Act of 2008," S3434, and HR6491 will be evaluated and plan to propose harsh remedy for those caught selling stolen products. The legislation proposed and backed by brick-and-mortar retailers such as Wal-Mart Stores and Target, would require that online marketplaces like eBay and Overstock.com promptly investigate and pull down listings when retailers or manufacturers provide "credible evidence" that merchandise is stolen. The bills also make it a felony to sell stolen items online and give retailers new rights to sue Internet companies in federal court if they fail to respond or promptly take down stolen merchandise from their sites.

Surprisingly enough, Steve DelBianco, executive director of Net Choice, an industry trade group whose members include eBay, AOL, and Yahoo, plans to testify against the legislation. He said his group was amenable to more severe criminal penalties for thieves and sellers who are fencing stolen goods online, but he was against the legislation. His contention is that there are other provisions of these proposed bills that amount to a creation of an "elite club of retailers that want to use their influence to bash their online upstart competitors." He felt that such legislation would enable traditional retailers to get information about their online competitors and this information could help to figure out where a competitor is getting his low-cost supply, or to harass that competitor by complaining their goods are stolen when they are not. No legislation is going to please everyone. However, without such remedy, theft just gets worse because we are not addressing the outlets or the source of the goods. These laws are also weak in addressing the remedy against the actual thief, for they only focus on the fencing and distribution components of supply chain theft.

The Organized Retail Crime Act focuses partly on creating penalties for organized retail crime by defining what it is. The bill also requires online marketplaces to "expeditiously investigate" reports of stolen goods and to maintain records of high-volume sellers. Both bills allow retailers to file civil lawsuits against the operators of online marketplaces that offer stolen goods for sale. These laws do not require victim companies to report their losses. Such reporting would further exacerbate the negative effect the original theft had on the brand owner. It does allow the retail industry to challenge the lineage of the goods for sale by e-tailers as previously stolen without connection to the original owner. For example, a retailer selling a product at $100 is competing with an online e-tailer on the same goods at $25. The retailer knows his base wholesale cost is $40 and yet his online competitor can sell it at retail way below his cost. His ability to challenge the e-tailer, as created by this proposed legislation, allows an investigation of the origins of these products without the involvement of the original brand owner. Since the original brand owner may have already been reimbursed by his insurance carrier, getting these goods back would not be desirable.

According to *Security Management* magazine, "Theft costs retailers around $104 billion a year," based on its annual Global Retail Theft Barometer. U.S. retail theft in 2007–2008 amounted to almost $45 billion, or the lion's share of retail shrink. Retailers reported that stolen merchandise accounted for 38.4 percent, or $14.6 billion, of internal fraud, while 23.8 percent of internal losses were in the form of stolen cash, coupons, vouchers, or gift cards comprising more than $9 billion. The Global Retail Theft Barometer is based on a survey of 920 large retailers around the world and is comprised of only reported data, both verifiable and unsubstantiated.

Employee theft is the leading cause of "shrinkage," or stock lost from crime in North America. Authorities caught around 5.3 million people stealing from retail stores between July 1, 2007, and June 30, 2008. This includes anything from diamonds to chewing gum, and it also includes both goods recovered and those actually taken. Although 84.6 percent of the thefts were perpetrated by customers, the average employee who was caught stole much more, and more often. Warehouse and general supply chain theft, as well as higher-bulk theft, are not reported as part of this data and remain at a speculative level. The value of these employee losses far exceed the more voluminous but petty thefts.

The most popular products for retail thieves included cosmetics, alcohol, electronics, and watches. Shaving products, cosmetics, meat, seafood, infant formula, CDs, DVDs, fashions, printer cartridges, shoes, computers, cell phones, MP3 players, computer games, and OTC drugs accounted for many other favorite targeted goods. Retailers estimated that they lost, on average, between 2 and 5 percent of new in-store product lines, while such popular products as Harry Potter books, electronic video games, and recent music CDs and DVDs collectively reached loss levels of up to 8 percent of stocked items.

Some, but not all, products that are sold online, in auctions, and by phantom e-tailers are in fact stolen goods. Police auctions, which legitimately remarket recovered products (previously stolen), and some brand owners, who sell their own diverted products, do so legitimately and through many of the same sources used by criminals. Bulk buyers who purchase goods recovered from insurance carriers and truckers are legally selling branded products (some of which were previously stolen) online at drastic savings. Even abandoned goods, resold by warehousemen to recover storage costs, find their way to online auctions and become great consumer deals. It becomes very difficult to differentiate between these legal business transactions and those done by thieves. It seems unfair to collectively conclude that auction "great deal" sales are all suspect and compounds the problem of legally enforcing online criminal activities.

Interestingly enough, there are means by which individuals and corporations can recover stolen property. Web sites and companies such as Just-Stolen.net and PropertyRoom.com provide a novel service. For a price, they will return recovered goods to their rightful owners. The mechanics of this operation are that one need only register the goods initially and then prove ownership of the goods either by a preregistration listing or by providing credible records to establish ownership, including police reports and transportation documentation.

The selling price of most legitimate products using this type of service incorporates the registration cost as well as insurance before items are even out for consumer sale. This increases the selling costs as a direct result of the perception of theft and inherent risk of supply chain loss but provides the buyer a sense of security that seems worth the cost.

As was previously mentioned, such recoveries en masse can be detrimental to the original owner, who may have already been paid for these goods by his insurance provider. This makes their return, in whatever condition they may be, an act of futility and results in an even greater loss to the original owner, thereby doubling his theft exposure. Because of this, many companies abandon their rights to the recovered property and allow them to be remarketed. The dichotomy is that the market wants laws to protect it, but fails to use the ones it does have because doing so is not in its best interest.

Despite the existence of viable legal remedies on the state and federal levels to ward off these conditions of theft, there has been no improvement in theft reduction over the last ten years. Property crime has in fact grown appreciably and diversified significantly to a point where even determining the economic scale is conjecture. Property crime is both lucrative, and participants are less apt to be prosecuted than violent criminals who use weapons or force. The lack of quantifiability of the actual theft-related losses, in terms of dollars, product volumes, and recovery costs is what makes law enforcement and lawmakers reluctant to address these matters more aggressively.

Most crimes are evaluated on an individual basis and not as a national economic threat. The futility of locating stolen goods makes attempts to do so truly a waste of resources for most police departments and federal agencies. Recovery is typically the result of luck or incidental to another unrelated criminal investigation. Goods such as food, drugs, refrigerated items, and many other types of time-sensitive materials are rarely, if ever, reported stolen and are almost never recovered. Many of the victims basically accept the loss and move forward. The reason, again, is that if you are lucky enough to be paid by insurance for the loss, recovery would mean that you would have to repay those funds and destroy the product anyway. If a food or an ingestible drug is out of the care and control of the owner, carrier, or recipient, if recovered, it legally must be destroyed. When such goods are inadvertently found and attempts are made at returning them to the rightful owners, most law enforcement agencies find corporate victims reluctant to accept their return because of these ramifications. Most of us will never know if we are eating evidence or watching a bootlegged film because the event is basically victimless and not viewed by the public as serious.

A COMPILATION OF FACTS

Kroll Associates is a large New York–based security and risk consulting company that provides investigative, security, and technology services. A recent analysis by Kroll outlined the risks companies face with their global supply chains and the amount of fraud, product tampering, and theft theoretically taking place today. The report dealt with a worldwide analysis of most forms of supply chain theft and included retail fraud in that calculation. The bottom line, as reported, showed that these vulnerabilities are equally common in the United States, Mexico, and Canada as they are in the EU and in Asia. According to the report, "The scale of supply chain fraud is difficult to measure and too broad in scope to estimate meaningfully." The Kroll report, like other studies, failed to state with any specificity the precise dollar value of theft and fraud but rather established the vulnerability of this form of loss to retailers, brand owners, and other supply chain components in terms of overall risk. Kroll data from its 2007/2008 "Global Fraud Report," which surveyed 892 global executives, showed just how large an issue it is. The report stated that 42 percent of companies worldwide had suffered from at least one incident of supplier fraud or the theft of physical assets; and while these are just two of the many ways to abuse supply chains, 9 percent of companies had suffered both types of loss.

According to their analysis, the more complex the supply chain of a company, the greater their risk of loss. "Fraud thrives on complexity," notes the report. "Modern operational complexities make companies vulnerable to frauds committed many links back in the chain and beyond the scope of most internal controls." Fraud can occur at any point in the shipment of goods including at the origin. Many companies use trust as the basis of imported shipments and fail to properly examine containers during stuffing or verify contents at delivery. Some companies become victims when goods are tendered to draymen and sit in unsecured yards prior to being loaded on to a ship. When inappropriate seals are used, domestic cargo can be removed easily by truckers from trailers and containers.

Once considered a mundane and victimless threat, cargo and supply chain theft has grown to almost 1 percent of the world GNP. Cargo theft has become increasingly well organized, sophisticated, efficient, and profitable. Few states have cargo theft–specific laws, so cargo and supply chain thieves are rarely severely prosecuted, making the reward far greater than the associated risk.

According to the Kroll report, one additional area in supply chain theft and monetary loss does not specifically relate to cargo or product issues but rather occurs through document manipulation. Weaknesses in information technology and the lack of appropriate auditing for payments and analyzing billing processes are all areas ripe for theft. Unless a company is diligent in monitoring paperwork anomalies, it can easily fail to detect fraudulent payment patterns or phantom orders. According to the report, "[w]hen controls around payment matching and approvals are weak, service providers will learn that a company does not notice when they are over billed, double billed, receive ghost bills, never receive product for bills received or they are billed for the wrong service or at the wrong price." It continues, "Falsified invoices, however, rarely follow the same patterns as those from honest suppliers." Most of these supply chain thefts are based on import or export operations of companies whose process controls and information systems are weak or poorly designed and monitored.

By its very nature, any freight conveyance, whether it is a truck, plane, railcar, barge, or ship is basically an unattended warehouse with one (or no) unarmed guards. It must be emphasized that most supply chain theft occurs when the cargo is unattended. The opportunity for thieves is almost overwhelming. The myriad of choices of different cargo is endless and the opportunities to take it plentiful. The risk of apprehension—much less prosecution—for cargo thieves, is extremely low, and the rewards are incredibly high. The notion of safety and security for most unattended goods in the international commercial supply chain is weak.

Regardless of shipped modality, the consistent lack of basic protection for the freight, both by the carriers and in the form of security procedures by the shipper, creates vulnerability. Shipped goods in the supply chain typically lack appropriate security measures. When these same goods are cross-docked in distribution centers, carrier terminals, or public storage warehouses, they become even more vulnerable to theft or manipulation. The easier the access is to cargo, the better the opportunity for thieves and employees of these facilities. The lack of recognition of the true threat of loss for cargo owners, warehousemen, and transportation providers causes little to be done by these supply chain components to protect goods when they are out of their care and control.

While the incentive and onus for cargo protection should rest with the owner of the freight, most shippers fail to apply appropriate security measures to the cargo. Most seek to meet minimum standards of security and fail to effectively contribute to the protection process. Carriers offer little to no effective remedy to theft, as they are not only protected by liability laws such as the Carmack Amendment when it comes to freight claims, but the exclusions in the shippers' own insurance coverage for theft losses make proactive security expenditures rare. Security countermeasures are typically the last expenditure carriers make to mitigate known risks of loss. Most even fail to adequately protect their own truck assets, which in turn would benefit their clients and further secure their cargo.

Since cargo moves anonymously across the nation's roads and highways, it is always passing through various state and local jurisdictions. Each state and local government has a different threshold for the investigation, apprehension, and ultimate prosecution of cargo thieves. Because of these known lax conditions, many cities and states become targets for thieves. Areas like Atlanta, Memphis, Los Angeles, Newark, New York City, Miami, and Chicago are prime examples of targeted cities for truck and cargo theft. The limited deterrent value of the threat from law enforcement to cargo thieves mitigates cargo theft risk to them. In addition, there is an escape hatch created by federal value limitation legislation. This condition creates a base threshold for prosecutors to accept or plea cases. For example, Newark, New Jersey, may have a threshold of $50,000 per incident, whereas Memphis, Tennessee may be $150,000, making a theft in Memphis less likely to actually be prosecuted.

Insurance coverage is typically ambiguous on cargo theft, and it creates a loophole for the nonpayment of claims. While most shippers believe that they have appropriate insurance coverage, many fail to recognize that in case of theft, the claim may not be paid. Rarely, if ever, do shippers request a copy of the tariff of the carrier to determine his limits of liability, insurance coverage, or any of the exclusions delineated in this document regarding freight liability claims.

TYPES OF THEFT CONDITIONS

Truck theft is by no means the only modality affected by cargo thieves. Aircraft, railway cars, and sea container loads are primary targets. In the late 1990s, a famous band of rail criminals known as the Conrail Boyz effectively stole millions of dollars worth of rail-shipped goods (piggybacked trailers on flatcars) in both large and small events. Modern-day criminals find that cargo theft represents easy money with little inherent risk of prosecution. The two-year Conrail Boyz investigation uncovered an extensive, well-coordinated, criminal cartel in the business of targeting freight trains carrying millions of dollars of consumer goods. These goods included designer clothing, electronics, cigarettes, and other merchandise. The investigation determined that members of the gang would leap onto the piggybacked trailers while rail cars were moving at a relatively slow speed. Then, using bolt cutters and other devices, they would breach the doors of the trailers or shipping containers holding the merchandise and extract it. As the train continued moving, the merchandise was thrown off the train onto the side of the tracks. Accomplices on the ground gathered the stolen items, which were then moved to a secret collection point. There the products were staged and organized to be sold to local fences.

From 1992 through March 2003, the Conrail Boyz were responsible for committing hundreds of cargo thefts totaling over $20 million in stolen merchandise, at manufacturer cost, including such articles as

- 17,496 Sony PlayStation electronic game consoles valued at more than $5 million
- Tommy Hilfiger clothing valued at more than $140,000
- More than 1,000 Jones of New York women's blouses valued at more than $49,000
- 1,800 cartons of Wave brand cigarettes valued at more than $500 each
- Approximately $7,000 in cash from the Metro Freight Line
- Numerous tractor-trailers for use in transporting stolen merchandise

The twenty-four gang members received thirteen years in jail apiece. The economic impact of their escapades wreaked havoc in the transportation industry as well as in retail and commercial trade in the Northeast for years.

Periodically gangs using cargo theft as their main source of revenue create a criminal enterprise that becomes too large for them to handle. Such gangs tend to break apart, fracturing into smaller and, at times, more violent associations. These turf wars escalate into uncharacteristic violence and can be extremely dangerous to commercial truck drivers, rail yard personnel, warehousemen, and other unsuspecting supply chain and retail personnel.

Because they begin to run out of unattended loads to target, many of these gangs raid working warehouses. In some cases, gang members infiltrate the company force in order to gain intelligence about the location of valuable products such as chips and electronics in these facilities. In many large, diverse warehouses or retail distribution centers, high-value goods are dispersed randomly to avoid such smash-and-grab operations, so location intelligence is paramount to a quick and fruitful robbery.

Most supply chain gateway cities such as Atlanta, New York, Miami, and Los Angeles experience tremendous levels of theft. Secondary air courier companies such as FedEx, UPS, and DHL have significant theft losses but limit their liability through their bill-of-lading and insurance requirements and exclusions. The random nature of courier goods makes specific product targeting difficult (although not impossible). Without specific knowledge of the shipper's packages and products inside, these packages become far more difficult to target for their specific goods.

Theft of goods from known shippers is relatively easy. However, even in supplied generic packages for courier cargo, the surreptitious opening up of these boxes and replacing of the package with an exact replica is a known benefit to thieves. Everyone has access to a new FedEx or UPS Box. Many high-value shippers—of jewelry, for example—try to disguise their products with pseudonyms and fake addresses, but since much of this theft is employee-based, such identification is easy, and the source of supply of these goods consistent and voluminous.

Also, because of the relative ease of hijacking and the lenient punishments associated with property crimes, cargo theft continues to grow each year. As this type of crime is not need-based, there is no correlation of theft with poor economic conditions. Regardless of the economic climate of a region or a country, theft continues to thrive. High-tech, high-value products, specifically consumer electronics, are always in constant demand. The demand for other less valuable goods is also continuous and consistent. So long as the outlet exists through the extensive fencing network, any goods can become targeted. Many fence operations have needs outside the high-value classification. Some of these are region-based. In Mexico, for instance, staples such as soap power and paper goods trump electronics in the barrio stores. Liquor, cigarettes, shoes, and clothing are as high on barrio store lists as food products and other basic need items. Because of specific demand for items such as food, paper goods, cosmetics, and convenience goods like razors, blades, and batteries, many less popular goods are now targeted throughout the United States. Theft has become far less opportunistic and more focused. Because of the dynamics of the world supply chain and consumer needs, a fence or reseller is rarely at a loss to find a buyer for almost any product.

In cases where specific product needs are internationally based, goods stolen in the United States may be exported by truck, sea, rail, or air based on the price buyers are willing to pay and the nature or timeliness of the item in its projected market. Many aircraft, automobile, and truck parts are exported regularly; so are heavy equipment, chassis, and construction items like generators and compressors.

Unattended theft is by far the method of choice. Larger items at construction sites are rarely guarded. Equipment is typically left unsecured, and drivers leave their equipment in areas that invite theft. Most construction equipment, such as backhoes, generators, compressors, and dump trucks, are stolen for parts or by demand. They are stripped for parts and rarely get recovered intact. These goods tend to exit the country in containers and are quickly disguised and reclassified as undistinguishable cargo. This happens on a regular basis through the port of Miami. Many of these goods wind up in South American countries, where they are sold or transshipped around the world.

Industrial pilferage is an organized effort to extract goods from manufacturers and warehouses and is also a crime of opportunity. In cases where manufacturers are lax in protecting the goods in their warehouses, thieves soon learn the necessary techniques to extract them surreptitiously. Once the pipeline is established and the technique becomes known by other employees, goods move freely from the building, especially during the workday and during shift changes. Goods can be staged for extraction if the volumes become more than one man can carry. Goods are placed in dumpsters for removal later in the evening or placed in trucks piggybacked with legitimate goods for distribution by the driver at a later date. Many times goods are put into black garbage bags and thrown away with the trash for later extraction by the courier. Even at this low level of sophistication, goods are extracted en masse from retailers, distribution facilities, and storage warehouses. Theft at this level is both systemic and growing. Because most of these small-volume losses are rarely discovered until year-end audits, they become simply a write-off adjustment to inventory and are never reported. The statistical data and economic impact of this scenario is even more difficult to quantify.

DIVERSION AND COUNTERFEITING

A diverter is someone who deals in the *gray market*. Although these are not criminal activities by definition, they do impact supply chain losses by providing authentic branded products to companies not authorized to resell them in certain areas or countries. Diverted goods may be overruns, slow-selling items, out-of-date designs, or excess inventory. Companies wishing to recover their costs will knowingly sell these goods to anyone willing to pay for them. Many times this is done outside the country in markets that are eager to get branded merchandise regardless of the material itself. Diverters can also be criminal enterprises disguised as legitimate companies buying products at lower costs, seemingly for legitimate overseas distribution. Once taking possession, they move these purchased goods at significantly lower costs back to the U.S. market and compete against the same branded item there.

A diverter is able to do this because he owns the product. Most often, brand owners require overseas companies to assure them that they will not remarket in the United States, but it happens continually nevertheless. Because the property was purchased legitimately, the buyer is within his rights to resell it whereever and to whomever he chooses. The brand owner can do little legally to prevent this from happening, even if a contract has been signed. Other gray marketers get overruns and out-of-style or out-of-date merchandise from brand owners themselves, who then become their own diversion source. In these cases, the approved supply chain is circumvented, which can change the complexion of the brands own rules of resale. The newly affected resale agents may become annoyed at this blatant competitive pressure and turn to criminal activities in order to get these same goods at lower costs to compete with the gray market items being sold against them in their own locale.

The world of theft is not limited to the illicit resale of stolen property. The nexus between counterfeiting and theft as well as terrorism funded by the sale of stolen goods is a major concern to every affected government, brand owner, and individual victim.

Terrorists and thieves have begun a working relationship with one another. Terrorists need clean cash to purchase materials and services, while thieves provide the commodity to generate these funds. Laundered money from the sale of stolen merchandise frequently funds drug smuggling operations. The surreptitious introduction of dope piggybacked into legitimate cargo provides free transit to market for millions of dollars in illegal drugs. This same system disguises the returning cash.

In the case of counterfeiters, supply chain theft serves as a great disguise to legitimize their products by combining them with legitimate goods in what is called *blending*. Blending makes it almost impossible for buyers to distinguish what is real from what is not. By aligning themselves with cargo thieves, whose focus is theft of large volumes of similar products, it is easy to provide them with a tremendous platform from which to inflate the value of their replicas into a far more valuable shipment. To mask counterfeit goods, many align with diverters (a different form of fraud), who then provide legitimate products to them, enhancing the value of their replicas. Diverters also use stolen goods to blend with their real products to make these goods more saleable through their distribution channels. In either case, the outcome is that unsuspecting buyers who purchase these products can wind up being burned. Regardless of the type of asset blending, stolen goods can find their way to any number of small and national retail store chains, Internet sales companies, and flea markets in all fifty states a matter of days after being released.

Since inventory of these stolen products becomes blended and redistributed through retailers' own networks of stores and distribution centers, locating stolen goods is all but impossible, and is highly improbable. For the most part, electronics, legal drugs, clothes, shoes, and other luxury items are unmarked and their serial numbers unrecorded. Surprisingly, resellers and agents who take possession of goods that are subsequently stolen do not keep specific data on the individual items. This makes recovery all but impossible. Many large-volume items such as razor blades, OTC drugs, cosmetics, and fragrances have standard packaging and crating and do not have any adequate means to identify individual units to their owner. Counterfeiters and diverters use the same blending method to mask their items with authentic products.

Counterfeiters are a major part of the world's supply chain. The fact that they have borrowed the owner's brand and replicated it makes them a primary contributor to the underground economy. These replicated goods provide a quick source of cash, but they are somewhat different from a conventional cargo thief. There are many reasons why both skills sets complement one another and why their respective supply chains for redistribution are almost identical. Profits made from imitations rival theft internationally. Depending on who you ask, product counterfeiting—not to be confused with currency counterfeiting—is a $300–500 billion criminal enterprise worldwide. For example, the World Customs Organization estimated the cost to brand holders for counterfeit goods is $512 billion for 2006. This is a complete economy that, combined with theft, has a greater negative impact on our economy than almost any other economic threat. The profits derived from criminal activities are larger than the GNP of many countries!

Products typically counterfeited vary from drugs to toys, from watches to art, from clothes to electronics, and everything in between. No item is sacred. Listed below are just some of the more common items counterfeited:

- Auto parts
- Aircraft parts
- Baby formula
- Toys
- Apparel
- Purses
- Jewelry
- Shampoo
- Cosmetics
- Sunglasses
- Software
- Movies
- Music
- Medical devices
- Consumer drugs and medicines
- Food products
- Cigarettes
- Razor blades

In order for counterfeiters to succeed, they need massive distribution networks and a seamless transition into a market. No reputable distributor or reseller would be fooled by a new company suddenly marketing a branded product at a better price. The way they instantly create their sales organizations is to partner with an authorized reseller who may have access into national retailers who would entertain price concessions and purchase in volume. Many distributors in the food industry resell to barrio stores and to other off-brand outlets that are not above accepting new brands to sell to their clients. Thieves who have these authentic but stolen goods will blend them with lookalike counterfeit goods and effectively double their volume to ship. The retailer will get a mixture of real and fake goods and sell these at discount prices in stores or flea markets, where buyers are not thoroughly inspecting products for authenticity but simply looking for a bargain. With both types of criminal activities working in concert, stolen and counterfeit goods enter the commercial supply chain quickly and invisibly. The invisibility of such transactions make source discovery by law enforcement almost impossible. Other ways counterfeit goods enter the market are through mail order scams, catalog sales, and Internet auctions. Here again, scrutiny of the delivered product is nonexistent, and the product sources and companies are typically post office boxes.

Counterfeit ingestible products such as legal drugs can kill for many reasons. Most of these counterfeit products have no efficacy—and surely no manufacturing standards, even if they do contain some of the main ingredients of the drug. Toys containing lead have been known to kill children who chew them, and children's swallowing small parts can cause serious harm. Not only is the person harmed—so, too, is the brand. The cost of losses associated with these negative experiences is incalculable to the brand owner.

CONVENTIONAL CARGO THIEVES

If anyone has ever thought that thieves are "stupid" or lack professional business skills, think again. If you ever considered the problem of the organized resale of stolen merchandise as a sporadic event, adjust your thought process. The business of stealing is alive, well, and firmly integrated throughout the world. Not only is it a daily occurrence and a 24/7 operation, it utilizes hundreds of thousands of people and millions of dollars in resources.

Fences, or middlemen, as they may be termed, run sophisticated operations that systemically offer a wide range of stolen goods for sale on an international basis to both legitimate and illegitimate enterprises. Their respective knowledge of business practices and their ability to avoid being noticed by the "tax man" is exceptional.

Thieves and fences must be equally connected to the community as well as to outlet businesses. They need to know the workings and operational needs of all clients and vendors as well as the system and personnel in each supply chain component. Their sophistication must go beyond normal business functions. Their offerings must be timely, their products marketable and available on a consistent and reliable basis. Yet their image must remain untarnished to sustain their honorable status among their peers and clients. The "honor among thieves" concept is most important to the middlemen because without this perceived integrity, deals of this magnitude would have to be done on a face-to-face cash transaction basis. The dynamics of a true fence operation relies on speed, anonymity, invisibility, and trust. Participants must stay clean in order to remain viable.

Just as in any normal enterprise, business through larger fences is typically done by cash, check, credit, wire, and, at times, even barter. Many companies use laundered funds, shell operations, untraceable accounts, and sophisticated smokescreens to transact business and move funds.

THE FENCING BUSINESS

The fence business is a way of life for the fence himself and his family. His business dictates his lifestyle and creates the basis of his associations and friends. To remain anonymous and innocuous in his community, successful fences tend to live under the radar. They avoid the appearance of opulence and questionable lifestyle. Even with the ability to 'live large', many choose a more reserved approach and stay out of trouble with the IRS or local law enforcement. This predatory and evasive lifestyle has to be adopted and maintained because it is easier to get involved in a criminal enterprise than it is to get out.

The complexity of a fence's personal finances and personal relationships, combined with the inventory and cash exposure in the criminal pipeline, keep them looking over their shoulders. The underworld associations needed to effectuate business and the overall daily risks of discovery and apprehension make this precarious career a permanent choice. Many who adopt this lifestyle have developed extensive networks and have a broad reach of clients and criminal associates. The fence's pipeline of goods to sell is his personal supply chain and constitutes his perception in the market to resellers and other types of clients. The larger the operation, the more sources he has for goods and the greater diversity of products he offers to prospective buyers. Fences control their environment, assuming a master role or a minor one. The master fence offers basically anything you may want to buy. Whatever he cannot get in the normal course of business, he orders from his network.

Good fences, especially larger ones, often have their own legitimate retail and wholesale businesses selling a variety of products. This helps create the cash resources needed to effectively pay for goods received at a moment's notice. These businesses also help to launder funds, mask activities, and confound investigations, outwardly legitimizing other activities and lifestyle and helping explaining income to close associates, family, and friends. These ventures also present a venue for distribution to effectively double-dip on the lucrative profits from the sale of stolen property. Without such diversionary tactics, the instant anomaly created by fencing activities would be a beacon for law enforcement. Typical fence businesses include all types of retail stores, bars, adult stores, restaurants, auto supplies, body shops, junkyards, pawn shops, and jewelry stores.

In an article on fences written by Darrell Steffensmeier about a convicted fence, a variety of theft activities were categorized. The exact nature of their individual activities differed, but what is remarkable is that even when dealing within the underworld, class distinction and business professionalism are recognized as an integral part of the business relationship and establish the hierarchy of criminal relationships. The categories of vendors, associates, and business partners included petty thieves, employee thieves, good (nonviolent) and bad (violent) thieves, burglars, walk-in thieves, gangs of thieves, in-between thieves (opportunists), first-timers, "criminal" thieves, organized criminals, and loners—to mention only a few. One must assume that each, by category, could deliver a particular volume and type of product and was somehow more suited in different cases to achieve the desired result than others. This decision matrix seems more complex than making a simple buying decision at a mall.

Those knowingly reselling stolen products are both cognitive and reactive marketers. The immediate availability of goods for sale is what drives their underground network. Supply and demand in both the legitimate and the illicit goods marketplace plays a tremendous role in determining sales outlets. With demand for a product being high, many fences are reluctant to offer certain high-end goods to certain resellers in highly scrutinized areas or situations where the anomaly of the sale of those products would be cause for law enforcement to investigate. Invisibility is a main marketing goal of both fences and resellers. Just as the brand owner may choose his markets, so, too, the fence controls his remarketing of these branded products. The irony here is that thieves' approach to market is essentially the same as brand owners'! In cases where need is the main sales driver, fences will create longer-term and more sophisticated contracts with resellers similar to a manufacturer's distribution agreement with a retail chain. Whether sold to a corner variety store or flea market or by Internet sales or mail order, fencing of stolen products requires consistency of supply. The parallels between both legitimate and illegitimate marketing tenets are surprisingly similar.

Honor among thieves is a question that is rarely asked since this entire activity is a criminal enterprise. Because of the dynamics and scope of theft distribution, the question of honor, reliability, honesty, and integrity of buyers and sellers is brought into question with each transaction. A thief or his fence just cannot guarantee trust in one another, especially if the relationship is new. Many cargo thieves are drug dealers, drug users, terrorists, mentally unstable individuals, violent people, or untrustworthy employees whose ethics are all but nonexistent. Because billions of dollars in cash and products are moving daily through their hands, you would think that the transition is seamless and consistent. This is true in only a small percentage of transactions. The inherent stress under which each transaction takes place, combined with the risk of discovery, the individual ethics of each participant, and the logistical difficulties associated with delivery, make the institution of criminal product sales less than desirable and not for the faint of heart.

Criminal enterprises operate in the moment. The path of least resistance can take what was a promise to deliver to a client into the wind in seconds based on events of the day.

The thief himself is tasked with finding specific goods ordered by his fence or handler and handling the actual theft. In some theft-to-order situations, goods can be easily located and stolen from distribution centers or from truck shipments. As previously mentioned, most sophisticated thieves know where to look for certain items. Many of these thefts are done at truck stops when drivers have left vehicles and trailers unattended. Because some products have extremely complex supply chains, locating the product source can be a difficult task that requires intelligence information on the part of the criminal enterprise. Such information is available from sources such as the Internet (for incoming cargo shipments), word of mouth, and drivers who have seen certain items in controlled public warehouses—as well as from many other underworld sources. In some cases, factories, warehouses, distribution centers, and even retailers are watched by cargo thieves to determine the volume of the targeted item in the location. After carefully checking the surroundings for local law enforcement patrols, private guards, and other deterrents, the location is hit on a weekend.

The default location for the theft of certain specialty items often winds up being the retail sort and consolidation level rather than at larger bulk distribution facilities. Many manufacturers use secondary distribution to move their products to retailers and break bulk multiple times, leaving any one truck or store with a limited number of that particular item. Usually, regardless of sources or volumes available, theft-to-order is far more prevalent than random product theft. Intelligence on the part of the thief or fence is untraceable, as everyone is rewarded for their part in identifying locations, volumes, items, and oversight. The information can come from drivers, dispatchers, and facility employees—even owners! Some information can come inadvertently from sales reps and others eager to identify such situations to establish credibility with legitimate buyers.

Fenced goods must leave thieves' hands within hours of receipt to avoid detection. Stolen trailers and tractors can be traced and are hard to hide, as are bulk shipments of most commodities. In rare cases, trucks stolen with cargo are relabeled and used by the thief to deliver the products to the fence. However, given the influx of RFID, GPS, and other covert security devices installed in tractors, containers, pallets, and trailers as well as on railway systems, rarely do thieves reuse original equipment.

Stolen vehicles and their cargo are quickly moved to public or private warehouses in the vicinity of the theft to maintain invisibility of the shipment. In more sophisticated thefts, these warehouses would be contracted well in advance by the thief or by the fence for cash. Most public warehouse facilities employ no guards, nor do they use any security measures to identify users—in this case, tenants. As unmanned public warehouses, they simply function as a drop-off point for the stolen goods, with no witnesses or scrutiny. Trucks and chassis arrive daily from everywhere, making the identification of any one particular trailer or its cargo almost impossible. Upon arrival, the awaiting teams, equipped with power equipment, strip out the truck or containers in just minutes while others disconnect the tractor and drive it as a bobtail or reattach to a different trailer to it as a disguise. Then the unit is taken many states away from the original site and dropped to avoid detection. Empty trailers are reattached to other stolen equipment and driven somewhere else and left to be discovered.

Although thieves may have goods to market, they will, more often than not, go through a fence to get quick cash and relieve themselves of the goods. Fences have the infrastructure and facilities to handle larger volumes of products. This is done as quickly as possible rather than have the thief locate a potential buyer. Fences play an integral, if not primary, role in the distribution and management of the underground supply chain. They bear the greatest initial risk, (after thieves themselves) by taking on volume commitments of random goods on a moment's notice and operating in the public arena. The conditions they face, which also include selling these products in light of market pressures, investigations, and law enforcement, make them essential to the orchestration of a successful criminal resale enterprise.

In defining the roles and functions of each participant in the enterprise, you will find that it takes many diverse skills to deliver a product. First and foremost, you need the thief himself. He makes relatively little from the actual theft in comparison to the value of the items taken yet assumes the greatest amount of initial risk from law enforcement. The thief may be organized or may act alone, but typically he is part of an organized crime family that may be comprised of anywhere from a few members to hundreds. Thieves may be contracted depending on the event, the risk involved, and the size and volume of the targeted goods. The area where they are to be hijacked or taken and the level of planning and equipment required to pull off the theft are significant factors.

When evaluating the underground supply chain, a major concern is that the players, although sophisticated, are in fact dangerous (and potentially violent) criminals. Just because their main focus is cash and they deal with inanimate products does not mean that they will not protect their turf, pipeline, sources, and clients from competitors. The inner workings of such criminal organizations are always violent, volatile, unpredictable, and dangerous. From organized retail theft gangs to criminal families of any size, violence is part of their reality. In many cases, this fixes their position and viability within their respective markets and against their competitors.

For a fence, distribution costs rival those of any conventional business. They have to secure immediate transportation, deliver timely to buyers, avoid law enforcement and corporate investigations, sell in regions outside their immediate area and the immediate area of the theft, and coordinate these activities in such a way as to be competitive against other fences. One main difference between conventional, legitimate business sales and the sale of stolen goods is that in the case of selling stolen goods, buyers (fences) are selected not only because of the price they are willing to pay the thief but also for their street integrity, loyalty, and trustworthiness.

The fence is the middleman who may or may not take possession of the stolen merchandise but who facilitates its resale through a series of distribution outlets. Many times goods stolen in bulk are divided into smaller units and moved independently to numerous locations, making traceability virtually impossible. Fences rarely get involved with the actual theft but rather are more hands-off organizers and developers of subsequent action. They create and respond to demand for products. Their distribution outlets, some of which are legitimate and some of which are not, can order goods specifically from the fence, who subsequently contracts for the theft. The fence is typically responsible for arranging for the logistics and storage of the goods, as well as the redistribution after the theft.

The fence needs to have a buyer in order to turn his venture into cash. The reseller, or "buyer," typically knows that he is receiving stolen merchandise from the fence but does not care what the source is—just that these goods are available for retail sales or distribution at the right price. The decision to purchase goods through these suspect channels is typically based on cost, demand, and instant availability. The ability of a fence to effectuate the instantaneous transshipment of stolen merchandise under the radar of law enforcement is a work of art. If industry was as efficient, millions of logistical dollars would be saved and delivery speeds would be improved.

TARGETED GOODS AND INDUSTRIES

The range of targeted stolen goods include such items as ingestibles, which encompasses all types of food, pharmaceuticals, alcohol, cigarettes, milk, beer, and soda. In all of these cases, improper storage can quickly contaminate the product, making it unsuitable for sale. The fact that the criminal supply chain handles these items with expertise, appropriate care, and speed speaks to its competence and focus. If the items stolen were not suitable for sale, fencing operations would quickly evaporate, and clients would seek new sources of supply. However, the unsuspecting retail buyer would not be aware of the storage condition, good or bad, and therefore accepts the product as new and in good condition when purchasing it from a reputable or perceived reputable source.

Resale of stolen goods is rarely limited to back-alley ventures. Because of the volume and profits available, resales are frequently done through established retail outlets, many recognized national names. Such incidents—in the case of prescription drugs in particular—can lead to sickness or even death in some cases, since the efficacy of the pharmaceutical can be lost quickly with improper storage and handling. This is prevalent in syringe-based vaccines, which require constant refrigeration and receive almost no validation before being used. Insulin and blood-related testing products are similarly vulnerable.

On one occasion, stolen vaccines were shipped to Haiti and used on over 3,000 children. At a significant cost to our government but with no benefit, these drugs had little to no effectiveness due to inadequate storage. Death or serious illness can happen in cases of buyers' purchasing fake cancer remedies.

Uncontrolled international distribution of branded items is extremely detrimental in certain industries. The fragrance and high-end clothing industries base their sales price on perception of quality and esthetics. The indiscriminate availability of their products through any available channel or reseller degrades the value of these goods and causes irreparable harm to the brand holder. The resale price is thus a major factor in eroding the perceived value of these goods and causes legitimate retailers to limit their stock. In turn, this reduces business and profits for the original brand owner. The competitive pressures of unauthorized resellers offering like kind goods for one-third of the normal price further cheapens the brand and causes incalculable financial harm to the manufacturer.

FOOD AND ALCOHOL THEFT

Food, alcohol, gasoline, and other bulk product theft all have one consistent characteristic associated with them. After they are stolen and consumed, there is no evidentiary trail. Food and liquor are repackaged, resold, and then consumed. Gasoline is introduced into large tanks. Bulk items such as seed, fertilizer, gases, and other commodity items are quickly blended to current stocks, leaving no trace for law enforcement to identify. Theft of these goods is totally invisible to any accounting audit and becomes a level of "corporate shrink" that is accepted and expected in all affected industries. In some businesses, an annual writeoff of up to 5 percent of gross sales is accounted for as shrink losses and deducted dollar for dollar from the company bottom line. In cases of companies that sell millions or billions in goods, such writeoffs deplete stock values and directly affect the value of the business.

INTELLECTUAL PROPERTY THEFT

There is yet another loss condition that negatively affects corporate profits to an even greater degree than the actual theft of finished goods. That condition is intellectual property theft or industrial espionage. IP theft constitutes the theft of a company's secret or proprietary materials, which can include designs, drawings, plans for new products, business strategy, financial data, client information, key personnel, sales databases, and the like. This information is also marketed (fenced) just as if it were more tangible physical property. Thieves are typically connected in some way to the targeted entity, but this type of theft has become a cyberevent with even more ramifications than the simple loss of trade information. In some cases entire databases are taken and sold throughout the world. This type of immediate-use data includes credit card numbers, personal data, and medical information on clients of the company. The marketing, regardless of the stolen IP, takes a far more sophisticated path than the simple fencing of stolen real products. Marketing is done at the white-collar level, and although "back room–oriented," the deals rarely involve violence and are typically well planned, organized, and executed. In most cases, the targeted data is requested rather than randomly taken, and the person stealing the items is typically a trusted employee. Some data—especially tactical information—stolen from defense contractors can lead to catastrophic results.

MORE OBSCURE COMMODITY THEFT ITEMS

Certain seasonal fruits and vegetables stored and shipped without maintaining precise refrigeration temperatures can spoil. These cannot ever be replaced, and entire earnings for owners can be lost by a single theft. This condition may not be apparent to buyers, who assume that the goods are fresh, but when they quickly spoil in a day or so after delivery the buyer is left a victim as well. Unsuspecting buyers quickly find out why purchasing goods from unknown sources can be a disaster. Many foods, such as soda and beer stored in extreme temperatures, are no longer suitable to drink yet appear good in their containers. Unknowing buyers eager to make a good deal for their business buy these goods in bulk for cents on the dollar and consequently expose the unwitting public to unnecessary risks. This can also have long-range negative consequences for retailers when customers begin to shop elsewhere.

When consumers register certain goods that were previously stolen with the vendor or manufacturer, these products become identified. When they reemerge on the commercial market or become serviced or pawned, the unsuspecting consumer can be identified as moving stolen property. Most vendors rarely prosecute those who purchase stolen goods when they register such products for warranty work. Bringing this to light to a consumer would further erode brand names and provide a negative image for the manufacturer or retailer. Many people purchase stolen products knowing they are probably stolen but rarely care. Those who purchase stolen goods unknowingly become irate when they are confiscated or fail to receive the service offered by the manufacturer to legitimate product owners. Most brand owners and manufacturers allow stolen goods to be registered and frequently afford the buyer the same rights and privileges as they would a legitimate owner to avoid the perception of negativity which comes with this type of punitive action.

Many other invisible thefts occur at the retail level, where the item itself is isolated to an individual user. These items can include theft of music, videos, software, prepaid telephone cards, and in-store gift cards as well as other (non-monetary) credit instruments. Such items are taken in bulk and then used individually, always making the retailer or manufacturer a victim at 100 percent of the face-value loss. These singular events, which result from larger-volume thefts, are a nightmare to locate and impossible to remedy. They can start as in-transit thefts or as shoplifted items. Their frequency and volume plague these industries and consistently erode the profits of all concerned. Trying to address these events using investigators accounts for another added cost to the brand owners and represents yet another invisible area of product theft loss. Because such items have smaller individual value, they are almost never traced or investigated. If the thief is discovered, he is not prosecuted due to the high cost of prosecution versus the actual amount of loss.

There are times when industrial theft is not asset-based. Service fraud and misuse of equipment, such as unauthorized trash collection and dumping, can account for millions in losses. These invisible conditions can rival product losses in many industries and are virtually undiscoverable unless the thief makes an error or the company is savvy to these potential threats. Retail and supply chain fraud also account for millions in lost profits.

Some examples of service fraud include employees upgrading purchased electronic components such as computers and cell phones with high-end memory, offering free features, or not charging for purchased goods. They then either pocket the fees or do not charge for them at all. This includes offering free extended warranties to friends and providing free upgrades of inventory components such as memory that are undiscoverable unless an audit is conducted. In the case of trash collection, dump fees rarely reflect consistent weights, and employees in this industry can make extra money by creatively misusing company equipment. Dump truck drivers can haul products for individuals with company-owned equipment, costing the owner fuel, time, wear and tear, and the salary of the employee while hauling cargo for personal gain. Over-the-road and local truck drivers can misuse equipment by integrating extraneous freight into their vehicle, including drugs and other stolen goods, and moving these loads throughout the country undetected.

The air courier business is not without fraud. Realizing that company-supplied packaging is exactly the same for all clients, courier agents can easily introduce contraband into these generic boxes and seamlessly ship them with conventional freight. This masks the use of the delivery service to move contraband to destinations without being detected. Drivers receive these items and simply repackage them with the same exact box, and no one is the wiser.

The construction industry also experiences invisible theft, as is the case with dumpsters. These expensive and valuable assets are frequently stolen from unattended job sites, repainted, relabeled, and then re-rented to unsuspecting clients. At the time of the theft, many of these dumpsters are emptied on the job site, causing site owners to pay fines and cleanup costs, which adds to their frustration as well as their loss.

Beside obvious credit card fraud and other currency theft conditions, these invisible thefts are surely an unrecoverable multimillion-dollar loss for many businesses.

METALS THEFT

Due primarily to the construction boom in China, the unprecedented demand for copper and other metals has fueled the metals market. These include bulk cable, manhole covers, scrap metal, copper pipe, construction equipment, and truck bodies. This newly developed demand has spawned a new breed of supply chain thief. Until just recently, this form of theft has never been on any law enforcement radar. Even though this commodity was vulnerable for years, the demand and prices paid for such items have now put them in their own category.

The metals thief can be a random opportunist or a burglar at the lower levels, rifling air conditioning systems, stealing gutters, and plumbing from home and factory construction sites, and stealing light and power poles as well as unattended railroad equipment, including wiring, that operates critical signals. At more organized levels, these people can be dangerous thieves targeting metals on a higher and more voluminous level, stealing steel, aluminum windows, copper, and other metals from distribution yards, construction sites, and flatbed trailers.

Demand for aluminum grew nearly 10 percent in 2004 and 4.6 percent in 2005. It has increased 4.5 percent each year since then. The theft of metal pipes, radiators, and wires out of vacant homes is nothing new. Copper is selling for about $3.90 a pound, and aluminum at about $1.45. Scrap copper, such as pipe and wire, is fetching between $1.30 to a $1.80 a pound, about double what it was a few years ago. Medium-grade scrap aluminum, such as siding, sells for $0.75 a pound, up $0.25 from 2005 levels. Authorities have long blamed it on drug addicts looking to pay for their next fix. Now police are being inundated with reports of metal thefts, but little is actually being done to recover any of it. Metals score low on law enforcement's list of sexy crimes to investigate. The interesting part of this form of theft is the sophistication needed to move these bulk products over the road and out of the country seamlessly.

Metal theft can wreak havoc in the construction and building industry. With long lead times for these custom-made goods, replacing stolen parts is extremely costly and time consuming. Losses of construction equipment such as dump trucks and other vehicles taken to be chopped cost the contractor and his insurance company significantly. When windows, beams, and doors are taken from jobs sites, the actual product replacement cost is far greater to the owner than the actual value of the items taken. The nature of this form of theft requires a considerable amount of logistical planning, because most metal products are very heavy, bulky and unidentifiable. In cases in which unattended switching facilities are robbed, knowledge of electricity and plumbing is critical in not getting the thief hurt during the extraction.

In cases in which dump trucks are stolen for their aluminum bodies and chassis, owners will never see their vehicles again in the same condition. Trucks' bodies are quickly chopped, reduced to container-sized parts, and shipped overseas. Metals, especially aluminum, steel, and copper, fetch high prices and are sought-after commodities in Asian markets. With virtually no way to identify most of these products in the field, the criminal fences of scrap metals are quickly generating tremendous profits without any real remedy for the original owners.

Just examining the logistical requirements of volume metal theft is a dynamic undertaking. Not only is the thief required to have a sophisticated operation to sort, chop, pack, and move these products, but he is also required to have them presold for quick distribution.

HAZARDOUS MATERIALS THEFT

Another issue with cargo theft involves hazardous materials. These items include gasoline, explosives, chemicals, and the like. Tandem tankers, railcars, and barges, which haul anything from corrosives to explosives, are equally vulnerable to theft. In some cases the stolen goods, like conventional cargo, are destined for resale. In some cases, these bulk items can be easily used by a terrorist. In certain cases, hazardous goods may cause tremendous collateral damage if used illicitly or inappropriately. Even mishandling, such as a spill or contamination of other products, can potentially cost the original owners millions in remedial actions or losses. There is never any ability to track or trace stolen bulk chemicals, so protecting these items over the roads, rails, and on inland sea corridors is extremely important. If conventional cargo falls into the wrong hands, companies loose money, but if hazmats fall into the wrong hands, the threat to the public is exponential.

The USA PATRIOT Act also has harsh provisions to find the original owner of certain goods liable if they are stolen and misused.

OTHER STOLEN GOODS

Certain goods are harder to steal than others. Cars, trucks, construction equipment, and certain electronics, including cell phones and computers, require activation, registration, monitoring, and repair. When transferred or repaired, notes are made on registration numbers. Items such as serial or VIN numbers are frequently compared electronically to lists of stolen goods. Many of these items contain computer global positioning systems, which also aid in tracing their locations. Once identified, many shops will seize the asset or notify law enforcement, who will recover the item for the rightful owner. In the case of pawned goods, owner (or transfer agent) photos are taken and research is done to validate the transfer. Pawn shops commonly aid law enforcement in recovering stolen property.

The newest loophole in the law for jewelry thieves is to offer stolen gold jewelry items to "gold buyers" who will turn your unwanted jewelry into cash. Gold jewelry taken in robberies of homes or business is easily converted to cash by these new fences, seamlessly and legally. Little effort is done to validate the ownership of the items; before long, these items are melted down and become lost forever to the rightful owners. Although this pennies-on-the-dollar buyback scheme is lucrative for the buyer, it becomes yet another means to convert stolen property to cash.

Certain items are easy to steal, because they are consumed or blended so well as to make the theft and the product taken invisible to any inspector or law enforcement agency. This does not, by any means, say that all goods have an equal propensity to be taken. It does, however, allow law enforcement to record and investigate the theft of certain goods through a wider and more sophisticated variety of means. Imbedded components that have to be turned on or validated electronically are good theft deterrents. These components aid in identifying stolen property. Serial number verification on diamonds and some jewelry as well as art can be a good means of recovery, but buyers of this merchandise rarely, if ever, allow the product out for examination. Many electronics providers have in the past considered adding secret imbedded electronic codes to turn on their devices such as cable boxes, plasma TVs, and sound equipment, but rarely have these been used effectively or consistently. These ideas have been discussed by manufacturing organizations and even by the FCC, but none have been implemented, primarily because of the costs involved and the inconvenience to legitimate buyers.

In retailing, where theft conditions are more visible than in the commercial supply chain, overt deterrent technologies such as radio frequency identification scanning and other on-product loss control technologies have blossomed in recent years. By using source tagging on packaging and small dye packs on garments, electronic alarms and chains, retailers have tried their best to address in-store theft by making goods more difficult to extract from stores.

Source tagging has a cost of almost $0.07, which is added to the resale cost of millions of items directly by the manufacturer. In some cases where multiple EAS tags are required to serve different retailers, up to $0.21 cents is added to the cost of goods.

Retail companies are more willing to address in-store product theft (shoplifting) with large-dollar expenditures versus spending these funds to address the greater issues of supply chain theft. According to all statistics, supply chain theft accounts for 98 percent of corporate product losses, whereas retail theft is less than 2 percent of product theft. It does seem illogical that shoplifting, or *boosting*, as it is now called, is a condition that both small and larger retailers understand with far more clarity than in-transit theft. Loss control products for retailers accounts for a $5 billion business on its own, thereby stimulating the economy! But the cost of crime to our economy is not offset by the profits or economic stimulus generated from use of these protective technologies. The development of the security industry specifically to address supply chain theft has spawned hundreds of new companies who manufacture electronics, cameras, devices, and the locks to address many common theft issues.

The reason that in-transit theft is of less importance to retailers is that much of the freight shipped to the retailer is f.o.b. (free on board) destination. This means that the cargo, although owned by the vendor and having been purchased by the retailer, is not legally the retailer's until it reaches its destination in good order. Since the cargo is owned by the vendor, little is done by the retailer to protect it during transit. The issue is that without the goods to sell, the retailer looses his client base but is still unwilling to participate in the protection of these goods to his door, since they are not his. This brings up the question of why the vendor is not actively participating in protecting these goods in transit. The answer is that shippers rely on the insurance of a carrier to protect their interests in the event of a loss. Many carrier insurance policies specifically exclude theft-related events from coverage. In some cases, the *employee infidelity clause* in most insurance contracts reduces the carrier's liability to that of the Carmack amendment's limit of liability. These limits are $0.50 per pound, regardless of the freight or commodity. Because of this misunderstanding, many shippers, carriers, and retailers become unknowing victims when their goods and vehicles are stolen in transit. Regardless of the downstream affect on the retail consignee, each participant in the supply chain seems to accept its chances and resist any change in security procedure.

Stolen products such as clothing, shoes, food, and OTC drugs make up a high percentage of products available on auction Web sites. On the other hand, goods from bulk thefts tend to be exported and resold in other markets around the world. In some cases, they are broken down and sold as units of measure (single items) rather than in the original bulk package. More clearly, items such as cigarettes, food, razor blades, and OTC drugs are frequently sold in small units to barrio stores, small-jobbers, and retailers on a cash basis. They are regularly moved within hours of the theft. Since availability of goods in certain markets is nonexistent, resales in smaller or single units is an acceptable means of redistribution.

For example, in some markets, the parts of a car are worth more than the assembled car. This adage applies to many redistributed products, which makes the spoils of cargo theft even greater than the original wholesale value of these items in bulk. Many fences specialize in smaller volumes that can be picked up and delivered locally rather than risking more sophisticated distribution. These cash transactions are highly profitable and mainly go undiscovered by law enforcement.

International distribution of stolen property is a mechanism that attracts all forms of criminal and terrorist enterprises. The resale represents instant untraceable cash without duty, tax, or government oversight. Little is done—or can be done—by the original intellectual property holder to protect his brand from being resold or redistributed in countries without laws to protect such brand owners. Most Third World countries have no restrictions on importation of branded goods. Because there is no basic tax structure or duty, there isn't any incentive for these countries to restrict imports. In the European Union, where importation is far more akin to the United States, much greater scrutiny is given to imported cargo. The issues in the EU with regard to inspection volumes, verification of shippers, and cargo are far more complex, but much illegal importation is still overlooked. Misclassified goods, no-hands-on examination of the cargo, payoffs, and still other factors permit the criminal enterprise to effectively move goods internationally.

Upon receipt of stolen products anywhere in the world, the new owner can typically operate his business or criminal enterprise with complete anonymity and obscurity. His choice of resale agents is unpredictable, and these new sales outlets are untraceable. The proceeds from the sale to the distribution channel and to the ultimate client are effectively laundered with no traceability for tax, VAT, or other governmental revenues.

The problem usually occurs when the brand owner finds his goods in unauthorized stores or areas and informs law enforcement. Once governments are made aware of these sales and their subsequent loss in tax revenue, they are empowered to shut down the reseller and trace the purchases back to his suppliers (fences). These situations typically result in identifying and arresting small operators, but before the ink has dried on the booking sheet, there is another fence and retailer to take their place.

THE SPOILS OF SUPPLY CHAIN THEFT

Profit calculations in legitimate businesses are derived from a great many factors. Each factor is a known balance-sheet component and has a traceable and predictable basis. In terms of selling or distributing stolen goods, profit is arrived at by a far more complex methodology, with none of the components being the same from year to year or, at times, from product to product. The diversity of market conditions, location, availability, and demand for certain types of products in a particular market directly impact the impetus for certain product to be stolen. Although none of these factors are predictable, they can be quantified.

It is essential that we obtain a picture of the size of the individual product market in terms of both dollar sales and utility. From that we can see which other factors stimulate the flux in supply and demand for those goods, and hence the selling price.

Just as in the legitimate market, customers must desire goods to create demand. Demand can be short- or long-term, and fences and redistributors understand these behavior-related market forces and plan accordingly. Items such as clothes (which are trendy and current) and baby formula (which is a staple) drive price and demand for theft-related sales. The fact that certain items are more easily fenced than others also contributes to their vulnerability. It is not a surprise that each commodity has a risk factor determined by need and desirability. The marketability of a product determines its price. The greater the desire, the less attention people pay to price. This creates a higher level of profitability for some products, which can be sold at equal or better margins than the legitimate product when sold by a retailer. This demand and reward fuels the market for certain goods to be stolen. This is especially true in pharmaceutical thefts with such products as Oxycodone and Viagra. The demand for these goods in the market, stolen or not, supersedes morality and makes availability the primary marketing factor in a consumer buying decision. New releases of toys around Christmas, DVDs of current cinematic releases, new book and CD releases, apparel, and electronics fall into this category. Staples such as cigarettes, shaving supplies, foods, OTC drug products, alcohol, and baby formula fall into the need category. They will always find an immediate sales outlet albeit at a lower margins, but with more consistency and availability on the street.

Fixed costs in both legitimate business and criminal enterprises are consistent and encompass components such as warehouse rentals, heat, light, power, sales and marketing costs, accounting, basic overhead, personnel, and handling equipment. In the criminal enterprise, the base cost of material, packaging, products, research and development, and insurance does not exist. Many shell corporations involved in the criminal transfer of goods do incur some of these costs, but at a fractional level when compared to legitimate manufacturers. The cost base for the transfer of stolen goods is predicated on the current market conditions. These components include the demand for the particular product, the location of the sale, the position or rank of the thief (in terms of trust from his fences), the goods themselves—their age, condition, and utility —and the unknown factors of risk that always plague thieves and fences. The riskier the transfer or transfer vehicle for the goods, the greater the resale price, and hence the higher the profit.

When companies become extremely successful in remarketing stolen goods, the profit from these sales grows exponentially. However, the cost of goods sold is disproportionate to reasonable revenues, and the money must be effectively laundered to fool the tax man and internal auditors. In effect, they need to obscure the origin of revenue to disguise the proceeds of the business. In order to remain undetected by authorities, they must show some way that they earned money, rather than having profits appear magically. The same situation is true with other criminal enterprises, such as drugs and prostitution, where cash is accumulated with no record of a product ever being bought or manufactured for resale. Since computer records are more available now, anomalies such as this are easier to find than in the past, and removals of large amounts of cash are traceable.

The criminal enterprise has certain costs of doing business. Shell businesses must offset their gains from the sale of stolen or counterfeit items they never owned or manufactured. Such activity now becomes part of the economy; taxes are paid to the government, and salaries are paid to employees. All of these expenses are aboveboard and on the record. Since the business of selling stolen goods is product-based and clients, in many cases, pay in cash, recordkeeping is a threat to the secrecy of the enterprise. Any overt disclosure of these funds to authorities would be an immediate cause for an audit. In many cases, these criminal groups establish secondary businesses that are known to deal primarily in cash, created to explain the large influx of cash in a way that is defensible in court and inconspicuous to authorities.

In a simple product business, the cost of goods is easily traced, and records always indicate the profits and expenses associated with running the operation. However, in a business dealing in stolen property, one must obscure this data. This is done with a parallel business, such as a bar, grocery, or restaurant, whose earnings are in cash, or which uses or sells the same type of product. This clouds any normal means to detect fraud. Most of these secondary business ventures are done legally. By blending the assets of both businesses, vast sums of cash can be effectively drained from one business to another and booked in any fashion desirable so as not to create a trigger for a federal or state audit. This is euphemistically known as *creative accounting*, but is, in effect, *money laundering*, and an effective way to hide and transfer wealth. Rarely are these businesses asset-based, for obvious reasons. Most rent commercial warehouse space, storefronts, and offices, which in itself offers another way to hide money. The monetary proceeds from both activities can then be paid in salaries to workers or to other bogus enterprises as payment for the receipt of goods when no goods actually change hands. Cash from these activities can be moved to accounts offshore or smuggled outside the United States. However, the federal government is more aware of these scams now and actively looks for Racketeer Influenced and Corrupt Organizations Act (RICO) violations to prosecute.

Many criminal enterprises pay funds in the form of employee benefits, 401(k) contributions, cash bonuses, and other innocuous payment transfers to members, most of which are aboveboard and visible. Surprisingly enough, many criminal enterprises are sophisticated and tend to filter funds locally, paying their taxes and staying under the radar screen.

Prices for stolen goods at retail are often lower or the same as those of normal goods, depending on the demand and sales outlet. CDs, video games, designer clothes, shoes, fragrances, cigarettes, and liquor are most often sold at normal competitive rates. Other items, such as jewelry, guns, steel, copper, aluminum, vehicles, and gasoline can be priced based first on market conditions and second on demand. The greater the products are sanitized, the more they are inherently worth. Items such as food, gasoline, or bulk commodities become invisible to any investigation as they are consumed and leave no evidentiary trail to follow.

There is an unspoken fair price standard among thieves, fences, buyers, and sellers that transcend traditional values. Thieves want to be paid but realize they need to get in and out of the goods quickly and quietly. Hence, their fair price standard varies with time-in-hand, risk, and logistic considerations.

Criminal enterprises do incur the costs of paying thieves, outside transportation, distribution, and storage suppliers. Even with the obvious legal risks, most operate profitably and effectively. The larger the criminal enterprise, the more akin to legitimate business it becomes. Many of these organizations have the same challenges and business parameters of legitimate businesses and also face similar competitive pressures as their counterparts. Many use front operations that are in fact legal, taxpaying entities. These front operations are needed to launder funds. Even in the criminal underworld, the skill of the entity's owner and staff will dictate the ultimate success or failure of the enterprise. And even in the world of criminal activity, the economic climate, both nationally and regionally, influences ability to serve clients' needs and grow business.

The price science of stolen goods is unpredictable and regionally and commodity-dependent. The actual thief reaps 5–10 percent on the dollar, while the fence would get upwards of 35 percent; the retailer gets the balance. There are no firm fixed numbers or benchmarks for this activity. However, the risk-versus-reward calculation stays constant: "the greater the risk, the greater the reward." In the underground economy, the costs of marketing, sales, logistics, and ultimate distribution are still a major factor in calculating a delivered price to a client even when nothing was paid for the original product.

HIDING THE MONEY

Money laundering is a method of concealing the identity, source, or destination of illegally acquired money. It is the means by which drug smugglers, organized criminal enterprises, counterfeiters, and conventional thieves filter their profits into what can be viewed as legitimate company revenues. This all starts with the original theft or unauthorized resale of goods or services. Stolen goods, as well as diverted goods and counterfeits, are typically the product base used to establish these businesses. The stores or distribution centers can be placed anywhere in the world. The retail outlets can be Internet-based operations, retail stores, or even flea marketers, furthering confound law enforcement efforts to track and trace sources. The world's free market status makes selling almost anything anywhere to anyone both easy and seamless. In some cases, goods stolen in the United States, Canada, and Mexico wind up in South American countries. These new owners can then find buyers elsewhere and, at times, reship these goods to legitimate businesses in the United States, Canada, and Mexico. Products originally stolen here can return to our shores in a matter of weeks.

Stolen goods that have been repacked and shipped through ports such as Miami are classified by the goods shipper as products other than what they actually are. This is done to avoid scrutiny by law enforcement and customs. These new classifications are rarely challenged by Customs and Border Protection and easily pass through the ports under normal documents that appear legitimate. Recipients in countries such as Ecuador, India, and even the UK receive the products, repackage them, and export them again as misclassified yet similar products. Since only 0.5 percent of containerized shipments in the United States are actually opened and verified, thieves and diverters have little risk of discovery.

The opening of a sea container is sometimes done arbitrarily but is most often done based on intelligence information and shipper anomalies. The chance of these previously stolen goods being opened for inspection is extremely rare. Importers and exporters are savvy on the criteria for inspection and are sophisticated enough to work under the radar screen of governmental scrutiny.

Upon receipt, the stolen goods are filtered back into the U.S. economy, where typically no tax liability is assessed or importation conditions implemented. If these goods are earmarked for resale in legitimate businesses, sales taxes are assessed at the time of sale, further obscuring criminal investigations. As the cost of the original stolen product was nil, any investment in ancillary costs such as overhead and taxes is moot based on the proposed profit from the sale.

The sophistication and business skill involved with managing an international criminal enterprise is equal to any international importer in any country. The infrastructure is such that it replicates a normal business. Typically the employees have no knowledge of the origin of the goods, and the validity of the enterprise is never brought into question. Simply put, it operates as any normal business would.

IT IS NOT A LOCAL PROBLEM

Dan Purtell, president of First Advantage, concluded in an article that international government-sponsored or -mandated security programs have unequivocally not diminished the level of cargo theft. Such efforts have only served to change the criminal's methodology in acquiring the goods. Purtell reported that "[r]egional hot spots such as Brazil, South Africa, Russia, the UK, and Mexico continue to be plagued by violent truck hijackings while violent crime here in the United States has drastically declined as compared to unattended product theft, which has increased almost 8 fold since 2004." He further reported that sea piracy incidents are growing in violence and are approaching an all-time high.

Sea pirates have the ability to steal entire container ships with all types of cargo on board. The ultimate distribution of that cargo can be devastating to brand owners and the recipients of those goods. In April 2009, an America flag ship owned by Maersk was hijacked off the coast of Africa, and the captain was detained by pirates. The U.S. Navy was forced to intervene and freed the captain after killing three of the four pirates holding him. This is a prime example of how high seas piracy is escalating throughout the world.

Targeted cargo can be anything from food to durable goods, from hazmat to tactical goods such as military equipment, guns, and ammunition. Cargo stolen in this method is rarely adequately insured and can be either lost at sea or moved to safer ports. Buyers for this cargo are plentiful throughout the world. Any commodity shipped by sea through highly vulnerable shipping lanes is at risk. The sheer volume of this form of product theft is in the hundreds of millions of dollars per event. In some cases, a ransom is paid to recover the ship, but much of the cargo reenters the world's theft pipeline and is absorbed with no compensation going to the goods owner, shipper, or carrier.

On land, facility-oriented security programs such as the Technology Asset Protection Association (TAPA) and the Customs Trade Partnership Against Terrorism (C-TPAT) are believed to have pushed risk to other parts of the supply chain but have in no way addressed it. Since TAPA's Freight Security Requirements (FSR) facility certification program was implemented in 2001, many carriers and shippers of high-value goods have benefited from tightening up security. The main flaw with this system was that it fails miserably to address the security of the truck itself, but rather focuses on warehouses and plants. With the current emphasis of organized crime on filling the pipeline with these products, such programs have had little deterrent effect. Although these limited loss prevention methods have fallen short of being effective, they have been catalytic to protecting those who avail themselves of the recommended techniques and technologies.

According to Purtell, "[i]n order to prevent losses in today's supply chain, corporations need to do more than baseline security procedures in higher risk locations to protect their interests." They also need to proactively add physical deterrent technologies to trucks and other unattended cargo containers. Such devices can include air brake locks, specialized door locks, door-to-door cables, and lock bar seals for international shipping. Wireless GPS in individual cargo pallets and other physical security tools for cargo and trailers are also among the best practices recommended by TAPA. The use of these devices makes it more difficult for the thief to penetrate or circumvent the targeted goods or containers. In most cases, the use of deterrent security tools hardens the target and protects the property owners and transportation providers from in-transit losses.

THE TRUE IMPACT OF CARGO LOSS ON THE ECONOMY

Because the numbers for the volume of cargo theft are calculated at the wholesale price level, the opportunity and related costs of loss are not part of the approximate $25 billion in goods stolen annually from trucks and containers in the United States. The exclusions in collateral sales opportunities, client loyalty, brand erosion, reseller competition, remanufacturing, and reshipping are not taken into account when determining the approximate cost of loss in stolen cargo.

In the last fifteen years, there have been very few verifiable reporting mechanisms for calculating supply chain theft losses. The reason is simply that most corporations with identifiable national brands regard theft losses and disclosure as the death knell for client confidence, brand reliability, and stock price valuation. In more practical terms, theft losses indicate that certain items such as prescription and OTC drugs have been out of the care and control of the vendor or his authorized agents, thereby giving way to potential product tampering issues, loss of efficacy due to improper storage conditions, and possible counterfeit product blending. "A lot of companies would not report cargo theft because they did not want their competitors to know they had a problem or that they had a loss," said William McLeod, senior special agent for the Department of Homeland Security's Immigration and Customs Enforcement (ICE) division.

The unfair competitive advantage that the resale of stolen goods poses in the market is significant. The retail client is affected not only by a lost opportunity to sell the product, but also by the ancillary costs of recovery, investigation, and remanufacturing associated with the theft. These ancillary costs dwarf the original cost of the manufactured goods.

Additionally, many insurance companies who stand to lose a great deal from these collateral events dissuade companies from reporting such losses to the general public. According to McLeod, "Insurance companies in some cases were not notified by the policy owner because these companies did not want their insurance premiums to go up." Theft-related events do affect insurance premiums. The all-important claims process is a factor that determines the risk associated with taking on insurance protection for a new client. In the insurance industry, such historic claims reporting is permitted by law, and any new provider can access loss data going back many years to determine risk and adjust premiums accordingly. The more risk involved with shipping the product, the higher the requirements are for stricter shipping parameters.

How many times have you heard on the national news that a truckload of some drug has been stolen? Surely not many, yet this happens weekly throughout the United States, Canada, Mexico, the EU, and South and Central America. Branding and consumer confidence are valuable assets to all large corporate entities, and losses associated with such brand erosion are almost impossible to quantify; hence they are blended into the cost of goods sold, causing unnecessarily inflated selling prices for these goods. The intangible costs of loss are never counted in any loss numbers, which makes the $25 billion a base rather than a gross assessment.

In a report by Thomas Ford in 2005, it was estimated that the real economic impact of cargo theft to the United States economy is in excess of 1 percent. And 1 percent of $11 trillion—the GDP (gross domestic product) of the richest, most affluent nation of the world—means that every man, woman and child in the United States pays in excess of $50 every year to make up for these supply chain losses.

The impact of this level of loss throughout the economy is significant. Many more people and companies are affected than meets the eye. Since loss data is so compelling, it makes sense to see a greater involvement by insurance companies and internal risk managers of affected companies than is actually the case. In most cases, supply chain theft losses are considered acceptable levels of business risk, so little is done proactively by most shippers to reduce this known peril.

It would seem that with the risk as high as it is for cargo theft, insurance providers would demand that shippers and carriers become more proactive in protecting cargo and assets from theft. The use of security technology would certain lessen financial loss while protecting client interests. Most insurance companies do not require and do not incentivize clients with cost reductions if they participate in reducing risk. The fact that no incentives are offered further reduces the propensity of shippers and carriers from participating in loss control programs.

In fact, the adverse economic impact of theft rarely concerns manufacturers, who they tend to apply these costs back into the wholesale and retail selling price of the product. For example, in computers, almost $100 of the sale price of every machine can be attributed to a loss condition! The costs of clothing, food, electronics, and other targeted items are inflated to offset the staggering costs of supply chain theft-related losses. Although no one is sure, it appears the cost of supply chain theft to each American is more—much more—than only $50 yearly. The cost of transportation is also affected in that many carriers have become reluctant to carry high-value or highly vulnerable goods into many areas, thereby causing prices to escalate and reducing carrier choices. Carriers can no longer afford to provide certain types of insurance, as they have become self-insured. Shippers can no longer get specific peril (theft) insurance for many product types and in many modalities and locations. All of these elements lead to a higher consumer cost.

Most people fail to understand the impact theft-related sales have on their cost of living. The products we buy, the insurance cost we pay, and the general nexus between gangs, terrorists, and organized criminal enterprises adversely affect us all.

The precise economic impact of supply chain theft is rarely effectively calculated for a number of reasons. These factors relate to intangible costs such as the true impact of theft to the brand owner, including the erosion of trust and the market pressures of competing against the resale of your own stolen goods. Other major areas of loss include remanufacturing and all associated costs with not having product sell, disruption of normal manufacturing activities needed to replenish supplies, higher insurance premiums, reshipping costs, and loss of sales opportunities, all of which tremendously impact a company's ability to stay viable in these tumultuous economic times. When a client is unable to restock your products due to theft, it may turn to your competitors' products to replace yours, resulting in lost sales and lost clients. Retailers must respond to demand, and demand can only be satisfied when the items are available for purchase. The cost of lost opportunity and of both collateral and ancillary sales cannot be quantified.

Losses and the threat of loss require dedicated security departments and personnel to manage, investigate, and administer loss claims, as well as customer service managers to run interference with angry and disappointed clients. Higher insurance premiums, which result from risk policies and the need to take out multiperil transportation insurance, increase the cost of goods and thereby adversely affect a company's ability to stay competitive. The basic cost of stolen property becomes a major financial burden that has to be added back into the product and passed along to all consumers. According to the Inland Marine Underwriters Association (IMUA) and many other insurance professionals, the replacement costs of stolen property can go as high as five times the value of the original goods. With just-in-time manufacturing schedules to contend with as well as long import times, modality, and speed, goods stolen in transit—especially seasonal or nonreplenishable items (such as fruits and meat)—impact the market and all participants extensively.

Security solutions for the commercial supply chain seem to be consistently funded as expense items. These remedies are based on conditions that have already occurred rather than included in a budget in advance of need. Such budget items would then become a cost of goods sold and be written into the base cost of the product. This would spread the cost of protection over all aspects of sales. General product theft and the risk of in-transit theft are clearly compelling reasons businesses need to dedicate security processes and personnel to any supply chain budget as a cost of goods sold. The paradigm must be created to ensure security is budgeted and considered in every aspect of manufacturing and logistics.

In the 2007 study "Better Security Drives Business Values," Dr. Barchi Gillai of Stanford University prepared to develop a basis for bolstering vulnerable supply chains from theft. The paper focused on the proactive use of supply chain security techniques, processes, and technology to address business losses in the supply chain. The study showed that despite the diversity of the companies that participated in the study, almost all of them realized major benefits in each of five areas: (1) inventory management and customer service, (2) product visibility, (3) logistic efficiency, (4) manufacturing resilience, and (5) customer relationships through controlling losses.

Given the broad range of products, each has significant direct and collateral benefits from security investments. The study participants concluded that "these investments should not be considered as a financial burden but rather as an opportunity for improving business performance and profitability." All of the companies that participated in the study took further security-related initiatives following 9/11 and continued to evaluate their supply chain security with time. Many were initially driven by government recommendations, but some entered into these programs proactively, due entirely to the threats surrounding their particular product, culture, brand vulnerability, and supply chain considerations. Company participants included hazmat materials, chemical companies, electronics manufacturers, and food and pharmaceutical suppliers.

These initiatives included measures that were taken to comply with government regulations resulting from the 9/11 report and included such security and safety regulations imposed by the U.S. Department of Transportation and those voluntarily recommended by TSA, DHS, and other government and industry security initiatives. These programs included U.S.

Customs Trade Partnership Against Terrorism (C-TPAT) and the Canadian Partners in Protection (PIP) security initiative. As pointed out by many companies who participated in this study, compliance with such voluntary initiatives was important for the manufacturing companies in order to prevent delays due to higher inspection rates and to speed up the clearance process for imported goods at the ports of entry. However, as they realized the tangible benefits of a proactive approach to supply chain security, their willingness and level of participation increased. The study pointed out that although most traditional business cultures believed that unless expenses can directly relate to marketable and profit-generating ends, such extraneous costs in areas such as security were frivolous and nonessential. The challenge of the study was to help associate proactive spending on security-related measures as justifiable in creating business wealth. Overall, the collective data was overwhelmingly in favor of securing company supply chain over and above any governmental mandates or suggestions.

In another recent worldwide survey of major international companies, it was clearly shown that supply chain security was a major component in the development of distribution strategies. More than 41 percent of respondents agreed that protecting cargo was a major component in their logistical planning efforts. The rating of supply chain security against other strategic components has grown from tenth to fourth place based on the criteria used by most companies to measure their overall supply chain vulnerabilities. Included in the data were areas such as brand theft, counterfeiting, diversion, product tampering, and hijacking, to mention only a few. As the world's supply chain gears up for more lean years ahead, securing unattended transported assets from theft becomes a priority. Limited supplies of items, smaller just-in-time (JIT) windows and changes in modality from air to sea, based on transportation costs, fuels the need to protect cargo. Since the ability to replenish and replace stolen goods is no longer a viable backup plan, only proactive planning can reduce this costly risk.

THE NEXUS OF TERRORISM TO CARGO THEFT

The chaotic and unpredictable behavior of street criminals creates a tremendous public vulnerability. In the terrorist arena, where motivation can be both economic and violent, the public risk further intensifies. Terrorists use stolen goods to fund their operations. Many terrorist operations have begun by first creating businesses with which a cell can generate legal earnings in an area of the country. Since many of these operations are legitimate fronts, stolen goods of all types can be channeled through them without notice. By their success in generating cash, they are successful in channeling funds back overseas to help run the terrorist operation.

Terrorists bent on disrupting the economic climate of the free world recognize that their criminal or terroristic enterprise must generate cash in order to perpetuate itself. By using this method of distribution and resale of stolen goods, terrorists can generate cash and send it back to their handlers. This attack is considered a weapon of mass effect as it creates a negative economic impact (unlike a weapon of mass destruction, which causes havoc on its targeted victims).

What better way than to create a source for cash than to move fake or stolen goods as both a fence and reseller? Criminals who steal are eager to turn a quick profit but have little use for the goods taken. In this scenario, terrorists masquerading as organized criminals offer to fund the activity and take possession of the goods, regardless of type or kind. This promotes random theft of truck trailers and other items such as cars. It promotes more brazen break-ins of warehouses, factories, stores and truck terminals. The goods taken are valued by bulk rather than by item description.

The going rate for a driver "truck give-up" is about $15,000. Thieves, smugglers, and terrorists have a distinct advantage over shippers, carriers and law enforcement in that they can easily attack any truck, trailer, railcar, or container when and where they wish, whereas no one agency or government can protect against all of these random attacks all the time. Terrorists need only to be able to succeed once to achieve their goal.

CONCLUSIONS

In effect, product theft control and preventative antitheft measures at the retail level have somehow been misdirected. This is due entirely to a gross misunderstanding of the problem. The National Retail Federation makes a point of promoting the use of antitheft technology but clearly fails to adequately educate its members on the bigger picture of supply chain theft. Regardless of the use of in-store countermeasures such as cameras, EAS, gates, and guards, the level of theft at the retail and warehouse levels has been consistently growing for the last twenty-five years.

Theft based demand for goods is a worldwide problem. Theft levels will escalate as the economy declines. Industry has been consistently myopic in dealing with the issue of cargo theft and fails to see the effect it has on the bottom line. This is primarily due to the fact that in larger companies, no one seems to take ownership of the loss condition or proactively assume the responsibility for the defense of the asset base. This also applies to brand equity issues, which include diverting and counterfeiting. At the transportation level, those who fail to recognize the nexus between their business prosperity and that of their clients become instant victims with no understanding why. By not being proactive in employing security technology or processes, logistical companies in all modalities become targets.

A cultural change is needed to begin the process to protect cargo, business assets, and profits for all concerned. Each employee must understand the need to protect company assets, brand, good name, and personnel from threats. Little is done by way of corporate education to help bolster a sense of morality thereby dissuading employees from turning to theft.

The understanding of *ownership and empowerment* is a means by which corporations can instill an esprit de corps among their employees. Ignoring the need to change cultural norms that accept theft as a condition of doing business is the single biggest threat to profitability a company can have.

Theft is unfortunately a condition that not only exists but thrives. However, losses can be made manageable by planning, education, and vigilance. Effective legal remedies to industrial theft can be only one factor in reducing the condition. Insurance is never a remedy, and technology without process can do little to help. Insurance falls far short of making up financial losses and can do little to relieve the basic problem.

Active participation against theft, and a keen understanding of its effects by all parties to the problem, is the most effective way to reduce the condition. It is plain to see that supply chain crime does pay remarkably well for little risk. Those sophisticated enough to manipulate the system with consistency can reap untold profits from every transaction. It takes a great many people, each playing a specific role in the business of supply chain theft, to make things work.

BIBLIOGRAPHY

I recommend the following sites, books, and articles that relate to the mechanics of supply chain theft. The list is eclectic, limited only by space.

Trade Associations

National Retail Federation Retail Theft Report
www.nrf.com/modules.php?name=News&op=viewlive&sp_id=522
American Trucking Association Loss Prevention Division
www.ata.org
The Global Retail Theft Barometer
www.retailresearch.org
Securing Pharma
www.securingpharma.com/40/articles/157.php

Governmental Web Sites

U.S. Department of Justice
www.usdoj.gov/ndic/pubs11/12620/pharma.htm
U.S. Drug Enforcement Agency
www.deaauctions.com/police_seized_property_auctions.htm
www.ustreas.gov/usss/counterfeit.shtml
Organisation for Economic Co-operation and Development
www.oecd.org/dataoecd/11/11/2090589.pdf
Interpol
www.interpol.int/public/financialcrime/intellectualproperty/default.aspe

Recent Articles and Reports

Bill Anderson, "Securing the Supply Chain: Prevent Cargo Theft." *Security Magazine*, May 1, 2007.
David Closs, Cheri Speier, Judith Whipple, and M. Douglas Voss, "Supply Chain Security: A Framework for Protecting Your Supply Chain." *Logistics Management*, September 1, 2008.
Jonathan Katz. "The Great Supply Chain Robbery." *Industry Week*, November 1, 2007.
Kroll Associates. Global Fraud Report. www.kroll.com/about/library/fraud/.
Robery McMillian. "Data Sharing Fight against Organized Retail Theft." *CIO Magazine Online*, January 10, 2009. www.cio.com/article/120705/Data_Sharing_Boosts_Fight_Against_Organized_Retail_Theft.
Charles Montaldo. "Organized Retail Crime on the Rise." June 11, 2009 [blog post]. http://crime.about.com/b/2009/06/11/organized-retail-crime-on-the-rise.htm.
Darren Parker. "Supply-Chain Theft on the Rise." *Engineering New Online*, January 30, 2009. www.engineeringnews.co.za/article/supplychain-fraud-on-the-increase-2009-01-30.
"Retail Theft Costs Industry, Consumers." *Apparel Magazine*, February 2, 2009. www.apparelmag.com/ME2/dirmod.asp?sid=&nm=&type=MultiPublishing&mod=PublishingTitles&mid=CD746117C0BB4828857A1831CE707DBE&tier=4&id=2C99A1012EA44FE18248A54998ACB291.

Books

John Fay. *Contemporary Security Management* (New York: Butterworth-Heinemann, 2005).
Robert D. McCrie. *Security Operations Management* (New York: Butterworth-Heinemann, 2006).
Philip Pupura. *Security and Loss Prevention*. (New York: Butterworth-Henemann, 2007).
Andrew R. Thomas. *Aviation Security Management: 3 Volumes* (Westport: Praeger Security International, 2008).

Legislation

"Carmack Amendment." Organized Retail Theft law, Chapter 277, Laws of 2006. www.csg.org/policy/pubsafety/documents/4OrganizedRetailTheft.pdf
The e-Fencing Enforcement Act. www.securitydirectornews.com/?p=article&id=sd200906FfECG2.

CHAPTER 2

Supply Chain Security and International Terrorism

John Harrison

> Amateurs study tactics; professionals study strategy.
> —General Omar Bradley

Terrorists and those who are tasked to prevent their operations share a common emphasis on tactics. Both sides fail to fully understand the importance of logistics—particularly of terrorist logistics, although that is beyond the scope of this chapter. Victory in war is often more dependent on the ability to deliver supplies efficiently. The modern globalized economy is no exception. The dependence of the international economy on a just-in-time delivery system allows the reduction in costly overhead common when large-scale warehousing was the norm. Given the weakness in the global economy and al-Qaeda's explicit strategy (called Bleed Business), the threats faced by the global supply chain and the wider economy appear to be greatly increased. However, outside conflict zones such as the Afghanistan–Pakistan border region and parts of India, little terrorist attention has been given to this critical economic activity. This chapter will attempt to address the reasons this is the case. However, it should be noted that although there is great concern around issues related to maritime piracy, particularly in the Gulf of Aden and the wider Indian Ocean, the chapter will not focus on that issue. Criminal activity, of which piracy is a dramatic example, is undoubtedly a threat. But the apolitical nature of the activity places it beyond the concerns of this paper.

ELEMENTS OF THE SUPPLY CHAIN

The complex network that constitutes the supply chain covers of the movement, assembly, distribution, and storage of people, goods, and services, and employs more than 4 million in the United States alone.[1] The broad definition could be taken to include public utilities, energy distribution, as well as cyber-networks. The focus of the chapter will be the transportation aspects—land, sea, and air—and the relevant infrastructure of the supply chain.

Land Transportation

This is by far the largest and most critical component of the supply chain, as well as the most vulnerable. Rail and road traffic and their supporting infrastructure stretch across thousands of miles of defined routes. While the vast majority of this system transits sparsely populated areas, critical dense networks are vital to urban existence. Many of the world's urban areas are dependent on bridges, tunnels, and rail and highway connections to their surrounding suburbs and hinterlands. The wide range of delivery vehicles traversing our cities is so common that they go unnoticed, making them perfect platforms for delivering nefarious packages to unsuspecting targets.

Maritime Transportation

The most important element of international trade is the maritime trade. Commodities such as energy, food, precious metals, and consumer goods travel the world's oceans daily. The large volume carried by ships and their cost-effectiveness make this mode of transportation highly desirable. The economic importance and the opaque nature of the maritime system would seem to make the system highly vulnerable to criminal and terrorist activity, yet while criminals routinely use shipping to smuggle goods and people, terrorist interference is rare.

Aviation Transportation

The age of modern international terrorism began on July 23, 1968, with the hijacking of an El Al Boeing 707 from Rome. It could be argued that one of the earliest events of global jihadi terrorism was the 1994 hijacking of an Air France Flight with the intention of using it in a suicide attack against Paris. The most dramatic terrorist attack in history was the aviation attack conducted by al-Qaeda on September 11, 2001. Thus civil aviation is intimately involved in the trajectory that has metamorphosed some of the traditional groups with specific and identifiable objectives—liberation from occupation, demand for separate homeland—to transnational groups with almost zero-sum objectives. One can trace the development of terrorism as a phenomenon and its tactical development through studying the interaction of terrorist groups with elements of the aviation, and more widely the international supply chain. Even as terrorism moves through its organizational evolution from highly structured organizations to the self-generated and -operationalized cells such as those that planned the 7/7 attack in the UK, the plot against JFK International Airport in New York, or the liquid plot originating in the UK, their focus remains on aviation.

The land transportation element of the supply chain is the most vulnerable to criminal and terrorist exploitation. The aviation sector has been involved for years in transborder criminality, including terrorism. Transnational criminal organizations use the aviation system to transport contraband—and, increasingly, people—across the globe. Cocaine smugglers used the FedEx air delivery system to transport their products across the United States; narcotics smugglers from Guyana used U.S. Mail pouches to smuggle millions of dollars of cocaine into the Unites States, which passed through JFK airport. Organized gangs of human smugglers use the aviation system to move people into North America and Europe as a matter of routine. Kenyans desperate to flee their home country have been found stowed away in the wheel wells of British Airways flights, arriving frozen to death at Heathrow.

This chapter will attempt to provide an evaluation of the operational environment that the logistics industry faces from crime and terrorism. The chapter will also examine the traditional responses to crime and terrorism. The argument of the chapter is that security education is reactive and lacking in a comprehensive approach targeted at addressing the current and evolving threat and risk environment. The chapter also argues that security education is capable of creating a professional cadre of motivated line staff and management.

THREAT VS. RISK

One of the ironic issues facing the logistics sector is that while the industry is advanced in evaluation of economic risks in its decision-making, and in taking the necessary steps to manage that risk, it is still focused on responding to security threats and appears to have great difficulty in developing and articulating a response. In most of the world, the service providers—with the exception of aviation—remain responsible for security. If criminals and terrorists, despite such measures, manage to carry out their activities, the industry bears the direct and indirect costs of both implementing security measures and the failures.

The suggestion here is that instead of looking at the threat, there needs to be a better system to evaluate and respond to risk. The first element in this approach is understanding what threat means. Threat is an exploitable vulnerability. When one examines the range of potential targets the modern supply chain offers to a perspective criminal and terrorist, the threat appears enormous and unmanageable. Theft and forgery of travel and shipping documents, smuggling of goods and people, attacks against land, sea, and air, and equipment theft are just a few examples of weaknesses and potential gaps that terrorists can exploit. And, as the IRA famously stated to British authorities, "We only have to be lucky once—you have to be lucky all the time." How does a society protect *everything* it values? What is needed is a shift from responding to the threat to examining the situation from a risk perspective.

There are many ways of examining risk, but the two critical elements include the examining of the probability of a given vulnerability being exploited and the consequences of that exploitation. This simple process helps to order the environment and allows limited resources to be deployed optimally. One can further refine this model by applying the threat structure to terrorist groups. Evaluating the threat posed by any given group rests on knowledge in three areas: (1) the intentions a given group has, (2) the group's capabilities to act on those intentions, and (3) the operational environment it faces. This additional step is critical to assessing the threat and risk environment. Without it, the security community will remain focused on the potential threat and will never grasp the actual threat and its accompanying risk. While the primary focus of security-related information has been on the users of the aviation system, there needs to be more awareness on those working within the system. The terrorist plot against JFK Airport, as well as the April 2004 arrest of twenty-five cargo and baggage handlers working for a Guyana-based cocaine smuggling ring,[2] illustrate that the threat comes from within as well as from outside. One critical element of security is the ability to conduct rapid and ongoing security checks on staff in all aspects of the supply chain. This is a necessary first step in protecting the system is currently being blocked by labor interests. It would seem that a reasonable compromise can be reached that both protects the employees and users of the system.

Critically, this is one area where industry is leading the government. The transportation industry has long understood the aforementioned model and most of the security courses offered to the industry, both pre- and post-9/11, have components of evaluating threat and risk.

TERRORIST TARGETING

Given the above, the most important question facing the supply chain is why it has not been a terrorist target for the last three decades. Terrorists are always looking for ways to inflict damage on their opponents far beyond the cost to themselves. Interfering with the supply chain seems to permit this, and yet it has not happened. The reasons terrorists choose a target are multiple and roughly classifiable as

1. Transportation can provide a powerful symbolic target.
2. It provides a unique multinational stage.
3. It offers unrivaled media exposure.
4. Operations against it are relatively simple.
5. It has enormous economic consequences for both the carrier and the targeted nation.
6. It can create political embarrassment for the intended targets.
7. It is a useful tool for revenge.
8. It is effective.

Reason 1. One of the most powerful stand-ins for a state is its national carrier, or what is perceived as a national carrier. For example, El Al (Israel's state-owned national carrier) is not just an airline, but also a demonstration that the state of Israel exists. Terrorist violence, at its root, is symbolic; until the last decade targets were selected not for the actual damage that could be inflicted, but for the message the attack sent. Terrorist hijacking or sabotage, even if not entirely successful, underscores the state's inability to keep its citizens secure. Air France, Egypt Air, Kuwaiti Air, Air Canada, and Swiss Air are just a few of the state-owned carriers that have been similarly objectified. Likewise, private carriers are vulnerable to this type of action: for the terrorist, they serve as a nation's proxy. Some of their names illustrate this point: Japan Airlines, British Air, American Airlines, and even Trans World Airlines (TWA) have all been all targets—not because of any particular business decision they have made, but because they carry the name and flag of the nation they serve. In the last decade, the desire of groups such as al-Qaeda to inflict massive loss of life, as well as to have a cascading effect on the larger economy of the target state, have magnified the threat to international civil aviation. Land and maritime transportation does not offer the same impact and is thus rarely used.

Reason 2. The multinational stage offered by international transportation yields particular benefits for terrorists in enlarging the bull's eye. The 1985 Hezbollah hijacking of TWA Flight 847 en route from Athens to Rome is representative of this. Israeli, American, Greek, and German passengers were on board. The terrorists were attempting to pressure Israel to release the 700-plus members of Hezbollah being held captive. They had assumed there would be Americans and Israelis, but the Greeks and Germans provided added leverage against the Israeli government. Another example is the so-called Dawson's Field hijacking in 1970, discussed below, which was designed to bring as many nations as possible into the crisis. A similar argument could be made for the maritime environment, where crews are from a wide range of countries.

Reason 3. As Brian Jenkins famously said, "Terrorists want a lot of people watching, not a lot of people dead." International civil aviation provides the window for the actualization of the desire for their "fifteen minutes of fame." Hijackings are the most "media-friendly" incidents imaginable, because hijackers hold hostages and provide deadlines that amplify the unfolding drama. During the TWA Flight 847 hijacking, the National Broadcasting Company, (NBC), one of the three major U.S. television networks, dedicated two-thirds of its half-hour nightly news broadcast to it.[3] *The New York Times*, *Washington Post*, and *Los Angeles Times* ran a combined 629 stories on the almost three-week hijacking.[4] But terrorists do not always handle the news media deftly. One press conference during the hijacking was canceled because of the media "near-riot" during what was supposed to have been a carefully staged event.[5] Aircraft sabotage has had similar coverage, where the media interviewed the grieving relatives rather than the hostages.

The December 1988 Lockerbie disaster was accorded saturation coverage. Few will forget the wrenching images of Susan Cohen being met at John F. Kennedy International Airport by a phalanx of media personnel as she collapsed, crying, "Not my baby." Although no terrorist group ever claimed responsibility,[6] the message was stark: another aircraft had been destroyed to achieve a political purpose, and during the immediate aftermath, this elevated various Middle East conflicts into major news stories.

Maritime and land transportation offers similar potential. An example is the hijacking of the "milk train" in the Netherlands in December of 1975.[7]

Reason 4. For all the devastation wrought by and media attention given to interference with transportation, it can be accomplished with a rather simple operation. A hijacking does not require special training or substantial personnel; most use two to four persons armed with easily obtained small arms and explosives. Fewer than twenty people were able to launch a coordinated attack against seven targets in the Mumbai rail infrastructure in 2006. Two dozen were involved in the Madrid bombings of March 11, 2004, that killed 191 and brought down the Spanish government.

Aviation is even easier. A small cell can control a multimillion-dollar aircraft, several hundred lives, and the agendas of governments and the media because it is in possession of the aircraft. Two young men hijacked TWA Flight 847.

Sabotaging an aircraft requires, at minimum, one person who can fashion the device but does not require that perpetrators board the plane before takeoff. The Lockerbie bombing was committed by two Libyan government intelligence agents; the November 1987 destruction of Korean Airlines (KAL) 858 was committed by two North Korean intelligence agents. Even the 9/11 multiple hijackings involved only twenty terrorists, about five per aircraft. None of these operations strained the disaffected organizations, yet all achieved major gains.

Reason 5. Terrorists want to make an economic impact on the target. The Popular Front for the Liberation of Palestine (PFLP) sought to undermine the Israeli economy so that Israel could not afford the cost of its security services. Although damage to the Greek economy was not the purpose of the TWA Flight 847 hijacking in June 1985 or the TWA Flight 840 bombing in April 1986, the Greek economy suffered a major downturn. The downturn occurred when, after the two incidents, the Reagan administration announced that the Greek government was failing to meet its international security obligations and advised travelers to avoid Greece. This naming and shaming by the United States cost the Greek economy more than $400 million.[8]

Al-Qaeda adopted the approach when it attacked the oil tanker MV *Lumberg* of the coast of Aden in 2002. The tanker lost some 90,000 gallons of oil and increased the price by $0.48 per barrel.[9]

Reason 6. Attacks on international civil aviation embarrass opponents. This is one reason that the armed forces of the Colombian Revolution (known by its Spanish acronym, FARC) began aviation hijackings in the late 1990s.[10]

And the Liberation Tigers of the Tamil Eelam (LTTE), the Sri Lankan terrorist group, attacked the Colombo International Airport in 2000 to put pressure on the Sri Lankan government to negotiate. The government had declared the airport one of the nation's most secure facilities, but the LTTE team infiltrated the perimeter easily and launched an attack that destroyed one-quarter of the Sri Lankan Air Force fixed-wing fleet and one-third of Air Lankan aircraft.[11] The message here was the same: an embarrassingly ineffective government.

Terrorists also use attacks to embarrass other factions in the struggle in order to gain predominance within the larger movement. A classic illustration of this is the Abu Nidal Organization's (ABO, named for its leader) December 1985 attacks against airports in Rome and Vienna. Abu Nidal wanted to derail the movement toward peace that was growing between the mainstream Palestine Liberation Organization (PLO) and Israel. The Italian and Austrian governments supported the PLO and the emerging peace.[12] The December 27, 1985, raids killed eighteen people and achieved what Abu Nidal had hoped: the peace process became moribund and remained so for many years.[13]

Reason 7. Terrorists employ attacks as a retaliatory measure for perceived slights or interference in sensitive policy matters. The 7/7 bombers wanted to punish the UK public for a range of injustices against the Muslim community. The GIA attacks on the Paris Metro system in 1994 was a response to the French involvement in the Algerian Civil War, and the plot against the New York Subway system, as well as the bridges and tunnels serving the system, had the same motivation.

Libya presents the classic example of this tactic. The state intelligence service is believed to have been behind the bombing of TWA 840 in retaliation for the U.S. raid on its compound earlier that same month. Still after revenge, Libyan agents placed a bomb on Pan Am 103 on December 21, 1988, killing all 259 people on board and 11 people in Lockerbie, Scotland—deaths that provided unintended revenge for the UK's having supported the earlier U.S. raid. Some observers believe that Iran was behind the bombing because of the accidental shooting down of an Iranian civil jetliner by the United States on July 3, 1988, killing all 290 people on board. Iran had announced that it would retaliate, and it appears to have done so five months later.

Irrespective of one's position on the actors involved in the attack on Pan Am 103, revenge was clearly the motivation. Libya, and perhaps Syria, struck again in September 1989, when agents destroyed an aircraft of the French carrier UTA Flight 772 over the Niger desert, sending the 170 on board to their deaths. The Libyan motivation was the French interference in Libyan interests in Chad during the early 1980s; the Syrian motivation was French involvement with anti-Syrian forces in Lebanon. Neither Libya nor Syria claimed responsibility for that attack, but the French courts eventually convicted Libyan intelligence agents for the bombing and exposed a possible Syrian connection.[14]

Reason 8. The terrorist targeting of transportation began and continues because it is effective, although not in the original strategic capacity for which it was developed. The PFLP tried to use attacks on civil aviation to undermine Israel's economy, and al-Qaeda is attempting the same strategy by attacking American aviation both domestically and internationally. While the strategic use of international civil aviation attacks has failed up to this point, the tactical use of aviation as a weapon has achieved notable success. Terrorists hijack aircraft to gain media exposure (as was the case with TWA 847). They use the lives of innocent civilians as bargaining chips for the release of comrades (TWA 847 or the October 29, 1972, hijacking of a Lufthansa flight by Black September that led to the release of the three surviving members of the Munich Olympic Games Massacre).[15] Their actions can be used to reveal a government's shortcomings vis-à-vis opponents, as with the FARC or LTTE, or to bring about change in government policy, as Pablo Escobar intended when he bombed a Colombia Airlines (AVIANCA) flight that was supposed to be carrying a presidential candidate advocating a strong position against the Escobar-led Medellin cartel.[16]

Terrorists can also gain influence by threatening actions against international civil aviation. Many experts believe that some terrorists and some states make mutual noninterference agreements that free each party to function independently and safely. Terrorists may extort money from the carrier or carriers of a nation in exchange for a hands-off stance. These are understandably controversial subjects that cannot sustain the light of investigation; hence, little is publicly available to corroborate the above beliefs. Even so, they are probably accurate. It is this latter extortion effort that is the primary motivation for the attacks against the Supper Ferry 14, as well as the attacks against the bus transportation system in the Philippines.

The above illustrates the reasons for attacking the logistics system. What is clear is that international civil aviation is the critical node for terrorists in the supply chain. However, it is passenger and not cargo aviation that serves as the primary target. Terrorist groups have desired to disrupt the economy of a state; al-Qaeda has a specific strategy for this, but while the intention is obvious, the capabilities remain limited. This is primarily due to the lack of attention given to the disruption of the supply chain by the general public. With the exception of oil, the public pays little notice to delays in the supply chain irrespective of the reason.

THREAT BY TRANSPORTATION SEGMENT

The above discussion raises the question of what are then the actual threats to the supply chain? Given the size and complexity of the system, there is no simple answer. The three categories, land, sea, and air, will each be addressed in this section.

From the terrorist perspective, land transportation offers a large and relatively well understood operational environment. Between 1968 and 2007 there were approximately 24,000 terrorist incidents, of which 1,267 were against land mass transit.[17] With the exception of war zones such as Iraq and Afghanistan, the targets were heavily against passengers.[18]

The above does not appear to apply to the landside of the maritime or aviation sector. There have been no notable attacks against ports, and only four notable attacks have taken place against landside aviation: the Japanese Red Army Attack on Lod Airport in 1972, the Abu Nidal attack on airports in Rome and Vienna in 1985, the Tamil Tigers attack on Colombo Airport in 2001, and the Glasgow attack in July 2007. One can argue that the more traditional terrorist organizations, such as those mentioned above, wanted to limit causalities and retain a moral legitimacy, whereas targeting large numbers of innocent passengers would undermine both objectives. New terrorist groups have none of these limitations, so it remains unclear as to why this has not yet occurred. Criminal activity is more common on the landside. This includes smuggling, theft, and other activities directly related to maritime and aviation operations, but also ancillary items such as identity theft from travel documents or airport-based hotels. This issue becomes more pressing as the industry moves to wireless travel, as envisioned by some Japanese airports.

Access control is a critical to landside areas is a critical issue for security. This not only includes both access to secure and secured areas (used to describe land, sea, and air) but includes the perimeter fencing as well. There are many countries where basic security is lacking or in poor repair, allowing for easy penetration for unauthorized persons to gain access to rail yards, ports, and aircraft as stowaways. While there is currently no evidence to suggest that terrorists are exploiting this weakness, the possibility exists. Although the current high-tech solutions offered by biometrics and other technology are encouraging, the best way to protect the supply chain is also the weakest. The need for trained and motivated staff that are encouraged and supported in their efforts to protect civil aviation is the most vital component. All the profiling and scanning equipment in the world will not stop a determined attacker if security forces are inattentive or corrupt. This is exactly what occurred in the suicide bombings targeting Russian aviation in August 2004. Thus, while the threat is potentially high, the risk posed by terrorist attacks on the landside remains, with minor exceptions, quite low. The criminal threat is higher, but risk is low, as the impact of criminal interference with landside transportation is marginal.

THREATS TO RAIL TRANSPORTATION

Rail transportation is a major component for much of the supply chain. The efficiency and ability to move oversized goods without disrupting other road transportation is critical. But, with the exception of passenger service, there has been little evidence that cargo rail transportation is a target. Since 1972, there have been a total of 498 attacks on rail and its related infrastructure (see Table 2.1).

As early as 1939, the IRA targeted the London Underground to disrupt passenger service, and continued to do so during the next sixty years. France, Spain, and the Netherlands have all experienced attacks on their mass transit systems. Globally, between 1972 and 2009, there have been a total of 498 attacks against rail transportation. Prior to 1998, the number of attacks per annum never exceeded six.[19] Since 1998, however, the number of attacks has averaged 36 per annum, never falling below fifteen in any year and thus far reaching a peak of eighty-seven in 2006.[20] There have been ninety-seven in Europe, and the worst terrorist attack in Europe prior to Lockerbie was the right-wing attack on the Bologna Railroad station in 1980, which killed eighty-five people.[21]

Attacks on rail outside Europe are more common. Tourist rail in Peru was disrupted by the Shinning Path and its remnants. Rail in Southern Thailand is frequently disrupted and suspended due to the insurgency in the region. The most persistent threat to rail traffic is found in South and Central Asia, with a total of 245 attacks occurring.[22] The majority have taken place in India, where a variety of groups from the so-called jihadi groups to the ethnonationalists groups in the Northeast of India have attacked or are currently attacking Indian Rail. The attacks are understandable, for much of India rail remains the primary means of transportation, particularly in rural areas.

Table 2.1
Breakdown of Attacks on Rail Transportation by Region*

Region	Number of Attacks
South East Asia	29
South and Central Asia	245
East Asia	2
Oceania	0
Middle East and North Africa	44
Sub-Saharan Africa	9
Europe	97
Commonwealth of Independent States	47
North America	5
South America	20
Total Number of Attacks	**498**

*ICPVTR Mass Transit Land Attack Project from MIPT database had data provided until 2007; Brigitte Nacos, et al., "Terrorism and the Print Media: The 1985 TWA Hostage Crisis," *Terrorism an International Journal* 12, 109.

It is critical to note that while attacks on mass transit, and particularly rail, are increasing, the targets are not freight, but passengers. For terrorists, a lightly defended, confined, densely populated environment offers a high-impact, low-cost spectacle. The visual impact of an attack on a freight train, let alone the minimal economic impact, tends to lower the threat and risk equation. The obvious caveat is an attack on a train carrying dangerous chemicals that if released could devastate an immediate locale or an entire community. Thus the focus of the response community should be focused less on security of the infrastructure and more on increasing the strength and safety measures on freight cars that carry chemicals and other risky items.

THREATS TO THE MARITIME SYSTEM

Piracy has become a topic of major concern over the last several years, first focusing on the Straights of Malacca and now on the costal waters of Somalia and, increasingly, beyond. While the events of the MV *Maersk Alabama*, including the dramatic rescue, attracted the attention of the United States, none of the pirate attacks are terrorist, or even political. One could argue that the rapid increase in piracy is linked to the inability of any authority in Somalia to enforce fishing and environmental regulations; there is no evidence of any link to terrorism. Since 1968, there have been a total of 162 maritime incidents that can be linked to terrorism. From these, only five groups—Hezbollah, Anti-Castro, Contras, PLASIRO, and the LTTE—can be linked to more than one incident,[23] and of these, Hezbollah and the LTTE are the only groups active today.[24] Al-Qaeda is very interested in attacks in this domain and has conducted operations against the USS *Cole* and the *Limburg*. Additionally, al-Qaeda and its acolytes have explored using divers to attack ships in harbor, but to date there has been little public activity. The diminished capacity of al-Qaeda, as well as the international attention to improved maritime security, has contributed to a limited threat.

THE TACTICAL ENVIRONMENT

Four terrorist tactics have been actualized against international civil aviation over the past three decades: hijackings, sabotage, shooting down aircraft, and assaults on airports and related ground facilities. Each has led to a response by the international civil aviation regime.

The most common terrorist tactic is hijacking, in which at least one person (and usually between two and five people) takes control of an aircraft in flight by brandishing real or supposedly real weapons. Hijackers have a political agenda and—at least prior to the early 1990s—wanted to survive the action. People were killed during some hijackings, and U.S. Navy diver Robert Stethem was murdered by the hijackers of TWA Flight 847, but a captive has greater chances of being killed in a rescue mission. On November 23, 1985, one such instance occurred during a rescue mission conducted by Egyptian commandos to rescue the ninety-eight hostages (including four security personnel) on Egypt Air Flight 648. The Cairo-scheduled Athens flight was diverted to Malta. The Elite Group 777 of Egyptian commandos were sent in to conduct this complex and dangerous rescue. A U.S. Army Delta Force operator was sent in to observe and support the commandos whom he had trained. The American-trained commandos had been replaced by an untrained group that was considered more politically reliable,[25] a decision that contributed to the death of sixty-eight of the people on the aircraft.

Terrorists' next most common tactic is the use of explosives against civil aviation, a tactic that "came of age" in connection with bombings during the post-1968 period.[26] Between 1949 and 2008, terrorists perpetrated eighty-nine of ninety-six sabotage bombings.[27] Nonstate groups were predominant in the cohort, but three of the most notorious attacks were carried out by states. In 1987, North Korean intelligence agents placed a bomb aboard KAL Flight 858, killing all 115 passengers and crew. Libya conducted two attacks: the December 1988 bombing over Lockerbie caused a total of 270 deaths, and the September 1989 attack over the Niger desert on UTA Flight 772 killed all 184 on board.

Political protest and retaliation seem to be the most common motivation for these kinds of attacks. Libya was protesting the dealings of the United States and France with itself; North Korea was protesting the awarding of the 1988 Olympic games to South Korea. Nonstate terrorists also make retaliatory use of explosives, as in the June 1985 destruction of Air India Flight 182 off the Irish coast by Sikh extremists attempting to avenge the Indian government's 1984 raid on the Golden Temple (this holiest Sikh shrine was occupied by heavily armed terrorists whose cause was an independent homeland for the Sikh faithful; upward of a thousand people, mainly Sikhs, were killed by the Indian government in the raid).

One of the more worrying developments over the last decade and a half has been the maturation of liquid explosives. The use of these explosives by terrorists was first introduced by Ramzi Yousef as part of his Bojinka Plot in 1995. Al-Qaeda linked terrorists would return to the use of liquids in August 2006 when authorities in the United Kingdom disrupted a plot to bomb as many as ten jetliners operated by United, American, and Air Canada, operating between London Heathrow and North America. Eight men—Abdulla Ahmed Ali, Assad Sarwar, Tanvir Hussain, Ibrahim Savant, Arafat Waheed Khan, Waheed Zaman, Umar Islam, and Mohammed Gulzar—were charged in the plot.[28] A UK court found Abdulla Ahmed Ali, Assad Sarwar, and Tanvir Hussain guilty of conspiracy to commit murder; the three had already plead guilty to the crime of manufacturing explosives.[29]

On March 7, 2008, the East Turkistan Islamic Movement (ETMI), a Urghur Turkic Muslim group fighting in China's western Xinjiang province, attempted to bring down China Southern Airlines flight CZ 6901 using an incendiary device.[30] The female bomber had soda cans filled with gasoline.[31]

Terrorists have found the use of explosives against carriers to be an effective way to make their political points. They are able to call attention to their grievances without risking their lives. Very small numbers of people—sometimes as few as two—have a limited likelihood of being stopped in the attempt or captured later. (Only 17 percent of attempts are halted prior the bomb's introduction into the aircraft).[32] Even when the accused bomber is identified, it can take years to bring him or her to justice.[33]

Legal and technical tools are already in place to prevent the introduction of explosives into an aircraft, but they are frequently ignored. The 1985 Air India bombing occurred because Air Canada ground staff allowed a bag with no confirmed seat holder to be checked through to its final destination.[34] It appears that a clerical error in Malta opened the door for a bomb to enter the aviation system and ultimately end up on Pan Am 103.[35] Pan Am was supposed to hand-check all interline transfer bags rather than use an X-ray machine. Its failure to follow FAA regulations very likely contributed to the subsequent destruction of the aircraft.

The bombings of KAL Flight 858 and Philippines Airlines Flight 434 could have been prevented had personnel been alert to the empty seats of passengers who failed to reboard the aircraft after a layover.[36] The KAL bombers were almost detected in Baghdad while passing through security. The Iraqi security officer was suspicious of the radio in the carry-on baggage. When asked to remove it, the male North Korean agent raised a ruckus and thereby avoided the search. Available technical countermeasures, such as the thermal neutron accelerator (TNA), are said to be a reliable detector of the presence of explosives, but as long as humans are involved in securing the aviation system, lapses are inevitable. Security could be avoided altogether if a terrorist were to smuggle weapons onboard an aircraft waiting on the taxiway. British Airways (BA) has been concerned about illegal immigrants (primarily Africans leaving Kenya) "hitchhiking" in the wheel wells of its aircraft. They position themselves while the aircraft is waiting to take off, only to freeze to death in flight in the pressurized but unheated wheel wells.[37] It is not beyond imagination that a suicide bomber might adopt the paratactic. The possibility could become reality by virtue of the presence of active al-Qaeda cells in Kenya.

A third tactical tool available to terrorists are the Man-Portable Air Defense System (MANPADS). Before November 2002, the threat of MANPADS in the hands of a terrorist group against a civil jet was only a spot on a distant horizon. Even the innovators, al-Qaeda, attempted then to bring down an Israeli airliner departing from Mombasa, Kenya, using a MANPADS in November of that year. It was a Soviet-manufactured SA-7 and, depending on the model, had entered service in 1967 (SA-7A) or 1972 (SA-7B). It had a range of 14,000–16,000 feet and an operational altitude of 9,000–14,000 feet.[38] The Soviets exported more than 100,000 of the SA-7s and the later-model SA-14. Many were supplied to Somalia, where, since the collapse of the government in the early 1990s, they are easily available to the militias that now control the country—where al-Qaeda has connections.[39]

The United States exported 9,000 of the highly capable Stinger MANPADS to the Afghan rebels during their war against the Soviet Union, and despite U.S. efforts to buy them back, not all were returned. Some may be in al-Qaeda's arsenal even today. It is unclear how well maintained the missiles used in the Mombasa assault were, but they were used to engage the target from the side and not from the tail (their proper method of use), rendering them ineffective.[40] A terrorist organization need not actually use a missile, but merely threaten to do so, in order to create potential havoc—witness the threat directed at London's Heathrow Airport in February 2003. The availability and dispersion of these weapons (at least twenty-seven terrorist and insurgent groups have access to MANPADS), makes them dangerous. DHL discovered how dangerous they were when on November 23, 2003, one of their aircraft was attacked with a MANPADS while departing Baghdad in Iraq. The three-man crew survived due to their incredible skill. Even with these two examples it is difficult to determine how many MANPADs have been used against international civil aviation.

The rush to mitigate this undeniable threat has obscured the actual threat. There are some who have rushed to adapt and deploy systems from the military to protect civilian aircraft from attack. The fact that over the last thirty years there have been thirty attempts to shoot down civilian aircraft, with twenty-four successes, causing 500 deaths, starkly illustrates the threat.[41] These numbers are not clear, however, and even if they are accurate, why has this longstanding threat not yet impacted international civil aviation? Some argue that the low probability of a missile attack—because of the difficulty of effective operation[42] and maintenance—does not justify the expense of installing defensive systems, but others argue the opposite.[43] The disputed nature of the threat should not be taken as an excuse for doing nothing. Placing monetary value on human life is a problematic undertaking, but the civil aviation industry has to account for its security expenditures based on the probability of potential threats. Unless a nation is willing to underwrite the costs, the costs are prohibitive for the industry.[44] Depending on many variables, $20 billion is not an excessive estimate. But if terrorists increase this activity, the equation will undergo revision.

The fourth terrorist tactic exercised against civil aviation has to do with ground facilities and can take two forms: terrorist attacks and insurgent attacks. The former specifically targets noncombatants at the airport and other ground facilities, whereas the latter targets military or government operations.

The first major attack against an airport terminal in many decades occurred on June 30, 2007, when two men, Kafeel Ahmed and Bilal Abdullah, drove their Jeep Cherokee into the terminal budding at Glasgow International Airport, killing Ahmed and injuring five others. This was part of a wider plot that included two failed car bombs meant to detonate in London on June 29, 2007, and is linked to al-Qaeda in Mesopotamia (Iraq).[45] Bilal Abdullah still awaits trial as of fall 2008.[46]

Attacks by the Japanese Red Army (JRA), the Abu Nidal Organization (ANO), and the IRA are examples of terrorist attacks. The JRA attacked Israel's Lod Airport in 1972, killing twenty-seven (including six Puerto Rican pilgrims) and wounding seventy-six. JRA members working for the PLFP had smuggled weapons in their hold luggage and then later fired on passengers who were retrieving luggage. The incident at Lod was an attempt to undermine Israel's tourist economy. The ANO's most infamous attacks were on the Rome and Vienna airports in December 1985 (previously discussed). The IRA fired mortars at London's Heathrow Airport's runways in two March 1994 attacks. The mortars failed to explode, but each disrupted operations at the world's busiest international airport. The attack on Glasgow airport would appear to have been the first vehicleborne improvised explosive device used against a terminal. The bombers were the only causalities in the attack. Although suicide-bombing inside crowded terminals has not occurred, the impact of a suicide bomber attacking Chicago O'Hare International Airport on a busy Friday, or on the Sunday after the Thanksgiving holiday in the United States, the busiest travel day of the year, is almost beyond imagination. The devastation wrought by a bus full of explosives or a small, coordinated suicide attack would bring the international civil aviation system to its knees and leave a nation substantially altered. Terrorists, chief among them al-Qaeda, are acutely aware of this.

Insurgents have targeted civil aviation throughout the developing world, primarily to assist in the isolation of sections of the population from government control. Guerrillas are attempting to develop both political and physical space to operate. Many developing regions lack sufficient roads to link hinterlands to the metropolis. And where roads do exist, they are frequently ambush sites. Governments are forced to rely on air transport to reach outlying areas that render airstrips primary targets.[47] Maoist insurgents in Nepal began to lay siege to remote airstrips in their struggle against the government in 2002[48] in an attempt to isolate the communities from the government.

Another Asian conflict provides the best example of targeting civil aviation's infrastructure: the LTTE assault on the Colombo airport in 2001. A team of LTTE suicide "commandos" infiltrated the Sri Lankan government's self-declared most secure facility and destroyed most of the Sri Lankan air force on the ground as well as several civil aircraft belonging to the state carrier Air Lanka.[49] The infiltrators were detected at least twice: first when perimeter security personnel discovered bags of discarded Sri Lankan security uniforms close to a breached perimeter fence but failed to notify anyone, and second when control tower personnel caught sight of armed men in the area between two runways but they assumed that the men were participating in a security drill and did not notify anyone. The LTTE's immediate military agenda was to destroy the air force aircraft on the ground, but its primary agenda was political. If the LTTE could infiltrate the facility undetected—at least that's what the commandos thought—how could the government protect any other location, let alone defeat the LTTE militarily? The LTTE scored a second unanticipated propaganda coup as well: just as the attack began, a planeload of UK tourists arrived from Mauritius. None were hurt, and all used their camcorders and provided incredible on-the-scene-footage to the BBC. This attack seems to have had the desired political impact, in light of the 2002 ceasefire.[50]

THE THREAT AND RISK TO THE SUPPLY CHAIN

The ultimate question remains what the threats and risks to the supply chain are. Thankfully, the question is that there is a low-to-medium threat and, at least for the short-term, a medium risk. The elements required for an attack to occur are intentions, capabilities, and opportunity. Some groups, such as the PLFP and al-Qaeda, have the intention to disrupt the supply chain. But no group appears to have the capabilities, and given the security and sheer size, no group seems to have the opportunity to achieve more than a short-term marginal disruption of the supply chain.

Recall that terrorists are at their core conservative goal seeking maximizers: they do what they do because they know it works. They are willing to risk a failed operation if they understand the potential consequences and are reasonably assured of success. Terrorists groups, including al-Qaeda, have limited resources and will attempt to conduct an attack that will reverberate beyond the victims of an attack. Thus, they seek targets with symbolic value. The supply chain does not provide this necessary element in the brutal calculus of political violence.

RECOMMENDATIONS

Even given the low threat and risk level, the issues described above need to be addressed at three levels: strategic, operational, and tactical. The strategic level involves the battle space of ideas. In general terms, we are not even engaged in this issue in any serious or sustained manner. While the international aviation system cannot be—nor should it be—involved in this directly, it can and must understand what the change in terrorism has meant and how it will impact its operations.

- A sustained research effort must be made by the industry to understand the trends in transnational threats and how they will impact its operations.
- The industry must invest in nontechnical research in order to support technical security efforts.

The above social science research is essential both to help understand terrorism and to counter the threat and mitigate the risk posed by terrorists. The enormous lead time and expenditure required to develop and deploy technology often means that it is redundant due to shifts in terrorist tactics.

By engaging with the existing threat research infrastructure, this continuing problem can be avoided.

This is most appropriate for senior managers. They need to be able to think about the trends across their industry, a skill they have developed quiet well in the business sense. But they need to apply this skill in wider areas of society that will impact the industry—something they do not do as well, if at all. They need to understand the strengths and limitation of the policy community, and vice versa. They can also cooperate to achieve similar goals. Training courses have to be designed to get senior management to think strategically, managing knowledge and understanding where to go for analysis.

The second level of analysis of terrorism is the operational level. This not only refers to both the organized groups, such as al-Qaeda, Hamas, JI, and others, but to also the response to these groups. The response community is doing exceptionally well in this area. Organized groups are finding their operational environment heavily restricted. The aviation environment has had some equal success. A commitment to multilayered approaches such as increase in access control, introduction of air marshals, locked cockpit doors, and programs like CTPAT are positive basic steps. But the international community needs to take a more active role in the critical area of standards and information sharing.

- ICAO/IMO and other UN bodies need to establish basic standards for cargo screening, document security, and other in-flight issues.
- The ICAO/IMO needs to have enforcement power that can and should include economic incentives for meeting required standards and recommended practices.
- The ICAO and IATA should establish a Joint Intelligence and Security Center (JISC)—and the maritime and land transportation sectors should do the same.

The international community is attempting to address the first issue, but powerful domestic forces that hinder these efforts. There are, for example, technology requirements for screening systems that are designed not to enhance security, but to protect domestic manufacturers from competition. This is understandable, but it is not acceptable. ICAO member states can currently opt out of security requirements by simply informing the ICAO that they are doing so, but they are not required to disclose which requirements they are not following, how long they intend to be out of compliance, and whether they have any intentions of regaining their former status. This ability is understandable, as states do not want to publicly disclose their vulnerabilities. Even restricting the information to member states is of limited value, given some of the connections member states have to terrorist groups. The difficulty is that carriers and passengers are not aware of the risk they face, making them thus unable to make informed business and travel decisions.

One way to provide enforcement is to work with the insurance industry to have adjustable rates for carriers and airports that are in various levels of compliance. Those in full compliance could get a reduction in insurance premiums, so long as they spend the savings on security. One can look at funding security through mechanisms such as infrastructure bonds as well.

The best way to defeat an asymmetric opponent is through information-sharing. The international aviation community can provide an example through merging the efforts of the ICAO and IATA by the creation of a Joint Security and Intelligence Center to leverage the laudable security efforts of both organizations through a central repository for the collection of information relating to terrorist and criminal interference with civil aviation. This will allow the industry to have both a tactical and strategic analysis capability addressing industry specific needs. The individuals at this level are the middle management, and they need to have the skills to be security managers—and potentially leaders. Thus, they need to know the elements of their job, but broader security issues as well. Courses should include analysis, introduction to intelligence, threat and risk calculation, terrorist operations, and perhaps a "red-teaming" module. These are all skills designed to help them to see various aspects of their job, understanding the strengths and limitations of intelligence as well as how to think about the field and, more important, how to understand how their opponents are thinking.

The final level of analysis is the tactical level. This is dealing with the increasing threat presented by the self-organized, self-radicalized, and self-operationalized cells, illustrated by the recent plots against the London Underground and JFK Airport. The general record against this threat is mixed. There are far more of these cells, so the threat is greater, but the risk they pose is substantially less, for they are more limited in their access to funding and training, to the extent that their skills are reduced. They are thus more likely to conduct London-, Madrid-, or Mumbai-style operations than they are to replicate 9/11. They still pose a potential threat to aviation, for it is relatively simple to hijack an aircraft—and only a bit more complicated to introduce—an explosive device. As this is the emerging trend, the industry can use the space to address existing weaknesses and develop a coherent proactive strategy to deal with current and emerging threats.

- Develop and implement a more coherent tactical response.
- Require regular and realistic training.
- Assist stakeholders in developing economically viable responses across the system.

The two critical elements in the first recommendation are staff and training. The industry must be involved again in its own security. This may require recruiting and training the proper staff. It also requires all staff in the industry to recognize their role in security and understand that they are empowered to act on their concerns. Staff must understand their operational environment and what aspect can easily be turned into a defensive tool in the event of an incident. For example, if there is an attempt to hijack an aircraft, the cabin crew must recognize that they have a nonlethal weapon readily available to disrupt an attacker—coffee, ideally hot. Ship crews are already using nonlethal weapons against pirates. Martial arts and other self-defense courses are useful, but unless there are going to be regular sessions in the gym, the likelihood of a martial arts approach working is limited. Using coffee or the food cart is much more effective in disruption of an operation.

The above illustrates why training is important. The understanding of how an event will take place and how to respond is not intuitive, but can be learned. It is believed that the first five to seven seconds in a hostage or other type of attack is the most critical. How one responds within that timeframe may determine the outcome for both the individual and all involved.

Any security program must be economically viable. This seems to be common sense, but frequently it is not. As can be illustrated with the debate over the protection against MANPADS or deploying sea marshals, the economic cost is prohibitive when looked at through a threat and risk assessment perspective. Just as important is that any security policy include inputs from the individuals who are going to have to implement them. They are the ones who will have to be able to understand the operational environment and the best and most efficient way to implement a new policy, dealing with the daily consequences of each new initiative.

This is the line-supervisor or junior manager level. Training for this position is very compliance-oriented. Those who hold it need to know how to spot surveillance, as well as needing to know basic compliance skills and other rudimentary management skills. Much of this is already being accomplished in training, but unless it serves as a basic building block for a continuing career path, the training is divorced from what the objective should be: creating professional security staff.

Critically, the training industry needs to move from its reliance on government. Undoubtedly, the above recommendations all rest on the ability of the stakeholders to have access to high-quality information and intelligence. While the cooperation between the government and industry is improving, there is still room for progress. One way to work around chokepoints within the system is to access information directly. Today, 95–99% of all information in the counterterrorism field is available in the open source domain. This includes both analysis and raw information that can help create realistic training as well as the framework that the industry needs to evaluate its risk. The supply chain industry does not need to invest in its own analytical capabilities; private-sector firms and academic centers can provide information and analysis.

The threat and risk facing international logistics is constantly evolving. It is now common for groups to have an evolutionary lifecycle of around six months, making response very difficult. The most effective security strategy is to develop a comprehensive layered security structure. The critical components in maintaining a robust and flexible response include staff, training, intelligence, and—most critically—will.

Terrorism and crime are human activities and thus can be reduced and perhaps prevented by human activity. But the move toward greater reliance on technology in all aspects of aviation and security may have a negative impact on security. Humans, with all of their limitations, are some of the best early warning detectors currently available. While the focus is identifying the correct personality type to work in security, one needs to understand that there needs to be an all-of-staff approach to make sure that everyone understands and is empowered to act in a potential security-related situation. This is not confined to the security and other ground staff. Ticket agents, sky caps, station staff, and anyone else in the industry needs to hold the investment in the notion that security is an all point's effort. The only way to protect the supply chain is to calibrate the response to the threat and risk posed by a given threat, allowing humans to remain engaged in attempting to reduce the threat.

NOTES

1. http://www.census.gov/epcd/cbp/view/us03.txt.
2. Deborah Fey Erick and Phil Hirschkorn, "Baggage, Cargo Handlers Arrested in Drug Probe: Smuggling Ring Accused of Importing 400 Kilos of Cocaine," CNN New York Bureau, Wednesday, November 26, 2003.
3. Paul Wilkinson, *Terrorism versus Democracy: The Liberal State Response* (London: Routledge, 2006), 180–181.
4. Brigitte Nacos, et al., "Terrorism and the Print Media: The 1985 TWA Hostage Crisis," *Terrorism an International Journal* 12, 109.
5. Capt. John Testrake and David Wimbush, *Triumph over Terror on Flight 847* (New York: Fleming Revell, 1987), 137–138.
6. As part of the legal settlement, Libya did eventually accept responsibility for both PA 103 and UTA 772.
7. http://www.time.com/time/magazine/article/0,9171,879514-1,00.html.
8. Spiros Kaminaris, "Greece and Middle Eastern Terrorism," June 28, 1999, http://www.ict.org.il/articles/articledet.cfm?articleid=403.
9. Akiva J. Lorenz, "Al Qaeda's Maritime Threat Intelligence and Terrorism Information Center," Israel Intelligence Heritage and Commemoration Center (IICC) May 3, 2007.
10. FARC was well organized; rather than return any of the hostages, it landed the aircraft in a remote landing strip and marched the hostages into the jungle, from which they were ransomed back to their families.
11. Dr. Rohan Gunaratna, "Intelligence Failures Exposed by Tamil Tiger Airport Attack" *Jane's Intelligence Review*, September 1, 2001, http://jir.janes.com/public/jir/terrorism.shtml.
12. Patrick Seale, *Abu Nidal: A Gun for Hire* (London: Hutchinson, 1992), 243–247.

72   Supply Chain Security

13. Patrick Seale, *Abu Nidal: A Gun for Hire* (London: Hutchinson, 1992), 243.

14. Syria may have been seeking revenge for what it perceived to be French interference in Syrian objectives in Lebanon.

15. Simon Reeve, *One Day in September* (New York: Arcade Publishing, 2006), 128–132.

16. Mark Bowden, *Killing Pablo*, New York; Penguin, 2002, 80.

17. ICPVTR Mass Transit Land Attack Project (from MIPT database) had data provided until 2007.

18. ICPVTR Mass Transit Land Attack Project.

19. ICPVTR Mass Transit Land Attack Project.

20. ICPVTR Mass Transit Land Attack Project.

21. http://www.nytimes.com/1981/09/13/world/suspects-in-bombing-of-italy-rail-station-captured-in-london.html.

22. Brigitte Nacos, et al., "Terrorism and the Print Media: The 1985 TWA Hostage Crisis," *Terrorism an International Journal* 12, 109.

23. MIPT database 2007.

24. PLASIRO remains an armed group but has not been involved in armed action since 1991.

25. Eric Haney, *Inside Delta Force* (Chicago: Delta, 2005), 277.

26. One of the earliest examples involved a woman in Canada who planted a bomb on a Canadian domestic flight in order to kill her husband in an attempted insurance scam. She succeeded in killing her husband and several others on board, but did not succeed with the fraud. See David Gero, *Flights of Terror* (New York: Haynes Publishing, 1997), 12.

27. Ariel Merari, "Attacks on Civil Aviation: Trends and Lessons," in *Aviation Terrorism and Security*, eds. Paul Wilkinson and Brian Jenkins (London: Routledge, 1998), 12, 13. Also see the Aviation Safety Network, Safety Issues page, Security, Sabotage Bombing link. http://www.aviation-safety.net.

28. Paula Newton, "Three Guilty in Airline Bomb Plot," CNN, September 8, 2008, http://www.cnn.com/2009/WORLD/europe/09/07/uk.airline.bomb.trial/index.html.

29. Paula Newton, "Three Guilty in Airline Bomb Plot," CNN, September 8, 2008, http://www.cnn.com/2009/WORLD/europe/09/07/uk.airline.bomb.trial/index.html.

30. Praveen Swami, "China's Mid-Air Terror Trail Leads to Pakistan," *The Hindu*, March 22, 2008, http://www.hindu.com/2008/03/22/stories/2008032254581200.htm.

31. Fred Burton and Scott Stewart, "China: An Outside-the-Box Terrorist Plot?" March 19, 2008, http://www.rightsidenews.com/index2.php?option=com_content&do_pdf=1&id=542.

32. Ariel Merari, "Attacks on Civil Aviation: Trends and Lessons," in *Aviation Terrorism and Security*, eds. Paul Wilkinson and Brian Jenkins (London: Routledge, 1998), 22.

33. It took more than a decade for the Pan Am 103 bombers to be brought to court; the bombers of UTA 772 have been found guilty *in absentia* by a French court but still have not been remanded to French custody.

34. Rodney Wallis, *Combating Air Terrorism*, London; Brassey's, 1993, 7. Air Canada was serving as a feeder for Air India, flying from Montreal to India with a stop in London. The Sikh passenger wanted his bag checked to India, even though he did not have a reserved seat on the Air India flight. The agent knew this was not allowed but was bullied into consenting due to the large crowd waiting to check in for the

Montreal leg. Further compounding the error, Air Canada did not offload the bag, even though the passenger never boarded. See Salim Jiwa, *Death of Air India Flight 182* (Toronto: Star Books, 1986) for a full discussion.

35. Rodney Wallis, *Lockerbie: The Story and the Lessons* (Westport, CT: Praeger, 2000), 74–79.

36. The Philippines Airline flight miraculously suffered only one loss of life; the skill of the flight crew allowed for a safe landing. Ramzi Yousef was the no-return passenger in this case; he was engaged in a practice run for the Bojinka Plot, which would have used the same type of liquid nitrogen explosive hidden in contact solution bottles.

37. David Sterland, "Stowaways Journey in the Wheel Bay," *Aviation Security International*, June 2001, 6–8.

38. Marvin Schaffer, "The Missile Threat to Civil Aviation," in *Aviation Terrorism and Security*, eds. Paul Wilkinson and Brian Jenkins (London: Routledge, 1998), 71.

39. In June 1989, a Somali militia shot down a Somali Air flight, killing all thirty persons on board. See David Gero, *Flights of Terror* (New York: Haynes Publishing, 1997), 116. The launcher used in the Mombasa attack was traced to Saudi Arabia. The launcher, and possibly the missiles, was traced to a cache that had been used in an unsuccessful and little-noticed attack against an American military transport aircraft landing at a Saudi air base.

40. Federation of American Scientists, http://www.fas.org/asmp/campaigns/MANPADS/MANPADS.html, Issue Brief 1: MANPADS Proliferation.

41. Fred Bayles, "Threat is 'no longer theoretical,'" *USA Today*, August 13, 2003.

42. The U.S. Army anticipates that a fully trained operator will only achieve a hit about a 30% of the time. Peter Harclerode, *Fighting Dirty*, London; Diane Publishing, 2001, 564. It's not clear how effective a poorly trained terrorist would be against an unprotected civil aircraft.

43. Thomas Hunter, "The Proliferation of MANPADS," *Jane's Intelligence Review*, November 28, 2002, http://jir.janes.com/public/jir/terrorism.shtml.

44. El AL has just introduced a flare countermeasures system that will cost about 600,000 pounds sterling per aircraft. The United States FAA will not allow the system to be used in the United States for fear of starting ground fires. *Sunday Times* of London, September 29, 2006.

45. Raymond Bonner, Jane Perlez, and Eric Schmitt, "British Inquiry of Failed Plots Points to Iraq's Qaeda Group," *New York Times*, December 14, 2007, http://www.nytimes.com/2007/12/14/world/europe/14london.html?pagewanted=1&_r=1&hp.

46. Mary Jordan and Craig Whitlock, "Rigged Vehicle Rams Terminal at U.K. Airport, British Raise Terror Alert to Highest Level," *Washington Post* Foreign Service, Sunday, July 1, 2007.

47. Fr. O'Riely, SJ, recounted his experience while on missionary assignment during 1987–1988 in Southern Sudan, where the Jesuit order ran a school and airstrip in the town of Wau. Both the insurgents of the Sudanese Peoples Liberation Army (SPLA) and the government wanted control of this vital location. Each side shelled the facility and adjacent school regularly, eventually driving the school out.

48. St. Andrews Domestic Terrorism database.

49. Capt. John Testrake and David Wimbush, *Triumph over Terror on Flight 847* (New York: Fleming Revell, 1987), 137–138. Air Lanka had three Airbuses destroyed and another three damaged. The air force had three fighter and three training aircraft

and two helicopter gunships destroyed. The air force also had six fighter aircraft and six helicopters damaged, two of them gunships.

50. It should be noted that since the ceasefire has broken down, the LTTE has been using light aircraft to attack government targets. It is not included as a terrorist attack, as the attacks do not fit the definition used in this work. To date, the LTTE is the only terrorist organization to have an air force.

CHAPTER 3

Legal Environment of Supply Chain Security

Mary F. Schiavo

WHO OWNS THE CHAIN?

In most of the developed world's legal systems, legal responsibilities and liability correspond with ownership, dominion or control, or the ability to affect the outcome of events.[1] Thus, to be able to understand what entity is legally responsible—and who is liable—for supply chain breaches, it is first necessary to consider what entities have ownership, dominion, and control over the supply chain. There are as many different opinions about who owns what part of the supply chain as there are entities involved in the supply chain. The Department of Homeland Security maintains that supply chains are owned by, or perhaps more accurately described as controlled by, an amalgam of private sector interests and are regulated by multiple international, national, state, and local government jurisdictions.[2] There are so many layers, objectives, players, programs, initiatives, and government agencies involved in supply chain security that the Department of Homeland Security itself resorted to a chart to attempt to list and provide order to the number of objectives, implementing programs, and government entities involved in each program or action. Those charts are reflected below in Tables 3.1, 3.2, and 3.3. Within this milieu of actors and facilities, there are overarching legal strategies and obligations that provide responsibility, liability, and some framework and structure to the emerging legal field of supply chain security law. For the United States, the National Strategy for Homeland Security (NASHS) provides the overarching framework. National Security Presidential Directives and Homeland Security Presidential Directives set the national policies and executive mandates for specific programs and activities.[3] While there were certainly myriad supply

Table 3.1
Strategic Objectives

Each of the three primary layers of the Department's approach to supply chain security is supported by a series of strategic objectives, implemented through programs, initiatives, and cooperative work in the international areana. Those strategic objectives are:

SO-1: Provide for end-to-end supply chain security by building trusted relationships and assisting trading partners and the trade community with enhancing their security systems.

SO-2: Provide incentives and benefits for supply chain partners who enhance their supply chain security, while recognizing that some benefits (e.g., increased security resulting in reduced cargo loss and/or reduced costs of doing business) are trade-driven issues.

SO-3: Advance security by promoting the development and implementation of international standards.

SO-4: Increase the availability and use of appropriate data in order to maintain complete awareness of the supply chain activities and target Department resources to the highest risk movements.

SO-5: Utilize provide WMD detection systems at ports of origin and entry, in order to provide for a defense in depth, layered system.[5]

SO-6: Expedite movement of low-risk shipments through the supply chain, while maintaining a level of detection such that even low-risk shipments are screened for high-consequence threats (e.g., WMD detection via RPMs).[5]

SP-7: Provide clear communications with the trade community and our international trading partners in order to facilitate recovery efforts.

SO-8: Ensure that data gathered during normal operations is also sufficient to allow for the management of resumption activities following a supply chain disruption.

SO-9: Promote technological development of detection sytems which increase the probability of detection, decrease "false positive" detections, and expedite processing times in order to promote rapid trade movement.[5]

SO-10: Leverage key nodes in the supply chain to provide for specific scanning, screening, and inspections activities in order to detect and deter illicit use of the supply chain.[5]

SO-11: Develop systems which automate and expedite the use of Department resources.[5]

SO-12: Provide, or support develompent of, a robust cargo security system that will withstand a supply chain disruption, and rapidly resume pre-incident or near pre-incident status.

SO-13: Provide for a flexible, standardized response mechanism which includes processes to facilitate trade resumption in short and long term recovery operations.

SO-14: Promote development of modal-specific technologies and systems to ensure security of cargo while in transit.

SO-15: Leverage agreements with foreign partners to facilitate investigative activities related to the detection of illicit material in the supply chain.

[5]Specific technology development initiatives are driven by DHS Science and Techonogy (S&T) based upon an Implemetation Planning Team (IPT) process in which S&T consults with customer bases and identifies targeted investment objectives. Specific information on IPT programs are protected information pending appropriate disclosure through contracting systems.

U.S. Department of Homeland Security, *Strategy to Enhance International Supply Chain Security* (U.S. Department of Homeland Security, July 2007), 13, http://www.dhs.gov/xlibrary/assets/plcy-internationalsupplychainsecuritystrategy.pdf.

Table 3.2

Table 1: DHS Supply Chain Security Strategic Objectives and Implementing Programs

Strategic Objective:	1	2	3	4	5	6	7	8	9	10	11	12	13	14	15	Pg
Customs-Trade Partnership Against Terrorism																64
Container Security Devices																66
24-Hour Rule																67
Container Security Initiative																68
Secure Freight Initiative																69
Automated Targeting Systems																70
DOE Megaports																71
Known Shipper Database																71
International Port Security Program																71
ISPS Code Implementation / Enforcement																72
Maritime Domain Awareness Program																72
Nationwide Automatic Identification System																72
Long Range Identification and Tracking of Vessels																73
Advance Notice of Arrival																74
Security and Response Operations																74
Domestic Maritime Security Regulations																75
Transportation Worker Identification Credentials																76
CBP Cargo Screening																76
Non-Intrusive Inspections and Radiation Scanning Technology																76
Certain Dangerous Cargo Tracking																77
Corporate Security Review (CSR)																78
HAZMAT Truck Tracking Program																78
Enhanced Security Measures for Highly Hazardous Materials																78
Federal Security Clearances for State Departments of Transportation																79
REAL ID Act																79
Hazmat Threat Assessment program																79
FLETC Training of Roadside Enforcement Officers																79
Freight Railroad Security Plans																80
Rail Protocols for Transportation of High-Risk Hazardous Materials																80
Air Cargo Security Programs																81
Strategy to Enhance International Supply Chain Security																NA
Participation in International Forums (e.g. APEC Trade Recovery Workgroup)																NA
ICE International Affairs & Trade Relations																NA

U.S. Department of Homeland Security, *Strategy to Enhance International Supply Chain Security* (U.S. Department of Homeland Security, July 2007), 14, 15, http://www.dhs.gov/xlibrary/assets/plcy-internationalsupplychainsecuritystrategy.pdf.

Table 3.3

Table 2: Principle Areas in which National Plans or Strategies Inform the Strategy to Enhance International Supply Chain Security

U.S. Department of Homeland Security, *Strategy to Enhance International Supply Chain Security* (U.S. Department of Homeland Security, July 2007), 18, 19, http://www.dhs.gov/xlibrary/assets/plcy-internationalsupplychainsecuritystrategy.pdf.

chain legal obligations, legal responsibilities and liabilities before September 11, 2001, the first directive issued after September 11 came on October 29, 2001, when Congress established the Homeland Security Advisory Counsel.[4]

HOMELAND SECURITY DIRECTIVES

There are a great number of federal government directives that are relevant in the national supply chain security—too many to cover in one chapter. The following are some of the major directives relevant to supply chain security. Homeland Security Presidential Directive 3 created the Homeland Security Advisory System to provide warnings to federal, state, and local authorities and to the American people in the form of graduated threat conditions that escalate as the government's evaluation of the risk of threat increases.[5] As the threat level increases, government departments and agencies are required to implement corresponding sets of increasing protective measures for additional response capabilities to match the perceived heightened threat. However, these security levels do not correspond directly with the more familiar code yellow, orange, and red that we are accustomed to seeing at our airports. For example, in the Marine security levels 1, 2, and 3, level 1 corresponds with conditions green, blue and yellow; level 2 corresponds with condition orange; and level 3 corresponds with condition red.[6] There are important legal ramifications as the threat levels are raised, be they MARSEC levels 1 through 3 or HSAS levels green through red. At each increased level of threat, additional requirements are triggered for inspections and other activities throughout the supply chain.

Homeland Security Presidential Directive 5 requires coordination of the government with the private sector to develop and implement the National Incident Management System (NIMS). NIMS requires governments, the private sector, and nongovernmental organizations to prevent, prepare for, and respond to, and, hopefully, recover from international supply chain security incidents.[7] Homeland Security Presidential Directive 7 identified the critical United States infrastructure as key resources to be protected from terrorist attacks. Within that framework is the National Infrastructure Protection Plan (NIPP) and the Transportation Sector Specific Plan (TSSP).[8]

National Security Presidential Directive 41/Homeland Security Presidential Directive 13 (NSPD-41/HSPD-13) established a maritime security policy and eight policy coordinating committees.[9, 10] In addition to intelligence integration and evaluation, these directives require a maritime operations threat response plan aimed at coordinating the United States government response to maritime threats against the United States. Included are the International Outreach and Coordination Strategy for coordinating with entities other than the United States, including foreign governments and international organizations, marine transportation security recommendations, a recovery plan in the event of security chain disasters, a commerce security plan to secure the maritime supply chain, and an outreach plan to engage nongovernmental entities in the development and implementation of marine security policies.

THE NATIONAL STRATEGY FOR TRANSPORTATION SECURITY

The Intelligence Reform and Terrorism Prevention Act of 2004[11] resulted in the development of the National Strategy for Transportation Security (NSTS). This strategy was also required by the 9/11 Commission.[12] Despite the fact that the document is a classified document and not available for public discussion, it requires action and coordination with private industry to secure United States transportation systems from terrorist threats and attacks. The NSTS is applicable to aviation, freight, rail, highway, maritime, pipeline, and transit, commuter, and long-distance passenger rail.

THE NATIONAL MARITIME TRANSPORTATION SECURITY PLAN, AREA MARITIME SECURITY PLANS, AND VESSEL FACILITY SECURITY PLANS

The Maritime Transportation Security Act of 2002[13] mandated the development of the National Maritime Transportation Security Plan (NMTSP). The NMTSP is a three-tiered maritime security planning system. The first tier is the National Maritime Transportation Security Plan itself, the second is the Area Maritime Security Plan developed by local U.S. Coast Guard Sector Commanders, and the third is composed of Vessel and Facility Security Plans developed by facility and vessel owners and operators in the private sector of course. The third tier is based on private sector assessments of the security risk.

COMPREHENSIVE ENVIRONMENTAL RESPONSE, COMPENSATION AND LIABILITY ACT

Predating the flurry of regulations and activity after September 11, 2001, were requirements for hazardous materials and hazardous materials response. The Comprehensive Environmental Response, Compensation and Liability Act of 1980 (CERCLA)[14] was intended to address all hazards and provide an approach for response and recovery. Hazmat responders under this statute were to harmonize their plans, coordination, procedures, and resources across various hazard categories to respond to a hazmat incident or threat.

Visualizing how the various laws of the many different countries and the responsibility of numerous governmental and nongovernmental entities may affect a single containerized shipment is perhaps better illustrated with a hypothetical transport of a container and shipment. The container at its point of origination will be subject to the business, transportation, taxation, and security laws and regulations of the originating nation where it is manufactured, containerized, and transported to an international port. At the international port, the shipment will move into the jurisdiction of that nation's customs laws. In the jurisdiction of that nation's customs laws, it will move through the customs laws to that of the originating nation's maritime administration's laws. As the container departs that nation's maritime jurisdiction and enters international waters, that container will be subject to multiple international agreements. The container could conceivably be under the control of a second nation which is serving as the carrying vessel's flag state: that nation's laws will apply to the ship and, potentially, the container on the ship. As the container on the ship moves into waters subject to the jurisdiction of the U.S. Coast Guard, the cargo (as well as the ship) will be subject to the jurisdiction of the U.S. Coast Guard. As the container arrives at the port and is transferred into the jurisdiction of the United States of America, the container will be subject to laws of the Customs and Border Patrol. Once the shipment is released by the Customs and Border Patrol for further transport within the United States of America, it does so subject to the jurisdiction of the U.S. Department of Transportation, the Transportation Security Administration, and any other relevant applicable federal laws (such as U.S. Department of Agriculture regulations, Food and Drug Administration regulations, Consumer Product Safety Commission regulations, Occupational Safety and Health Administration regulations, Center for Disease Control regulations, and so forth). Finally, upon release by the Customs and Border Patrol and any other federal agency, the cargo becomes subject to state and local jurisdictions.

As can readily be seen by this example, there are myriad places a private shipper can run afoul of laws. Not surprisingly, supply chain security law is a rapidly developing, highly technical, and largely unsettled area of the law. One of the easier ways to find and identify applicable statutes and regulations is to determine which government agency is responsible at any given point in the supply chain. Once the cognizant government agency is identified, its applicable federal regulations will determine its responsibilities and the reach of its powers. The Department of Homeland Security has at least seventeen components or directorates, including the Transportation Security Agency, the Customs and Border Patrol, Citizen and Immigration Services, Immigration and Customs Enforcement, the U.S. Secret Service, the Federal Emergency Management Agency (FEMA), the U.S. Coast Guard, and several other entities. The Department of Homeland Security has attempted to delineate the various government agencies and their responsibilities on a chart, which (subject to change and availability on its Web site) is reprinted here:

Figure 3.1
U.S. Department of Homeland Security, *Strategy to Enhance International Supply Chain Security* (U.S. Department of Homeland Security, July 2007), 39, http://www.dhs.gov/xlibrary/assets/plcy-internationalsupplychainsecuritystrategy.pdf.

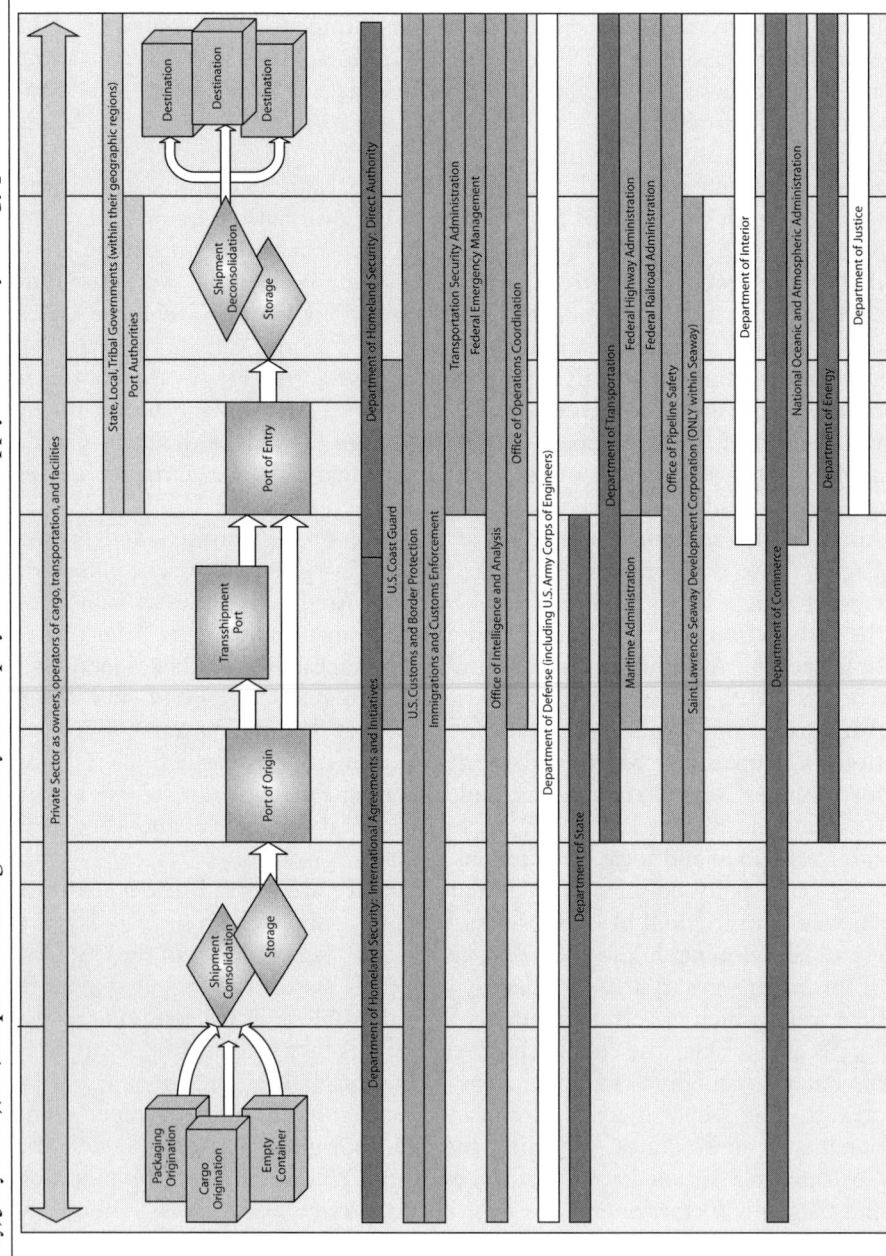

THE U.S. COAST GUARD

The U.S. Coast Guard, formerly part of the U.S. Department of Transportation, is one of the five services of the nation's armed forces. It has a law enforcement role as well as an environmental and security role in international coastal port and inland waterways of the United States and various locations around the world. The U.S. Coast Guard has to perform at least five very different jobs related to maritime safety—or, more particularly, the safety of persons involved in everything from sport boating to commercial fishing—maritime security, aids to maritime navigation to maximize the access to and transportation in waterways, national defense, law enforcement including drug and other criminal interdiction, and protection of maritime natural resources, including maritime wildlife. To carry out these various responsibilities, the U.S. Coast Guard necessarily has broad legal authority. That legal authority is expanded through Captains of the Port (COTP), which is designed to provide Coast Guard support to the Customs and Border Control in screening and evaluating cargo movement into and out of the United States.

CUSTOMS AND BORDER PROTECTION

The U.S. Customs and Border Protection screens and evaluates cargo, crew and passenger movements into and out of the United States, conducts hands-on physical boarding of vessels, inspects and searches vessels, persons, and cargo within the customs territory of the United States, can detain and seize vessels, cargo and contraband, can determine the admissibility of persons arriving in the United States, and can take actions to detect and identify chemical, biological, radiological, and nuclear materials through appropriate detection technology. Customs and Border Protection supports the U.S. Coast Guard in its functions.

ICE, TSA, AND OTHERS

Immigration and Customs Enforcement's (ICE) job is to protect national and border security through enforcement of economic transportation and infrastructure security. The Transportation Security Administration (TSA) provides oversight of the security for highways, pipeline, mass transit systems, ports and the over 450 U.S. commercial-use airports. The Federal Emergency Management Agency (FEMA) coordinates the response to disasters that have occurred within the United States and that overwhelm the resources of state and/or local authorities. The governor of the state in which the disaster occurs declares a state of emergency and formally requests that the President of the United States direct FEMA to respond to the disaster (unless the disaster occurs on federal property). The Department of Defense (DOD), at the direction of the president or the secretary of defense, may assist in the event of a supply chain disruption. Local military commanders and other DOD components are authorized to take necessary action to respond to save lives, prevent suffering, and mitigate great property damage as deemed necessary in an immediate response. The U.S. Department of State (DOS) assists U.S. citizens traveling or living abroad and U.S. businesses in international marketplaces. In the event of supply chain disruption, the DOS coordinates transportation assistance from foreign governments.

THE U.S. DEPARTMENT OF TRANSPORTATION (DOT)

Even though after 9/11 the DOT shrank to a fraction of its former size and power, the U.S. Department of Transportation can still, in the event of a supply chain disruption, prioritize and allocate transportation capacity; manage hazardous materials, containment, and response (but only in coordination or delegation by the U.S. Coast Guard); provide expertise and financial assistance, as well as orchestrate the repair and restoration of the transportation infrastructure; and direct and command the operations of the Federal Aviation Administration and other Department of Transportation entities.

THE MARITIME ADMINISTRATION (MARAD)

The Maritime Administration can provide transport of critical supplies, goods, and equipment in the event of a supply chain disruption or national disaster through the use of its national defense reserve fleet. It can also obtain priority use of port facilities and services, shipping services, and containers under the Defense Production Act.

THE FEDERAL HIGHWAY ADMINISTRATION (FHWA)

The Federal Highway Administration's chief mission is to provide money for construction and maintenance of the national highway system. In the event of a transportation system disruption, the FHWA is likely to be the banker for any improvements, repairs, and reconstruction of highways.

THE FEDERAL RAILROAD ADMINISTRATION (FRA)

The Federal Railroad Administration provides direct rail loans and guarantees to rehabilitate rail equipment and facilities.

ST. LAWRENCE SEAWAY DEVELOPMENT CORPORATION (SLSDC)

The St. Lawrence Seaway Development Corporation operates and maintains the St. Lawrence Seaway between Montreal and Lake Erie. It is empowered, in the event of a transportation system disruption, to operate and maintain vessel traffic services on the St. Lawrence Seaway.

THE OFFICE OF PIPELINE SAFETY (OPS)

The Office of Pipeline Safety is the federal safety authority for the nation's 2.3 million miles of natural gas and hazardous liquid pipeline. While woefully understaffed, and largely unable to provide much in the way of manpower, OPS can provide emergency funds or loans for repair or reconstruction of pipeline and respond to requests for emergency waivers to keep pipelines operating in the event of a national disaster or emergency.

THE U.S. DEPARTMENT OF ENERGY (DOE)

The Department of Energy is responsible for securing America's nuclear security and works to ensure that seaports are not unwitting highways for importation of nuclear and radioactive materials. The DOE and the National Nuclear Security Administration secure ports from nuclear and radioactive materials through provision of detection equipment, training, and enforcement.

THE U.S. DEPARTMENT OF JUSTICE (DOJ)

The Department of Justice enforces the law and prosecutes those who break the law and endanger the security of the transportation modalities and any other federal law violations.

OVERARCHING LAWS

This complex network of interlocking jurisdictions, governments, authorities, nations, actors, and powers and their corresponding vast collection of laws, regulations, responsibilities, and liabilities at federal, state, and local levels impacts supply chain security. In the eight years since the September 11, 2001, attacks, hundreds of thousands of pages of regulations—and millions of pages of recommendations, guidelines, and commentary—have been generated. This chapter can only touch on a very few of the primary laws but will hopefully give at least an initial starting point and a framework for the comprehensive network of regulations.

Homeland Security Act

The Homeland Security Act of 2002[15] established the Department of Homeland Security with broad powers to address the threat of terrorism. The Critical Infrastructure Information Act of 2002[16] protects the private sector from public disclosure of information it submits to the federal government.

The Aviation and Transportation Security Act of 2001 (ATSA)[17], granted broad powers to the federal government, and more particularly the Transportation Security Administration, as delegated by the Department of Homeland Security for security in all modes of transportation, including civil aviation security. Those responsibilities covered cargo as well as passengers, background checks for transportation security personnel, implementation of security measures at transportation facilities, intelligence functions, threat assessment, law enforcement related to security functions, research, and development of new security technologies.

The Robert T. Stafford Disaster Relief and Emergency Assistance Act (the Stafford Act)[18] provided the authority for government agencies to respond to emergencies and disasters both natural and intentional. This act provides the legal empowerment to provide medicine, food, and other goods, take necessary action to save lives, remove debris, provide emergency care, provide temporary facilities for schools and other community services, demolish unsafe structures, and repair and replace facilities, among other emergency services.

The USA PATRIOT (Uniting and Strengthening America by Providing Appropriate Tools Required to Intersect and Obstruct Terrorism) Act of 2001[19] empowered domestic policies relating to deterrence and punishment of terrorists and information-gathering.

The Maritime Transportation Security Act of 2002[20] put in place requirements governing transportation security and crew member identification.

The Ports and Waterway Safety Act (PWSA)[21] granted the U.S. Coast Guard broad authority to respond to safety and security issues. The Coast Guard is also authorized to control vessels and facility operations to ensure safety and security.

The SAFETY (Support Anti-Terrorism by Fostering Effective Technologies) Act, part of the Homeland Security Act of 2002,[22] authorized the Secretary of Homeland Security to limit the liability of sellers of Qualified Anti-Terrorism Technologies (QATT) to zero for certifications and to the amount of the insurance coverage required by the government for designations or developmental test and evaluations designations, an amount established by the federal government. The SAFETY Act also protects other entities in the supply and distribution chain. The liability limitation is distinct from indemnification, which involves defending against claims brought by others and satisfying any resulting liability. Concessions granted by the SAFETY Act are lost if the technology has been changed or modified without Department of Homeland Security approval or in the event of fraud or willful misconduct or the failure to maintain insurance.

Federal Preemption

While many presume the preemption principles enumerated by the Supreme court in *U.S. v. Locke*, 529 U.S. 89 (2000) concerning federal preemption of state vessel safety equipment and operating requirements obviate significant attention to state and local regulations, a recent Supreme Court decision[23] makes doubtful the assumption that federal preemption is an all-encompassing escape from state and local requirements and liabilities.

Agency and Court Interpretation

Because the laws and regulations are so new, and propounded by the government almost faster than the Government Printing Office can reproduce them in the *Federal Register*, there is little court opinion and case guidance, and little published agency determination, to guide supply chain security lawyers through the millions of words of regulations, guidelines initiatives, programs, recommendations, obligations, requirements, and suggestions. In the coming years, transportation security law will develop as a specialized area of practice and the various fits and starts of the ever-changing landscape of government agencies' supply chain security requirements will settle and sift out with more defined guidelines and regulations. Until that time, petitioners of supply chain security law will be well advised to watch the *Federal Register* and stay in close contact with the general counsel at their respective government agencies. In the event of a supply chain security disaster, the federal government will likely be able to escape responsibility and liability, but the private sector will not.

NOTES

1. Notable exceptions include modern responsibility burden and wealth-shifting vehicles such as uninsured or underinsured motorist coverage and government victims funds such as the 9/11 Victims Compensation Fund.

2. U.S. Department of Homeland Security, *Strategy to Enhance International Supply Chain Security* (U.S. Department of Homeland Security, July 2007), 5, http://www.dhs.gov/xlibrary/assets/plcy-internationalsupplychainsecuritystrategy.pdf.

3. U.S. Department of Homeland Security, *Strategy to Enhance International Supply Chain Security* (U.S. Department of Homeland Security, July 2007), 20, http://www.dhs.gov/xlibrary/assets/plcy-internationalsupplychainsecuritystrategy.pdf.

4. George W. Bush, "Homeland Security Presidential Directive 1: Organization and Operation of the Homeland Security Council," U.S. Department of Homeland Security, October 29, 2001, http://www.dhs.gov/xabout/laws/gc_1213648320189.shtm.

5. George W. Bush, "Homeland Security Presidential Directive 3: Homeland Security Advisory System," U.S. Department of Homeland Security, March 11, 2002, http://www.dhs.gov/xabout/laws/gc_1214508631313.shtm#1.

6. The various levels of the Homeland Security Advisory System (HSAS) may be of marginal utility, because since the implementation of the HSAS, the threat level has remained at yellow or orange. Only for three days in 2006 was the threat level raised to red for flights originating in the United Kingdom and bound for the United States. At all other times, the threat level was yellow and orange, never falling lower and never again rising to red. U.S. Department of Homeland Security, "Chronology of

Changes to the Homeland Security Advisory System," U.S. Department of Homeland Security, http://www.dhs.gov/xabout/history/editorial_0844.shtm.

7. George W. Bush, "Homeland Security Presidential Directive 5: Management of Domestic Incidents," U.S. Department of Homeland Security, February 28, 2003, http://www.dhs.gov/xabout/laws/gc_1214592333605.shtm.

8. George W. Bush, "Homeland Security Presidential Directive 7: Critical Infrastructure Identification, Prioritization, and Protection," U.S. Department of Homeland Security, December 17, 2003, http://www.dhs.gov/xabout/laws/gc_1214597989952.shtm.

9. Department of Homeland Security, "National Security Presidential Directive 41/Homeland Security Presidential Directive 13," U.S. Department of Homeland Security, http://www.dhs.gov/xprevprot/programs/editorial_0597.shtm.

10. George W. Bush, "Homeland Security Presidential Directive 13: Maritime Security Policy," U.S. Department of Homeland Security, December 21, 2004, http://www.dhs.gov/xabout/laws/gc_1217624446873.shtm.

11. *Intelligence Reform and Terrorism Prevention Act of 2004*, Public Law 108–458, 108th Cong., 2d sess. (December 17, 2004).

12. *The 9/11 Commission Report: Final Report of the National Commission on Terrorist Attacks upon the United States* (New York: W.W. Norton & Company, 2004), 391.

13. *Maritime Transportation Security Act of 2002*, Public Law 107–295, 107th Cong., 2d sess. (November 25, 2002).

14. *Comprehensive Environmental Response, Compensation and Liability Act of 1980*, Public Law 96-510, 96th Cong., 2d sess. (December 11, 1980).

15. *Homeland Security Act of 2002*, Public Law 107–296, 107th Cong., 2d sess. (November 25, 2002).

16. *Homeland Security Act of 2002*, Public Law 107–296, 107th Cong., 2d sess. (November 25, 2002), Title II, Subtitle B.

17. *Aviation and Transportation Security Act of 2001*, Public Law 107–71, 107th Cong., 1st sess. (November 19, 2001).

18. *Robert T. Stafford Disaster Relief and Emergency Assistance Act*, Public Law 93–288, as amended, 42 U.S.C. 5121–5207.

19. *Uniting and Strengthening America by Providing Appropriate Tools Required to Intersect and Obstruct Terrorism Act of 2001*, Public Law 107–56, 107th Cong., 1st sess. (October 26, 2001).

20. *Maritime Transportation Security Act of 2002*, Public Law 107–295, 107th Cong., 2d sess. (November 25, 2002).

21. *Ports and Waterway Safety Act*, 33 U.S.C. Sec. 1221, et seq.

22. *Homeland Security Act of 2002*, Public Law 107–296, 107th Cong., 2d sess. (November 25, 2002), Title VIII, Subtitle G.

23. *Wyeth v. Levine*, 129 S.Ct. 1187 (2009).

CHAPTER 4

The Complexity of Assessing Supply Chain Risk

James R. Bradley

Events such as the West Coast dock strikes in 2002, the closing of the U.S.–Canada border subsequent to the 9/11 attacks that shut down manufacturing plants for lack of parts transported by trucks, and the earthquake in Taiwan in 1999 have exposed vulnerabilities of supply chains to disruptions in supply networks.[1] The importance of such disruptions to particular companies can be found in the often-cited story that involved a ten-minute fire in 2000 at a Philips Electronics wafer fabrication facility in Albuquerque, New Mexico, which produced cell phone parts for Nokia and Ericsson.[2] The production outage, which persisted much longer than Philips forecasted, caused Ericsson to lose hundreds of millions of dollars and to delay the launch of a new cell phone model that was critical to its competitive position because Ericsson did not arrange for an alternate supply of parts. One might argue that this incident contributed significantly to a weakening of Ericsson's competitive position and to its subsequent merger with Sony's cell phone business in 2001.[3]

The significant impact of these recent supply chain disruptions have focused the attention of managers and academic researchers (including Kleindorfer and Saad; Handfield, Blackhurst, Elkins, and Craighead; Green; Elkins, Kulkarni, and Tew; and Elkins, Handfield, Blackhurst, and Craighead) on measuring risk and implementing tactics to mitigate the risk of future disruptions.[4] Concern over supply chain disruptions is heightened by two realizations: (1) global supply chains are exposed to a greater number of risks than are more localized supply chains,[5] and (2) inventories, which can cushion the effect of supply chain disruptions to some degree, have been reduced with the widespread adoption of just-in-time inventory management practices.[6] Kleindorfer and Saad summarize these observations by saying that "longer paths and shorter clock speeds" present "more opportunities for disruption and a smaller margin for error if a disruption takes place."[7]

Professor Yossi Sheffi of the Massachusetts Institute of Technology depicts a two-by-two matrix that characterizes supply chain risks in terms of the likelihood of supply chain disruption (high versus low probability) and the impact of disruption (large versus small).[8] Sheffi argues that managers need only be concerned with two of the four quadrants, one of which denotes high probability disruptions with low impact, which are the types of risks that academics in the operations management field and practitioners have studied and managed for a long time. These day-to-day fluctuations in supply and demand and variability in inventory replenishment lead times, for example, are fairly well understood. The remaining relevant quadrant, which depicts events with a low probability of occurrence but a large impact on the supply chain, have been studied to a much lesser extent and are the current focus of supply chain risk management, and of this paper. Although unlikely, these catastrophic occurrences, like the Philips fire, can potentially jeopardize the existence of a company if they do occur. In a similar supplier outage (due to strike) GM recently lost production of 330,000 vehicles and an estimated $2.6 billion in profit.[9]

Sheffi argues that an accurate assessment of risk is needed just as Kleindorfer and Saad argue that "risk has to be quantified through a disciplined risk assessment process" in order to manage supply chain risk.[10] Elkins, Kulkarni, and Tew have noted a deficiency in industrial companies' enterprise-wide capability to assess supply chain risk.[11] Our goal is to explore in fine detail the task of measuring supply chain risk in an environment of realistic complexity. This goal is an end unto itself, because top-level managers are increasingly requiring such an assessment. A risk assessment is also a precursor to mitigating risk: the measurement tool can be used to compare and select among competing alternatives for mitigating risk. By evaluating the complexity or risk assessment in a realistic environment, we hope to evaluate the prospects for such a full-scale decision support tool. We also hope to make a fundamental contribution in exposing the terrain of supply chain risk, which will provide a foundation for researchers and analysts to structure effective risk assessment and decision support tools.

Many papers in the supply chain management and procurement literatures have analyzed the effect of supply network disruptions. For example, Tomlin investigates the effectiveness of extra capacity and extra inventory in buffering against the effects of disruptions in a setting with one manufacturer who buys a part from two suppliers.[12] Tomlin also evaluates disruption management tactics for a firm that sells two products and that has two suppliers.[13] Tomlin and Snyder analyze the value of a signal that indicates the likelihood of a particular catastrophic disruption at a supplier that supplies one part to a manufacturer.[14] Ross, Rong, and Snyder analyze supply chain disruptions where the probability of disruption is not constant.[15] Tomlin and

Wang analyze the value of flexibility and dual-sourcing with multiple suppliers of one manufacturer that sells many products in a context with one buying opportunity and one selling opportunity (e.g., a short-life seasonal product).[16] Zsidisin and Ellram analyzed procurement managers' methods of managing supply risk, and Zsidisin categorized supply risks, although the risk factors addressed in both these papers might be fairly categorized as more frequent and less severe types of disruption rather than Sheffi's low-probability, high-impact disruptions.[17] Graves and Tomlin investigate flexibility in a multistage supply chain where multiple products are produced.[18] Their analysis encompasses a broader view of a supply chain than many papers but is geared more toward analysis of frequent disruptions of smaller magnitude than of catastrophic disruptions. While making important contributions into effective risk mitigation, these papers entertain different problems than we do in this paper. First, some of the papers address day-to-day, low-impact disruptions, whereas our main concern is more with catastrophic disruptions. Second, whereas most of these papers encompass a small part of a supply chain, or a subset of a company's products, or a subset of a company's suppliers, or a subset of the parts that a company purchases, or a subset of the disruptive events that a company might face, we instead wish to comprehend all parts, products, suppliers, and potential disruptive events in order to entertain a comprehensive assessment of risk and evaluate the feasibility of a risk measurement and decision support tool for the entire supply chain. A CEO should want such a comprehensive assessment of his or her enterprise.

We consider a model similar to that of Deleris and Erhun, but our context and goals are different.[19] Deleris and Erhun analyze a portion of a company's supply chain, including five products, one part used in those products, five suppliers, and four disruptive events. Our goal is to evaluate the feasibility of such a risk assessment for a company's entire supply chain that comprehends all risks. Also, rather than analyzing a particular supply chain, our goal is to provide a foundation for future models and supply chain risk analysis techniques by explicating in fine detail the dynamics of supply chain disruptions. In exposing the sources of complexity in assessing supply chain risk, we reveal avenues for simplifying risk assessment models and how those simplifications might affect the accuracy of the risk assessment. We evaluate the efficacy of assessing supply chain risk both with a direct analytical approach and with simulation.

In the sections that follow, we construct a model to analyze supply chain risk, describe probability distributions that are particularly relevant in describing infrequent disruptions with large magnitudes, and describe the constituents of a supply chain risk model and how each component adds to the complexity of an analytical assessment of supply chain risk using probability theory. The goal here is not to suggest that such a method be considered in practice, but to better understand the elemental attributes of supply chain risk models and their complexity. In so doing, we demonstrate that such an approach is probably not viable even if significant simplifications are made. We next evaluate computer simulation as a method for computing supply chain risk, evaluate the efficacy of various simplifying modeling assumptions using the foregoing assessment of complexity, and, finally, summarize our findings and suggest alternate methodologies for assessing and mitigating supply chain risk.

A MODEL OF SUPPLY CHAIN RISK

Our representation of a supply chain is the same as in Deleris and Erhun, where we represent the supply chain as a network of nodes and arcs.[20] Each node represents a facility where manufacturing or distribution activities occur. Each arc represents the transportation of parts and products between two facilities. A simplification of General Motors' (GM's) supply chain is as shown in Figure 4.1. We have drawn only one arc between any two nodes, although in reality, there often could be multiple arcs, each one representing the path of a specific part that is transported via a particular mode. Note that while our nodes denote facilities, an alternate model could have just as well been drawn in which nodes specify production departments within plants, or even individual machines or work stations. In this more detailed representation, transportation would include material handling activities within facilities, and the model would obviously have a great many more nodes and arcs.

Figure 4.1
GM Supply Chain Network

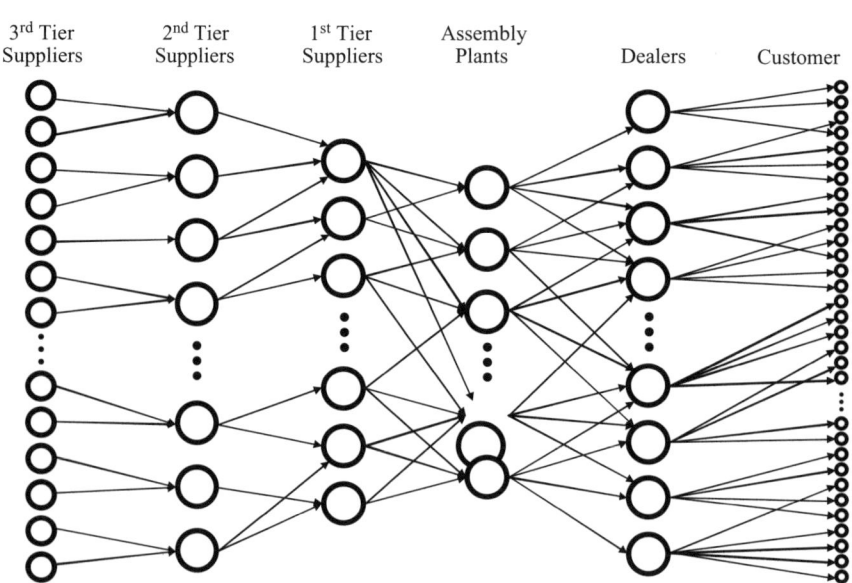

For the final goods that GM ships to its immediate customers (car dealers), the bill of material specifies the many ingredient parts that are necessary to make those products. One can identify the nodes and arcs associated with each part required for a particular product, and the disruption of any of those nodes and arcs will reduce or halt production if an alternate source cannot backfill the requirements completely. Note that the disruption of any one node or arc can disrupt the flow of many products where parts and logistics paths are common. A recent example of a supplier plant (node) disrupting many products and plants is the strike at American Axle and Manufacturing Holding, Inc., which idled 30 GM assembly plants.[21] That strike certainly represented a large impact, causing GM to lose production of hundreds of thousands of vehicles, take a $1.8 billion loss, and pay American Axle $215 million to help settle the strike. Similarly, a recent strike at a carpet supplier (node) idled one GM plant in Lansing, MI.[22] Arcs are also affected by disruptions, as was the case with the 2002 West Coast dock strike that disabled many transportation arcs. Our modeling framework will consider the full incapacitation of flow through a node or arc and also partial shutdowns, as occurred recently when some truck drivers either slowed down or stopped their trucks in protest of high fuel costs.[23]

Our assessment of supply chain risk is based on probabilistic risk analysis, which characterizes the risk of uncertain events using probability distributions. Probability functions are well suited to this task because they incorporate both the likelihood that an event will occur and the impact if it does. Figure 4.2 is an illustrative example for a plant fire that might occur at a particular manufacturing plant. Within a particular year, there is a probability that no fire occurs. If a fire does occur, the lost profit could be either small

Figure 4.2
Illustrative Probability Distribution Function for Plant Fire

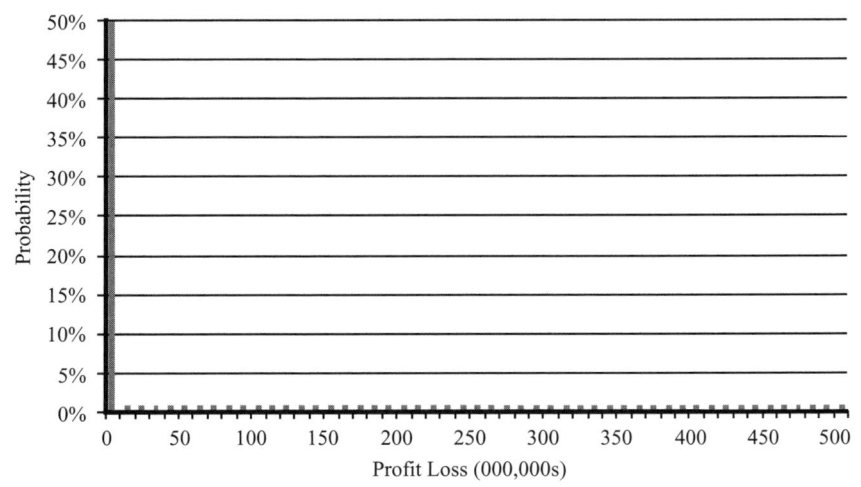

or large, depending on the magnitude of the fire and where it occurs in the facility. This range of possibilities for monetary impact is shown along the x-axis of Figure 4.2. The likelihood, or probability, that each outcome might occur is determined by the height of the corresponding bar in relation to the y-axis. For this example, we show a 50% chance of no fire (we should hope that this probability is larger, although this particular value was selected for clarity of the illustration). The probabilities of all other possible monetary impacts from $10,000,000 to $500,000,000 are uniform at 1% and, in total, constitute the remaining 50% of the probability distribution (the sum of probabilities of all events must equal 100%).

The ultimate goal of a probabilistic risk analysis is to combine probability distributions for *all possible* disruptive events into a comprehensive probability function that describes risk for an entire supply chain or company. Such an analysis would thus start by identifying all possible events that could disrupt a supply chain and specifying a probability distribution for each event. The mathematical computation that combines those probability distributions for individual events into a comprehensive probability distribution is called convolution: it is not important to understand the details of this calculation for this chapter, but it is important to recognize that such computations are cumbersome, especially when many probability distributions must be combined.

Determining the effectiveness of various risk mitigation tactics requires that we compare two probability distributions for risk: one without mitigation and one with mitigation. Such a comparison determines the benefits in a cost–benefit analysis. Comparing two graphs such as Figure 4.2 is a conceptually difficult task, and for that reason, various statistics are used to summarize salient aspects of probability distributions. One candidate statistic that we might consider is the mean of the probability distribution, which, when applied to a probability distribution for a disruptive event, indicates the average loss we would experience over a long time period. The mean is perhaps a necessary statistic, but other statistics are more sensitive to catastrophic events such as the fire in the Philips plant, which are the focus of supply chain risk assessment—the numerical values of these statistics increase more significantly than does the mean when events with the possibilities of catastrophic impacts far out along the x-axis. These are so-called statistics of dispersion, which measure the range of monetary losses possible, from the least to the greatest. As this range of a probability distribution increases, then so, too, must the magnitude of the worst possible monetary loss. Typical summary statistics that are used to describe the existence of the possibility of these catastrophic events are (1) standard deviation, (2) value at risk (VaR), and (3) conditional value at risk (CVaR).

We will focus on measuring risk with the standard deviation and VaR. The numerical value of the standard deviation increases as the largest possible monetary impact increases and, desirably, it also increases as the probability of events with the largest economic impact increase. VaR is monetary loss such that for 95% of years we would expect a monetary loss less than its amount. (VaR can be defined for probabilities other than 95%, although 95% is commonly used.) We do not discuss CVaR as a measure of risk, although it is also subject to the same issues that we discuss for the standard deviation.

PROBABILITY DISTRIBUTIONS FOR DISRUPTIONS

In this subsection, we first discuss probability distributions that describe the likelihood of an occurrence of a disruptive event, and then probability distributions that describe how large events tend to be if they do occur.

Asmussen and Glynn describe rare events as those that have probabilities of occurrence that range from 10^{-3} to 10^{-9} or less.[24] This value corresponds with the height of the bar for a particular event in a distribution such as that shown in Figure 4.2. Thus, if a risk assessment were conducted for a one-year period, we should be able to accurately assess risk due to events that are likely to occur in one out of every 1,000,000,000 years (corresponding with a probability of 10^{-9}). We will discuss problems in both accurately estimating probabilities that are so small and in making accurate computations in this case.

Sheffi discusses the nature of accidents in a company where the impact of a very small number of accidents constitutes a vast majority of the total impact of all accidents.[25] Sheffi also notes that natural disasters follow this same pattern: a small percentage of natural disasters cause a majority of all damage due to natural disasters. A type of probability distribution that exhibit this behavior are called power law distributions or heavy tail distributions, which Willinger, Alderson, Doyle, and Li analytically show represent the occurrence of natural disasters in the twentieth century.[26] Practically, we can describe these types of distributions as having the possibility of extreme impact, or outcomes of nonnegligible probability far out on the right-hand side of the x-axis of the probability distribution. In fact, there can be many such extreme outcomes for any type of event. Although each of these outcomes may have very small probability—such that they might be described as rare events—the impact is so large that when an event does occur, it dwarfs the cumulative impact of many preceding and smaller impact events.[27] These are precisely the low-probability, high-impact events of which Sheffi and others warn us—the Philips fire, for example.

Figure 4.3 compares a heavy tail distribution (Pareto) with other distributions that do not have heavy tails (exponential, normal, etc.). (Note that Figure 4.3 shows probability distributions plotted as continuous lines rather than as a column chart. We will not discuss the technical differences in these two types of probability distributions, although the height of the line in Figure 4.3 can still be interpreted as the relatively likelihood of the corresponding monetary loss on the x-axis.) In the first pane of that figure, it is not clear how a heavy tail distribution might differ from other distributions or be problematic in any way. Only in the second pane of that figure, which looks at more extreme values ($5 \leq x \leq 15$), does it become evident that the tail of the Pareto distribution decays less quickly than the tails of the other

Figure 4.3
Light Tail Distributions versus a Heavy-Tail Pareto Distribution with Enlargement of the Right Tail

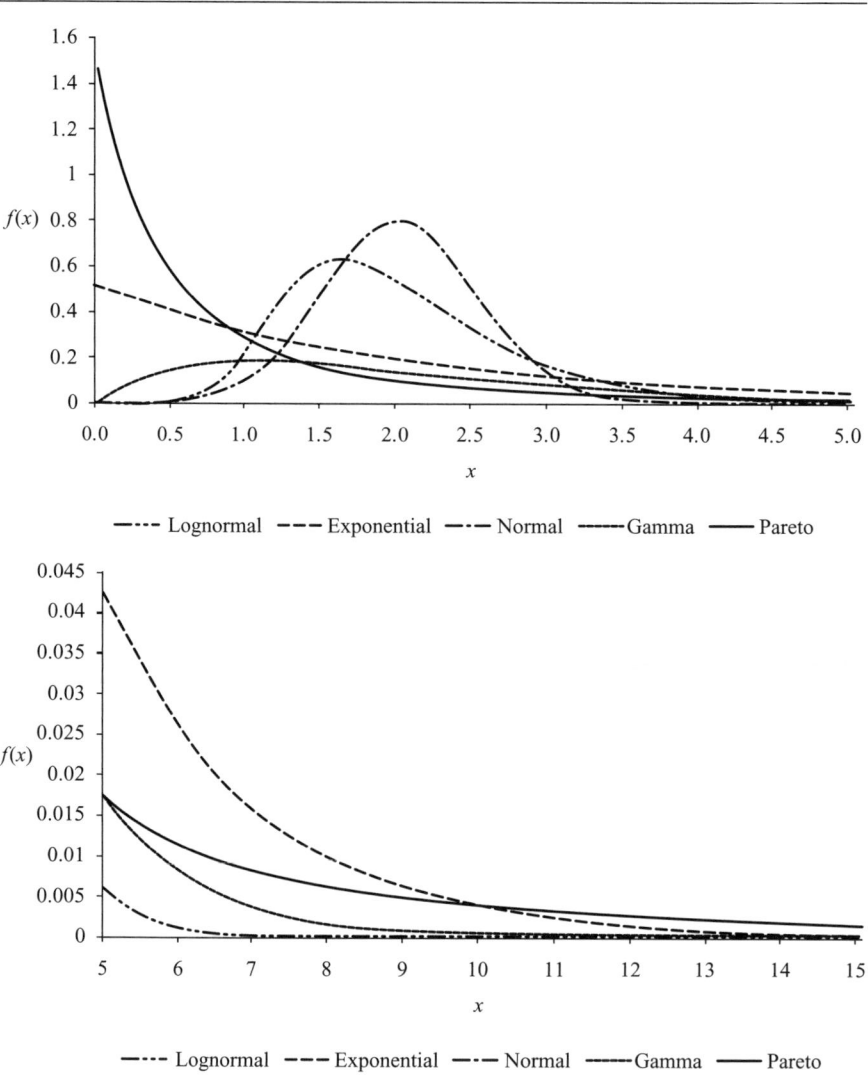

distributions. Even then, the implications of the heavy tail, which demonstrate greater probabilities for extreme events than for the other distributions—but still low probabilities in an absolute sense—may not be apparent. However, this subtle difference causes significant issues with supply chain risk measurement, because the standard deviation of heavy tail distributions is infinite (and the mean may be infinite also), which renders the standard deviation ineffective in measuring the amount of catastrophic risk a supply chain might face when such heavy tail distributions affect supply chains.

In the next section, we discuss the problem of computing a comprehensive probability distribution for a supply chain, which might be useful when no heavy tail probability distributions apply, or if one wanted to compute it even if the standard deviation cannot be used to summarize it.

THE COMPLEXITY OF MODELING SUPPLY CHAIN RISK

In this section, we investigate the analytical computation of supply chain risk, whereby a probability distribution for monetary loss is computed from many probability distributions, one for each possible disruptive event. We show how attributes of supply chains and their models affect the complexity of that computation. Furthermore, we will note assumptions that can be made regarding each attribute that simplify the analysis at some possible loss of accuracy. Throughout this section, we use GM's supply chain as an example, partly because estimates of its "size" are available. GM is a larger company than most, however, and so we will comment on the implications that our analysis has for smaller companies, as well as purposefully underestimating the complexity of GM's problem to bring our assessment of complexity more in line with the complexity that smaller companies face.

The Number of Possible Disruptive Events

In this section, we approximate the number of catastrophic events that would need to be considered to compute supply chain risk based on these dimensions of GM's supply chain:

1. General Motors makes dozens of car models.[28]
2. GM has approximately 139 manufacturing plants in 33 countries.[29]
3. Parts for GM products are supplied by approximately 3,200 companies worldwide, from as many as 10,000 facilities.[30]
4. GM sells vehicles in 200 countries.
5. GM has 7,500 dealers.
6. A typical vehicle has 14,000 parts.[31]

The plant census figure above includes only manufacturing plants, and it excludes GM-owned distribution centers that supply parts to assembly plants and that supply service parts to dealerships. We must also consider the transportation links that connect each supply chain facility. We assume two transportation modes leaving the assembly plants (truck and rail) and, for the sake of understating the number of disruptive events, we will assume only one mode of transportation between any two facilities in the remainder of the supply chain.

Table 4.1
Possible GM Supply Chain Disruptions

GM bankruptcy	Product recall for supplier's part	Building subsidence
Logistics provider failure	Product recall for GM error	Building structural collapse
Supplier bankruptcy	Raw materials shortage	Building fire
Service provider failure	Equipment fire	Boiler explosion
Severe hot/cold weather	Equipment mechanical breakdown	Compressed air failure
Blizzard/ice storm	Accidental equipment damage	Utilities failure
Hail storm	Accidental plant damage	IT software failure
Heavy rain	Labor shortage	IT hardware failure
Flooding	Union/labor strikes	Denial of service attack
Tsunami	Terrorism	Pollution
Hurricane/typhoon	Sabotage	Hazardous waste spill
Tornado	Vandalism	Asbestos exposure
Other wind damage	Theft	Mold exposure
Lightning strike	Workplace violence	Logistics mode failure
Volcano	Geopolitical risk	Logistics route disruption
Earthquake	Epidemic	Distribution network failures
Wildfire	Pandemic	
Animal/insect infestation	Access/egress restriction	

General Motors has identified 100 potential causes of business disruption, as reported by Sheffi.[32] We culled that list by focusing on (1) events that disrupted the flow of goods through GM's supply chain, (2) catastrophic events that could disrupt facilities for one day or longer, and (3) disruptive events in the supply network. Thus we exclude "demand-side" disruptions (e.g., a precipitous drop in demand) and disruptions of a purely financial nature. (The intent of this paper is to focus on the physical flow of goods through supply chains, although financial catastrophes seem to be an especially pertinent topic in light of the economic crisis at the time of this writing.) We then added to GM's list some disruptive events that any company might face, bringing the number of events on the final list to 52 (see Table 4.1). This list is clearly neither complete nor sufficiently specified. We are confident that it is not exhaustive—many events are undoubtedly omitted. Also, it will be suggested in a later section that some of the events listed in Table 4.1 would need to be disaggregated into greater granularity to perform the computations that we will discuss. Thus, a comprehensive analysis would require a list longer than this (possibly much longer).

To compute the number of distinct ways that each of the 52 disruptions could affect GM's supply chain, we categorized the disruptions by *mode* and *scope*, as shown in Table 4.2. The mode describes the affinity group of the

Table 4.2
Disruptive Event Categorization: Scope Descriptors for Disruption Modes

	Mode			
Geographic	Company	Part	Product	Logistics
Machine	GM	Raw materials	Car models	Transportation node
Plant	Parts supplier	Part		GM facility
City	Service provider	Subassembly		Route
Intracountry region	Logistics provider			Mode
Country				
Intercountry region				
Continent				
World				

affected subset of supply chain nodes and arcs; specifically, the disrupted links might be within a geographical region, belong to a certain company, be associated with particular parts or products, or be a logistics function. Disruption scope describes how widespread the disruption is. (Note that "machine" is included as one possible scope within the geographic mode; while it is not a natural geographic concept, it serves as a natural extension of the other geographic scope descriptors.) Table 4.3 shows the categorization of several example disruptions for clarification.

This categorization, along with the quantification of the dimensions of GM's supply chain (above), allows us to compute the total possible number of distinct events. To illustrate, note that GM has 139 plants and that Table 4.1 contains 26 geographical disruptions that affect the supply chain on a plant-by-plant basis. There exist, therefore, 3,614 distinct disruption events (139 × 26) that affect single plants. If we (conservatively) assume that there are 10 machines in each plant that could suffer catastrophic failure, then GM has 1,390 machines that are subject to three events in Table 4.1, which implies 4,170 distinct events (1,390 × 3). Similar computations were performed by mapping the remaining categorized failures to the dimensions

Table 4.3
Categorization of Example Disruptions

Example	Mode	Scope
Supplier bankruptcy	Company	Parts supplier
Pontiac Fiero engine fire recall	Product	Car model
West Coast dock strike	Logistics	Transportation network node(s)

of GM's supply chain, which, when summed together, resulted in 300,993 distinct events.

In GM's case we should, therefore, be prepared to assign probability distributions for the likelihood of occurrence and magnitude of impact to 300,993 distinct events. This suggests a large data collection task, which, for reasons we will show, is even larger than the population of possible events suggests. Alternatives for simplifying the model and reducing the data collection effort here would be to simply omit some events from consideration, or to specify a small number of generic probability distributions, each of which could be applied to many events (e.g., distributions for probability and impact of a fire might be applied similarly to all plants). The former method would understate risk and, because we tend to specify mitigating efforts only for the risks that are specified, might leave some important risks unmitigated. The latter approach is an approximation whose accuracy would need to be evaluated.

Aggregation of Events

In specifying probability distributions for the likelihood of a disruption and its impact, one must ask: "Do all the instances that we are including within a particular disruptive event (e.g., union strikes) always follow the same probability distributions for likelihood of occurrence and magnitude of disruption?" If the answer is no, then the specification of this type of event is an aggregation of multiple different types of events, which must be split into multiple event categories for maximum accuracy.

We demonstrate the inaccuracy caused by aggregating events using a simple example with fictitious probability distributions. Specifically, we will consider the aggregation of two types of labor strikes that cause a unionized manufacturing plant in the automotive industry to shut down. The United Auto Workers (UAW) union has local leadership at the plant and a national leadership over all such plants. The first type of strike is a "wildcat strike," where the plant union leadership calls a strike at one plant based on a local incident at that plant, without approval from the national union.[33] The second type of strike is a national strike against all UAW-represented plants in the United States, which is endorsed by the national union leadership and occurs most often in conjunction with the negotiation of national UAW–GM labor contracts.[34] Labor contract negotiations reoccur at fixed intervals of time, depending on the industry and, in the automotive industry, have historically been held every three years. Unauthorized wildcat strikes, which can occur at any time, tend to be short, because the national union often urges the local union to go back to work in relatively short order. National strikes tend to be longer and vary in duration to a greater degree than wildcat strikes.

For this example, we will assume that the probability distributions for how many of each type of strike occur in a given year and for the duration

Table 4.4
Frequency and Impact Probability Distributions for Wildcat and National Strikes

Wildcat Strikes				National Strikes			
Frequency		Impact		Frequency		Impact	
Annual # of Strikes	Probability	Strike Duration	Probability	Annual # of Strikes	Probability	Strike Duration	Probability
0	0.90	0	0.00	0	0.72	0	0.000
1	0.05	1	0.85	1	0.28	1	0.000
2	0.04	2	0.10			2	0.000
3	0.01	3	0.05			3	0.020
						4	0.050
						5	0.150
						6	0.150
						7	0.200
						8	0.150
						9	0.100
						10	0.075
						11	0.050
						12	0.020
						13	0.020
						14	0.015

of each type of strike are as given in Table 4.4. (For those familiar with probability, we will assume that the occurrence of strikes are statistically independent.) Let's assume that we want to characterize the risk of strikes by computing the mean (average) and standard deviation of the number of days lost to strikes each year, and that toward that end we have collected data on strikes for a number of years that reflect with reasonable accuracy the data in Table 4.4. Computing the mean and standard deviation can be done in two ways. First, the mean and standard deviation could be computed for all of the data which combines national and wildcat strikes. The second way would be to separate data for national and wildcat strikes and compute the summary statistics separately. Subsequently, the two sets of summary statistics would need to be combined using laws of probability (which we do not discuss in detail here). The first method would yield a mean of approximately 2.697 days on strike per year and a standard deviation of 4.26, while the second method would yield a mean of 2.697 and a standard deviation of approximately 3.61. Thus, using the first (and incorrect) method we would find the correct mean, but we would be tempted to use a probability distribution in our analysis that was approximately 18% too large in terms of the standard deviation. Furthermore, it can be shown that not separating the data for events with distinctly different characteristics in this case also overstates risk as stated in terms of VaR. The correct 95% and 99% VaR values are 10 and 13 days, whereas treating the data in a pooled fashion yields values of 11 and 18 days.

Thus, aggregating events with dissimilar probability distributions for disruption duration can be misleading, and furthermore, this error repeated over many different risks that a supply chain faces could yield substantial error in our assessment of risk. If we were to assess GM's supply chain risk, the most accurate analysis would be one that carefully considers whether every event classified within each type of disruptive risk truly has the same underlying causes and dynamics, as reflected in the probability distributions, or whether dissimilar events have been aggregated and thus must be separated into different categories. Such a careful analysis might well result in more than 300,993 events, and in greater complexity.

In the event that one might want to simplify an assessment of risk by aggregating events, our example suggests that any aggregation should be done carefully and be accompanied by an analysis that ensures the desired level of accuracy. In particular, our example suggests that events should be aggregated only when they share similar probability distributions for disruption duration. Further, if one were to aggregate event types, then it is likely that one should aggregate events whose mode and scope are the same and, moreover, that affect the same supply chain entities; otherwise, disruption probability distributions for a particular set of supply chain entities would be based on data that was not pertinent to it.

In passing, we note a mistake in our example possibly more significant than that caused by aggregation. Specifically, national strikes tend to occur when national contracts are negotiated, which the data might suggest in this case is every three years. The original probability for occurrence of national strikes is thus inaccurate, because it is already aggregated. In reality, the probability of a national strike is essentially zero in every two out of three years, and highly likely every third year. A less aggregated and more accurate assessment of risk would disaggregate the data between contract years and noncontract years, necessitating two analyses: one for contract years, and one for other years.

The Likelihood of Concurrent Disruptions

We would never need to consider the circumstance in which a supply chain was simultaneously disrupted by two or more of the 300,993 distinct disruptive events that we previously cataloged under these three conditions:

1. The duration of impact of any disruption was infinitesimally long.
2. No two disruptive events could commence at precisely the same time.
3. The occurrence of no two events was correlated.

However, we should expect none of these three conditions to hold in real supply chains, so we must consider the coincidence of multiple disruptions. In fact, GM suffered multiple concurrent disruptions recently, when simultaneously a carpet supplier to a Lansing, MI, assembly plant went on strike April 17–May 2, 2008, as the plant it supplied went on strike from April 17–May 19, 2008. Other significant disruptions to GM's supply chain occurring during this same timeframe included a strike by American Axle and Manufacturing (February 26, 2008, through late May 2008) and a strike in a Fairfax, KS, assembly plant (May 7–23, 2008). The two Lansing strikes affected the same assembly plant, whereas the other two strikes affected distinctly separate GM plants. The impact of concurrent disruptions may sometimes increase disproportionately with the number of disruptions (e.g., where reserve capacity was sufficient to cover for the first disruption but not the second), or the effects may simply sum (e.g., if two events affected a disjoint set of supply chain links such as the Fairfax and American Axle strikes), or the effect may be less than if the two events had occurred separately (e.g., two parts shortages that affected exactly the same products or the two strikes that affected Lansing plants from April 17 until May 2).

We now compute the number of concurrent events that are possible in GM's supply chain, all of which would need to be comprehended in our calculation of GM's risk probability distribution. To make our analysis tractable and to be conservative in our estimate of that number (i.e., to compute a lower bound), we make three additional assumptions:

1. Each event cannot occur again before its disruption has been resolved.
2. No event cannot occur more than once in the time horizon of interest.

3. The high-frequency, low-impact, day-to-day fluctuations and uncertainties of demand, materials supply, transportation, and production can be safely ignored because their effects are dwarfed by the impact of catastrophic disruptions.

Of the 300,993 events, the disruptions due to any two events could occur concurrently, or the disruptions due to any three events could coincide, and so on. The disruptions due to any number of events, up to 300,993, however probable or improbable, could occur concurrently. This is the probability notion of *combinations*, and (for example) the notation for the number of different combinations of GM's 300,993 events involving two events is expressed as $\binom{300,993}{2}$, and similarly for other numbers of concurrent events. With the assumptions above, the number of possible scenarios is the sum of all the combinations involving one or more events:

$$\sum_{n=1}^{300,993} \binom{300,993}{n}. \tag{1}$$

Interestingly, this number is too large to be computed in Excel; only the first 76 terms can be computed, which equals 1.2×10^{305} combinations. Even the consideration of single, double, or triple events represents approximately 1×10^{13} scenarios. Besides the collection of 300,993 probability distributions for the likelihood and impact for each of the 300,993 events, we therefore need to be able to describe the probability distributions for the practically uncountable number of multiple-event scenarios. To accomplish this, we would need a description of how each of the 300,993 events affected the physical flow through the supply chain, for each of many possible levels of severity with which each event might occur, and a description of how the physical disruption of each individual event was interrelated with the physical aspects of disruption for all other disruptions. Included in specifying the impact of each combination of events would be the determination whether the aggregate impact of multiple events was subadditive, additive, or superadditive. This observation greatly increases the chore of collecting data for a risk assessment.

A further complication is that the disruptions from any combination of events that occur over a timeframe can overlap in different ways, or not at all. The typical method for computing a probability of a particular magnitude of disruption from multiple events would be to use calculus. Thus, for each of the practically uncountable number of possible combinations of disruptions, we must also perform multiple calculus computations, one for every possible sequence of the multiple disruptions of each combination, and for different modes of overlap. The total number of computations when N events are possible can be expressed as

$$1 + N! + \sum_{n=2}^{N} \binom{N}{n} \left[n! \left(1 + \sum_{i=2}^{n} (n-i+1) \right) \right], \tag{2}$$

where the subscript n represents the number of events that occur, and i represents the number of overlapping events. Recall that $N = 300,993$ for GM.

While understanding the details of the mathematical expression above is unimportant, perhaps its visual complexity serves as an exclamation point on the observation that taking into account the possibility of concurrent disruptions greatly increases the complexity already reflected in the practically uncountable number of combinations in (1). We have performed the calculus required for concurrent disruptions under the most amenable mathematical circumstances (for those interested in mathematics, we assumed a homogeneous Poisson process for occurrence of a disruptive event and an exponential disruption duration). These computations are arduous for the favorable assumptions that we made and, in most cases, are not tractable.

Note that calculations such as in (1) and (2) for smaller companies are likely to result in the same conclusion that we made for GM: that an analytical assessment of risk is intractable. Before moving on, we underscore that claim by noting that our assumptions that led to our less than encouraging analysis cause our estimates for the number of computations and the quantity of data required to be conservative. For example, if the same event could occur multiple times within the time horizon of interest, then more disruptive scenarios are possible than indicated by (1). Moreover, if we acknowledged this possibility, then we would need additional information in order to specify how each event could reoccur: (1) nonoverlapping impact durations, or (2) overlapping durations. Making the assumption that durations due to the same event reoccurring cannot overlap is valid for some types of events, such as when a machine breaks down: it cannot break again until it is fixed. This is not always valid, however; for example, although a plant might burn to the ground, it can burn again during reconstruction without ever becoming operational again, which is one example of concurrent events of the same type. Additionally, our conversation has been put in the context of independent statistical events. Acknowledging the possibility that the occurrence of disruptive events are positively correlated or dependent increases the complexity of the analysis required for a risk assessment, and, perhaps, the data requirements.

Moreover, by assuming that we do not need to model the effects of high-frequency, low-impact, day-to-day fluctuations in the supply chain, we need no mechanism to keep track of the state of the supply chain (for example, how much inventory exists of each item), which varies from moment to moment. Realistically, the impact of a disruption varies with the current state of the supply chain, and it is less when, for example, more inventory exists to buffer the impact. Ignoring the computations necessary to represent a probability distribution for the various possible states of the supply chain when disruptions occur is to avoid a problem that is most likely on par in complexity with the task of assessing supply chain risk. It is not clear, however, whether this simplification is one that is likely to significantly compromise the accuracy of a risk assessment. Today's global, multiple-party supply chains are indeed complex systems, as described by Charles Perrow, who warns us that the confluence of many small factors can cause large, catastrophic impacts in which case the state of the supply chain when disruption occurs might be a critical factor.[35]

While one might want to simplify a risk assessment by ignoring the possibility of concurrent disruptions, a philosophical argument for not making that simplification is that although the occurrence of concurrent disruptions is even less likely than a single disruption, their combined effect could be much worse. Thus, if the domain of supply chain risk management is the mitigation of rare but catastrophic events, then concurrent disruptions are members of the category of risks that we seek to control. A rough quantitative argument for not dismissing these possibilities proceeds as follows (in which we assume that all events occur independently). Consider 2 of GM's 300,993 disruptive events, both of which occur within a given year with the same probability, which we vary in three scenarios from 10^{-3} to 10^{-6} to 10^{-9}. Roughly 4.5×10^{10} combinations of two events $\binom{300,993}{2}$ exist, each of which has a probability of occurring in the three scenarios of 10^{-6}, 10^{-12}, and 10^{-18}. It is possibly surprising that with 4.5×10^{10} combinations, the probability that one of these two-event combinations will occur in one year is roughly 4.5×10^4, 4.5×10^{-2}, and 4.5×10^{-8}, respectively. (For positive exponents, these results can be interpreted as the expected number of combinations that occur in one year.) The corresponding probabilities for any one single event occurring in GM's supply chain are 301, 0.3, and 0.0003, so that it is more probable to experience multiple events than a singular event within a year's time when singular events have probabilities of approximately 10^{-5} or more. These calculations are too rough to determine the degree to which disruptions would be likely to concurrent, because the events might happen sufficiently far apart that their durations did not overlap, although it is perhaps nonetheless motivation for carrying out a careful analysis before dismissing consideration of concurrent disruptions in a risk assessment. A similar analysis for other circumstances suggests that events need to be sufficiently rare, and the number of possible events very small, before we might be able to safely omit the consideration of concurrent events. Thus, dismissing the impact of concurrent events is one possible simplifying assumption, but successfully implementing it requires an appropriate definition for "sufficiently rare" and "very small."

Dependence of Disruptive Events

We have thus far assumed that all disruptive events are independent of one another and uncorrelated in terms of the probability distributions for occurrence and durations of events. This, however, is unlikely to be the case in all cases. For example, Stephen Flynn, the Ira A. Lipman Senior Fellow for Counterterrorism and National Security Studies at the Council on Foreign Affairs, suggests that terrorist attacks might be fairly likely to be correlated because of their intentional nature.[36] For example, four airliners were destroyed on 9/11, whereas not one airliner had been affected in this way before 9/11. From a company perspective, two American Airlines airliners and two United Airlines airliners were involved in the 9/11 attacks. Another example of dependent events was a United Auto Workers (UAW) strike on a Dayton, OH, parts plant in March 1996 over outsourcing, the timing of which may have been for the purpose of communicating a hard line on outsourcing in advance of national contract talks later that same year.[37] That strike also idled a number of assembly plants that depended on it for parts. Still another example of dependence occurs when two disruptions are caused by the same event, as in the case of an earthquake that damages a factory as well as the surrounding infrastructure that provides utilities to the factory and transportation in and out of the factory. The factory would not be back online until both disruptions are resolved.

Positive correlation among events such as the GM example can greatly increase the variability in losses due to disruptions and the probability of long disruptions. The effect of dependence among events complicates the analysis of supply chain risk, potentially significantly, by requiring that a dependence structure be specified for occurrence among all possible events and for the duration of any two events that occurred concurrently.

Exhaustive Specification of Disruptive Events

If we do not comprehend the possibility of a particular event, then we obviously will not include it in our risk assessment, which will therefore underestimate risk. The accuracy of a risk assessment is thus dependent on an exhaustive list of disruptive events, including even those that have never before occurred. It is most likely impossible to prove that there exists an event that nobody comprehends; to do so would most likely require that we identify the event of which we do not aware, which is a contradiction.

Requiring that an event exists that nobody has comprehended is a more restrictive condition than necessary for proving that any particular analysis would likely underestimate risk; rather, we must prove only that a particular analyst has not thought of every event for *his or her* supply chain. As an example of omitted events, Dr. Helen Peck, who is a Senior Lecturer at Cranfield University in the United Kingdom found that managers in the aerospace industry did not include in their risk framework the catastrophic events that are the focus of this paper.[38] We can also offer an imprecise qualitative argument in the form of a thought experiment composed of two questions. First, entertain the question: "How many people would have foreseen the possibility of the events that took place on September 10, 2001?" Nassim Nicholas Taleb discussed the possibility of a plane crashing into *his* high-rise office building in a 2005 book that he reported in his 2007 book as being (originally) published a week before 9/11.[39] (This author cannot confirm the exact publishing date of this book, which Amazon.com lists only as October 2001.[40]) Even more notably, best-selling author Tom Clancy ended his 1994 novel *Debt of Honor* by describing a suicide attack in which a fully loaded airliner is used to destroy the U.S. Capitol building, in which the Congress is in session, with the president in attendance. So some people, although perhaps only a few, might have included this event in their risk assessment.

A second question in our thought experiment is: "How many people who do not work in a high-rise office building would have considered an event where a plane crashed into a high-rise building in their analysis before 9/11?" We cannot answer this question—for one reason, because it is unfair to assess people's pre-9/11 knowledge in the years after 9/11. But it seems plausible that very few, if any, companies or facilities residing in low-slung buildings in the heartland of the United States would have had such an event on their event list. The aftermath of 9/11 unfortunately included the cessation of air traffic and border crossings, which did affect many companies with no direct linkage with the World Trade Center or any other high-rise building. For example, Ford shut down five of its assembly plants after the 9/11 attacks due to delays in crossing the Canada–U.S. border.[41] Thus, risk assessments must consider events whose initial impacts are not directly on the supply chain under consideration. Taleb argues that humans tend to focus on particular types of rare events only after they have occurred: since 9/11, we will include similar events in our analysis.[42] But the author hypothesizes what he cannot prove—that other potential disruptive events remain that are not conceived by many managers. If true, a probabilistic risk assessment would always underestimate risk, possibly significantly so, leaving us at the peril that our models are dangerous, self-fulfilling instruments that lead us to focus mitigation efforts only on the most obvious disruptions. Kleindorfer and Saad remind us of the oft-used adage: "You cannot manage what you do not measure."[43]

Availability and Accuracy of Data

Deleris and Erhun have pointed out the difficulty of analytically estimating probability distributions for disruptive events because of lack of data. In this section, we discuss in detail difficulties presented when data for rare events are sparse or unavailable.[44] Moreover, we discuss the difficulty in estimating probability distributions when impacts have heavy tail distributions. In addition, even when data is available, it must be transformed from raw form to a form appropriate for risk analysis.

Although some events have not yet occurred, a probabilistic risk assessment requires probability estimates for those events nonetheless. For example, we have not yet suffered an avian flu pandemic, but its possibility is widely entertained. In the absence of historical data, expert judgment might be the source of probability estimates for the occurrence and duration of such an event. Deleris and Erhun have suggested the use of expert judgment and incorporated it in their models, as do Elkins, Kulkarni, and Tew; McCormack; and Handfield and McCormack.[45] Moreover, probabilistic risk analysis has long relied on eliciting probability data from experts and managers. Philip E. Tetlock's research, however, casts suspicion on the accuracy of experts' forecasts in the realm of politics.[46] If experts' probability estimates are also unreliable for rare events in supply networks, then the accuracy of supply chain risk analysis would be suspect.

Historical data sometimes exists, but is insufficient for facilitating accurate probability estimates of rare events. For example, Melvin Hinich observes that estimating probabilities accurately for rare events with Bayesian updating requires many observations.[47] His analysis extended to our problem indicates that data for 876,000 years would be required before the estimation error for a probability of 10^{-5} was on the order of the true probability. This puts verifiably accurate empirically derived probability estimates out of reach in our lifetimes, and perhaps forever; one might wonder after 876,000 years whether the causal factors that determine that probability might have changed, implying that the estimate would still be inaccurate. We might still trust probabilities deduced regarding earthquakes and the shifting of tectonic plates after 876,000 years, but we should not trust probabilities regarding those events whose dynamics change more quickly—terrorists, for example, adapt their tactics on a short time scale.[48]

Estimating probability distributions for duration of disruption is also difficult when the impact has a heavy tail. Use of techniques for identifying a distribution as having a heavy tail rather than a light tail is difficult, but more reliable than use of techniques for estimating the parameters; it is perhaps fair to say that this science is still in its infancy.[49] Estimating distributions is compounded in our context because the rarity of heavy tail events implies that we accumulate data very slowly, so developing reliable estimates of heavy tails is difficult, if not impossible. Thus it is conceivable that empirical data from a heavy tail might be mistaken as having a light tail, something that could yield a grossly inaccurate model.

We also note that although probability estimates are sometimes available for potentially disruptive events, this does not occur in the form required for a supply chain risk assessment. For example, Sheffi shows maps of earthquake and tornado frequencies.[50] This data needs to be transformed, however, from data on *events* on a broad geographical basis to data on *damage* to specific supply chain facilities and the infrastructure that serves those facilities. For example, data is available from the United States Geological Survey on peak ground acceleration: specifically, thresholds for ground acceleration are specified that will be exceeded with probabilities of 2% and 10% for earthquakes of frequencies 1 hertz and 5 hertz.[51] This data might be used to inform engineering judgment (akin to expert judgment) on the distribution of damage that might be expected to a particular supply chain facility and the surrounding infrastructure. Possibly more accurate damage assessments might be possible with an extrapolation from these data to all magnitudes and frequencies (using the assumption, among other assumptions, that earthquake magnitudes follow power laws), which could then be translated into probability distributions for damage to facilities. Even for the latter (presumably more accurate) method, one relies upon forecasts that are not 100% accurate, as well as much analytical work in translating earthquake statistics into terms useful for risk analysis.

It appears that whether we like to or not, data regarding likelihood and magnitude of damage and disruption will necessarily be approximate, perhaps with considerable error, especially for events where data is sparse and impacts have heavy tails. When raw data about events must be transformed into data about supply chain disruptions, one may choose to do less computation and use possibly less accurate assessments of likelihood or magnitude. While some choice regarding accuracy of data exists in this regard, the approximate nature of the data and the necessity to engage expert judgment suggests the necessity of investigating the effects of inaccurate input data on the accuracy of the risk assessment. However, sensitivity analyses to assess the effect of inaccurate probability distributions will likely pose significant difficulty given the large number of possible disruptions.

Model Scope and Fidelity

We tried to comprehend the entirety of GM's supply chain and all possible disruptive events in the foregoing analysis of complexity. If we had considered a smaller subset of events, considered only a subset of supply chain links, or considered the supply chain for only a particular product or product family, then the analysis would have been simplified. One must gauge, however, whether the simplifications render an analysis tractable, and how they would affect accuracy.

Recognizing the rate at which the number of possible concurrent events increases in (2) as a function of the total number of events N suggests that one might reduce the number of events comprehended in the model. For GM, restricting the supply chain model scope might mean that it considers only their first-tier suppliers. This tack would reduce the number of events by the number associated with the omitted suppliers so that this, in essence, might also be fairly viewed as a way of reducing the number of events that are considered. The downside of omitting events is that disruptive events that are important to mitigate might be inadvertently omitted, as might the combinations of events be that might significantly affect risk; risks not comprehended in the model are not likely to be mitigated.

Restricting the supply chain model to a particular set of products while taking all foreseeable risks into account may be a more prudent tack for simplifying assessment. This approach would be more accurate, however, where the supply chains for various products did not interact—for example, where suppliers and back-up capacity were not shared among product families (i.e., where supply chains were separable).

We view network nodes as facilities, while a more granular perspective would view network nodes as production departments within plants, or specific machines. Taking a more granular approach would complicate the analysis. Taking a less granular view would most likely require aggregation of events, possibly to the extent that the accuracy of the result would be suspect.

Conclusions on the Analytical Modeling Approach

The analysis in the preceding sections might fairly suggest that an analytical approach to computing supply chain risk is likely to either be intractable or inaccurate; the sheer number of complex calculations that are required, the large number of probability distributions that must be specified, and the difficulty of accurately estimating probability distributions for rare events of large magnitudes together seem sufficient to suggest the intractability of such an approach. In addition to these barriers, we still must consider the difficulty of identifying all possible risks, which leaves us vulnerable to unforeseen risks.

These observations are not surprising; perhaps all researchers and analysts would, frankly, intuitively comprehend the complexity of a full-scale analytical approach to quantifying supply chain risk and avoid such an endeavor even without considering the problem at such a detailed level as is done here. Hopefully, however, those sections provide a better understanding of the supply chain risk problem, the various sources of complexity, and possible simplifying assumptions that can be a basis in pursuing more tractable assessments. We investigate one such candidate methodology in the next section: simulation.

ASSESSING SUPPLY CHAIN RISK WITH SIMULATION

Computer simulation is an assessment methodology alternative that is often used in circumstances in which computations cannot be made directly with mathematics. In our case, simulation allows us to avoid the calculus required to combine all the probability distributions for individual events into probability distributions for combinations of events and, finally, a comprehensive assessment for an entire supply chain. We do not delve into the details regarding the structure of what type of simulation methodology (there are many) might be used (e.g., Monte Carlo simulation, discrete event simulation). However, we note that an additional benefit of simulation is that it allows an assessment to more easily consider (1) events whose probabilities change over time, (2) easier computation of monetary loss than with analytical computations, and (3) easier computation of transient effects of material pipelines that empty and refill.

While simulation offers the potential advantage of avoiding many intractable calculations, some of the same difficulties that we encountered with an analytical analysis remain, such as defining an exhaustive list of events, choosing an appropriate level of event aggregation, accurately specifying a large number of probability distributions for rare events with heavy tail disruptions, determining whether keeping track of the ongoing state of the supply chain is important, and specifying a mathematical structure for the dependence among events still are required for a simulation analysis. We will not revisit those issues, but rather focus on a disadvantage of simulation that results from its being an approximate mode of numerical rather than analytic analysis. Specifically, care must be taken to ensure that the results of simulation analyses are of sufficient accuracy, which generally entails simulating a model for a period of time long enough that it can be statistically verified that the numerical results are an accurate representation, within some tolerance, of the true answer. We investigate how long a simulation might need to be run in order to obtain an accurate assessment of risk and, indeed, whether that task is feasible at all if the number of disruptions is practically uncountable or if the probability distributions associated with any disruption are of the heavy tail variety.

Rare Events without Heavy Tails

When disruptions are rare, simulation techniques (i.e., variation reduction techniques) have been developed to reduce the simulation run time required for accurate results.[52] While the literature has developed efficient algorithms for estimating performances measures with a single rare event, the author knows of no well-developed methodology that might be efficient with the millions, or perhaps more, of rare events that must be considered in a supply chain risk assessment.

Rare Events with Heavy Tail Impacts

When disruption impacts are described by heavy tail distributions, whether disruptive events are rare or not, then additional difficulties are encountered. Specifically, it can be shown by mathematical proof that if the impact of only one possible disruptive event is described with a heavy tail probability distribution, then the standard variance of monetary loss is infinite, as its mean might also be. The practical implication of this result is that while the mean and variance of disruption impact could be calculated numerically at any point in a simulation run, those values could never be trusted to be accurate. Therein lies a pitfall by which one might be tempted to believe that the simulation had converged to reliable estimates when in fact it never would.

To illustrate the potential pitfall, consider a disruptive event with a probability of occurrence of 10^{-3}. Consider this to be the probability of a disruption over a one-year period. Then a simulation analysis might consider many years in succession, some in which the event would occur and some when it would not. In the years that the event did occur, its monetary effect would be derived from a heavy tail distribution. The mean and standard

Figure 4.4
Mean and Standard Deviation of Monetary Loss from Simulation

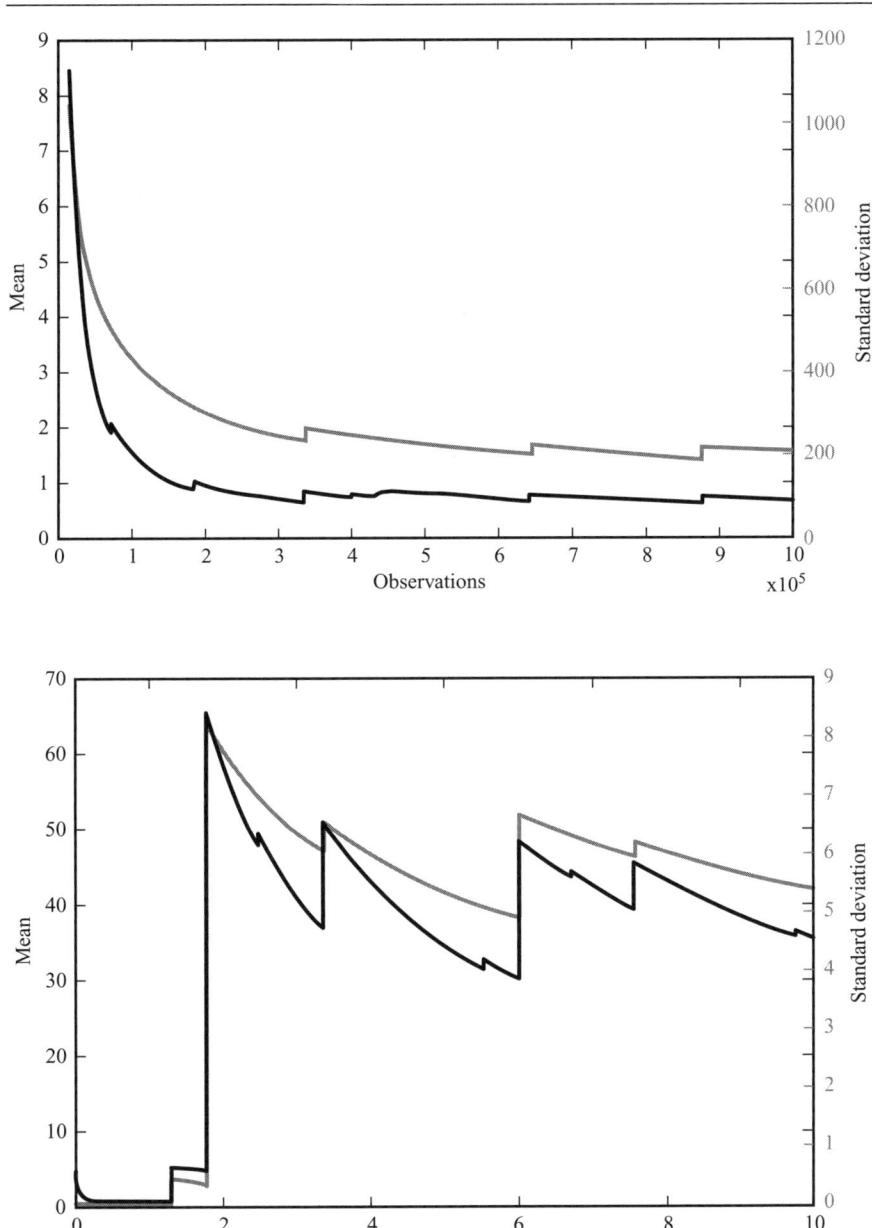

deviation could be computed after each year, as shown in Figure 4.4. If we observed Figure 4.4(a), we might be convinced that are simulation had "settled down" (converged in technical terminology) to values that were representative of the true mean and standard deviation of monetary loss after observing results for 1,000,000 years. If we were to observe a greater number of years, as shown in Figure 4.4(b), however, we would observe that convergence has not occurred: after approximately 2,000,000 observations, the mean and standard deviation make a sudden and dramatic jump. This is precisely the effect created when the magnitude of any one disruption impact can dwarf the cumulative effect of many or all preceding disruptions. In this example, we would witness such wild excursions indefinitely, and the simulation results would never settle down to reliable values.

When we are interested in measuring risk using VaR rather than the mean and variance, the difficulty may be even greater. For example, Asmussen and Glynn discuss the difficulty of estimating the tail of the heavy tail distributions.[53] Existing simulation technology thus does not provide us with adequate capabilities to assess accurately the mean, standard deviation, or VaR of monetary loss and supply chain risk.

One can argue that the potential financial loss at a facility or in a company does not practically extend to infinity as a theoretical heavy tail distribution would reflect. Instead, the monetary loss due to any disruption would be capped by the value of a company: no monetary loss could exceed that amount. This observation relieves the computation problems somewhat, but it can be mathematically shown that the reliability of measurements of the standard deviation of monetary would still likely be unreliable. Simulation is a useful approach, because it most often allows the analysis of problems that are intractable analytically. Our analysis, unfortunately, forces us to conclude that the utility of simulation is greatly diminished when rare events are possible and the magnitudes of impacts have heavy tail probability distributions, even when heavy tail distributions for impact magnitudes are truncated.

THE EFFICACY OF POSSIBLE SIMPLIFYING ASSUMPTIONS

We know of corporations where CEOs use a probability distribution to describe the risk in their company's supply chain. If such analyses are to become increasingly in demand, then the obstacles identified in the foregoing analysis must somehow be surmounted. In the short term, simplifying the calculations or simulation analysis is perhaps the only avenue available. Our foregoing analysis offers an initial analysis on which simplifying assumptions might be viable without introducing significant errors in accuracy, and which might induce gross inaccuracies. All of the possible assumptions discussed below warrant further analysis to see which might indeed be viable methods and how they might be implemented so that they do not induce too much inaccuracy.

The possible simplifying assumptions that we have mentioned include

1. Aggregating events
2. Ignoring initial conditions upon disruption due to high-frequency, low-impact events
3. Ignoring concurrent disruptions
4. Simplifying data collection/estimation by using rough probability estimates
5. Limiting the number of disruptive events included in the model
6. Restricting the number of supply chain links in model

Other simplifying assumptions that might be possible include

1. Representing heavy tail impacts with a light tail probability distributions
2. Assuming deterministic demand

Data collection and estimation of probability distributions present a great burden. One possible simplification to make that task easier would be to purposefully use rough estimates of probability distributions (although we would still need the capability of distinguishing between heavy and light tail distributions). If rough estimates suffice, then the data estimation task might be simplified by specifying a small number of probability distributions that are applied to the events as most appropriate.

Substituting light tail distributions for disruptions with heavy tail impacts is likely to be a fatal flaw in an analysis, leading us to believe that our analysis is accurate when it is not as well as giving grossly inaccurate results due to the very different characteristics of distributions in these two categories. Furthermore, a worse error might be when a light tail distribution is used in error, because heavy tail distributions are difficult to identify from empirical data.

Omitting some possible disruptions from consideration in a risk assessment, whether intentional or not, seems inevitable. Purposefully doing so and omitting events of a potentially significant nature seems unadvisable unless analysis could confirm the degree to which accuracy would be compromised.

Assuming deterministic demand, as we have essentially done in the analysis contained in this paper, reduces the computational load, but it is not clear to what degree it compromises accuracy.

CONCLUSIONS

We have demonstrated the potential complexity of models and analysis for assessing supply chain risk, which is a requirement for rigorously evaluating which mitigation tactics are best in terms of cost–benefit tradeoff. Our conclusion is that a rigorous and accurate assessment of risk using either analytical probability distributions or simulation analysis is not possible due to the complexities that we have discussed. Perhaps the biggest challenges are dealing with the scale of the problem (e.g., the many possible disruptive events, the interaction among the events, and the related data collection), estimating the probabilities of rare events with scarce data, and doing calculations with probability distributions for disruptions that have heavy tails, or to be better able to determine when it is appropriate to use heavy tails and the extent to which they are appropriate to use in supply chain risk assessment. We have identified various ways that such analyses could be simplified and, indeed, have done some preliminary research in the efficacy of some of these approaches, although much more research is necessary to identify the best simplifying assumptions that simplify risk assessment the most while reducing analysis accuracy the least. However, many obstacles to an effective risk assessment exist, and so we must hope for the feasibility of many simplifying assumptions or methodological advances.

However, even if those technological hurdles are surmounted, many difficulties persist unabated, including the inability to comprehensively list all possible disruptive events, and the subsequent data collection and specification. One might conclude that the path going forward for assessing supply chain risk and determining mitigation tactics is one that must consider that we cannot know all the risks facing a supply chain and that the rigorous description of those risks in terms of probability distributions is not possible. Short of a complete and rigorous assessment of supply chain risk, we might alternately strive for methodologies that identify the most critical risks or that identify mitigation tactics that are robust in they reduce the disruption due to many types of events, perhaps even unforeseen events.

One such specific approach is to focus not on the events that cause disruptions, but rather on the modes and effects of disruptions. Failure Modes and Effects Analysis (FMEA), for example, is a methodology that focuses on failure modes in product design and process design and improvement, prioritizing which failure modes are most critical (thus prioritizing them for mitigation). FMEA bases its prioritization on *estimates* of (1) probability of a failure mode occurring, (2) impact of the failure, and (3) likelihood of detecting an imminent failure before it occurs in order to mitigate the impact effectively. Applying FMEA to supply chains, a failure mode would be a description of which nodes or arcs were inoperative in a particular scenario, and for how long. Further, FMEA might be appropriately adapted to supply chain risk by emphasizing the impact of failure modes, which might more readily be ascertained than the probability of failure modes. Although FMEA can be fairly described as an approximate method because it is based on approximate data, our foregoing analysis suggests that approximate data may be the best that is possible for supply chain risk management. Therefore, the accuracy of FMEA is commensurate with the data that is available.

NOTES

1. Ann Zimmerman, Amy Merrick, and Queena Sook Kim. "Retailers Scramble to Keep Stores Stocked," *The Wall Street Journal*, October 21, 2002; Martin Mittlestaedt, "Truck Traffic Snarled at Border," *The Globe and Mail*, September 14, 2001; Hiawatha Bray, "When 'Just in Time' Isn't: Factories Return to Stockpiling as Deliveries Suffer," *The Boston Globe*, September 25, 2001; P. Porter, "Lack of Parts Shuts Down Auto Plants," *Dispatch Business Reporter*, September 14, 2001; Jody Snider, "Ford among Companies Feeling Pinch from Grounded Airplanes," *Daily Press*, September 13, 2001; Ioannis S. Papadakis, and William T. Ziemba, "Derivative Effects of the 1999 Earthquake in Taiwan to U.S. Personal Computer Manufacturers," in *Mitigation and Financing of Seismic Risks*, ed. Paul R. Kleindorfer and Murat R. Sertel (Boston: Kluwer Academic Publishers, 2001), 261–276.

2. Almar Latour, "Trial by Fire: A Blaze in Albuquerque Sets Off Major Crisis for Cell-Phone Giants," *The Wall Street Journal*, January 29, 2001.

3. Sony Press Release, "Sony and Ericsson to Create World Leader in Mobile Phones", *Sony Press Release*, April 24, 2001, http://www.sony.com/SCA/press/010424.shtml.

4. Paul R. Kleindorfer and Germaine H. Saad, "Managing Disruption Risks in Supply Chains," *Production and Operations Management* 14, no. 1 (2005): 53–68; Robert B. Handfield, Jennifer Blackhurst, Debra Elkins, and Christopher W. Craighead, "A Framework for Reducing the Impact of Disruptions to the Supply Chain: Observations from Multiple Executives," in *Supply Chain Risk Management*, ed. Robert B. Handfield and Kevin McCormack (New York: Auerbach Publications, Taylor & Francis Group, 2008), 29–49; Meg Green, "Loss/Risk Management Notes: Executives Rank Fire, Disruptions Top Threats," *Best's Review* 105 (September 1, 2004): 105; Debra Elkins, Devadatta Kulkarni, and Jeffrey Tew, "Identifying and Assessing Supply Chain Risk," in *Supply Chain Risk Management*, ed. Robert B. Handfield and Kevin McCormack (New York: Auerbach Publications, Taylor & Francis Group, 2008), 51–56; Debra Elkins, Robert B. Handfield, Jennifer Blackhurst, and Christopher W. Craighead, "A 'To-Do' List to Improve Supply Chain Risk Management Capabilities," in *Supply Chain Risk Management*, ed. Robert B. Handfield and Kevin McCormack (New York: Auerbach Publications, Taylor & Francis Group, 2008), 57–63.

5. Robert B. Handfield, "Consumers of Supply Chain Risk Data," in *Supply Chain Risk Management*, ed. Robert B. Handfield and Kevin McCormack (New York: Auerbach Publications, Taylor & Francis Group, 2008), 1–28; Robert B. Handfield, Jennifer Blackhurst, Debra Elkins, and Christopher W. Craighead, "A Framework for Reducing," 29–49.

6. Debra Elkins, Devadatta Kulkarni, and Jeffrey Tew, "Identifying and Assessing Supply Chain Risk," in *Supply Chain Risk Management*, ed. Robert B. Handfield and Kevin McCormack (New York: Auerbach Publications, Taylor & Francis Group, 2008), 51–56.

7. Paul R. Kleindorfer and Germaine H. Saad, "Managing Disruption Risks in Supply Chains," *Production and Operations Management* 14, no. 1 (2005): 53–68.

8. Yossi Sheffi, *The Resilient Enterprise: Overcoming Vulnerability for Competitive Advantage* (Cambridge, MA: The MIT Press, 2005).

9. Glenn Brooks "US: Full Production at GM plants for First Time after AAM strike; Lordstown to Build More Small Cars," *Automotive World* (June 17, 2008): 7; Harry Maurer and Cristina Linblad, "More Dents in Detroit," *BusinessWeek* (June 9, 2008): 3.

10. Yossi Sheffi, *The Resilient Enterprise: Overcoming Vulnerability for Competitive Advantage* (Cambridge, MA: The MIT Press, 2005); Paul R. Kleindorfer and Germaine H. Saad, "Managing Disruption Risks in Supply Chains," *Production and Operations Management* 14, no. 1 (2005): 53–68.

11. Debra Elkins, Devadatta Kulkarni, and Jeffrey Tew, "Identifying and Assessing Supply Chain Risk," in *Supply Chain Risk Management*, ed. Robert B. Handfield and Kevin McCormack (New York: Auerbach Publications, Taylor & Francis Group, 2008), 51–56.

12. Brian T. Tomlin, "On the Value of Mitigation and Contingency Strategies for Managing Supply Chain Disruption Risks," *Management Science* 52, no. 5 (2006): 639–657.

13. Brian T. Tomlin, "Selecting a Disruption-Management Strategy for Short Life-Cycle Products: Diversification, Contingent Sourcing, and Demand Management" (working paper, Kenan Flagler Business School, University of North Carolina at Chapel Hill, 2008).

14. Brian T. Tomlin and Lawrence V. Snyder, "On the Value of a Threat Advisory System for Managing Supply Chain Disruptions," working paper, Kenan Flagler Business School, University of North Carolina at Chapel Hill, 2008, http://public.kenan-flagler.unc.edu/faculty/tomlinb/working%20papers.html.

15. Andrew M. Ross, Ying Rong, and Lawrence V. Snyder, "Supply Disruptions with Time-Dependent Parameters," *Computers and Operations Research* 35, no. 11 (2008): 3504–3529.

16. Brian T. Tomlin and Yimin Wang. "On the Value of Mix Flexibility and Dual Sourcing in Unreliable Newsvendor Networks," *Manufacturing and Service Operations Management* 7, no. 1 (2005): 37–57.

17. George A. Zsidisin and Lisa M. Ellram, "An Agency Theory Investigation of Supply Risk Management," *Journal of Supply Chain Management* 39, no. 3 (2003): 15–27; George A. Zsidisin, "Managerial Perceptions of Supply Risk," *Journal of Supply Chain Management* 39, no. 1 (2003): 14–25.

18. Stephen C. Graves and Brian T. Tomlin, "Process Flexibility in Supply Chains," *Management Science* 49, no. 7 (2003): 907–919.

19. Léa A. Deleris and Feryal Erhun, "Risk Management in Supply Networks Using Monte-Carlo Simulation," in *Proceedings of the 2005 Winter Simulation Conference*, ed. M. E. Kuhl, N. M. Steiger, F. B. Armstrong, and J. A. Joines (Piscataway, NJ: IEEE, 2005), 1–7.

20. Léa A. Deleris and Feryal Erhun, "Quantitative Risk Assessment in Supply Chains: A Case Study Based on Engineering Risk Analysis Concepts," to appear in *Handbook of Production Planning*, ed. K. Kempf, P. Keskinocak, and R. Uzsoy, Norwell, MA: Kluwer International Series in Operations Research and Management Science, Kluwer Academic Publishers, 1–7.

21. Reuters, "Strike at Supplier Leads G.M. to Idle 3 More Plants," *The New York Times*, March 1, 2008; Shawn Langolis, "G.M. Sees $1.8 Billion Loss in Wake of Supplier Strike," *MarketWatch*, May 23, 2008, http://www.marketwatch.com/news/story/gm-sees-18-billion-loss/story.aspx?guid=%7BC7BABC8B-23E5-4972-8263-EB9E024898EE%7D.

22. Michael Murphy, "GM Delta Township Plant Affected by Carpet Supplier Strike," *Automotive World*, April 16, 2008.

23. Jeffrey Gold, "US Truckers Pull Rigs Off Road, Others Slow to Crawl in Protest of Fuel prices," *Associated Press Release*, April 1, 2008.

24. Soren Asmussen and Peter W. Glynn, *Stochastic Simulation Algorithms and Analysis* (New York: Springer, 2007).

25. Yossi Sheffi, *The Resilient Enterprise: Overcoming Vulnerability for Competitive Advantage* (Cambridge, MA: The MIT Press, 2005).

26. Walter Willinger, David Alderson, John C. Doyle, and Lun Li, "More 'Normal' Than Normal: Scaling Distributions and Complex Systems," in *Proceeding of the 2004 Winter Simulation Conference*, ed. R. G. Ingalla, M. D. Rossetti, J. S. Smith, and B. A. Peters (Piscataway, NJ: IEEE Press, 2004), 130–141.

27. This effect is discussed in the following two references: Yossi Sheffi, *The Resilient Enterprise: Overcoming Vulnerability for Competitive Advantage* (Cambridge, MA: The MIT Press, 2005); Nassim Nicholas Taleb, *The Black Swan: The Impact of the Highly Improbable* (New York: Random House, 2007).

28. Yossi Sheffi, *The Resilient Enterprise: Overcoming Vulnerability for Competitive Advantage* (Cambridge, MA: The MIT Press, 2005).

29. General Motors Web site, http://www.gm.com/corporate/about/company.jsp.

30. Tom Murphy, "Strategic Sourcing," *Ward's Auto World*, July 1, 2007, 20; Konicki, S. "EDS Tools Tie Suppliers to GM Design Network," *InformationWeek*, http://www.informationweek.com/story/showArticle.jhtml?articleID=6502093.

31. Pat Snack, Mike Comerford, Marianne Grant, and Tim Thomas, "Building the Standards Foundations for Global Enterprise," presentation at 6/12/2007 *DAMA Meeting*, http://www.dama-michigan.org/21%20AIAG_Overview%20Jun07.pdf.

32. Yossi Sheffi, *The Resilient Enterprise: Overcoming Vulnerability for Competitive Advantage* (Cambridge, MA: The MIT Press, 2005).

33. An example of a wildcat strike is a strike called at the Lordstown, Ohio, GM plant in 1996, as described in Keith Bradsher, "Wildcat Strike Shuts Down a G.M. Plant," *The New York Times*, April 16, 1996.

34. An example of an authorized UAW strike is discussed in Sholnn Freeman and Frank Ahrens, "Workers at GM Walk Off the Job: Union Strikes to Keep Work in United States," *Washington Post*, September 25, 2007.

35. Charles Perrow, *Normal Accidents: Living with High-Risk Technologies* (Princeton, NJ: Princeton University Press, 1984).

36. Steven Flynn, *America the Vulnerable* (New York: HarperCollins, 2004).

37. Keith Bradsher, "Automobile Workers Strike Shutting 2 G.M. Parts Plants," *The New York Times*, March 6, 1996.

38. Helen Peck, "Drivers of Supply Chain Vulnerability: An Integrated Framework," *International Journal of Physical Distribution Logistics Management* 35, no. 4 (2005): 210–232.

39. Nassim Nicholas Taleb, *Fooled by Randomness: The Hidden Role of Chance in Life and in the Markets* (New York: Random House, 2005).

40. The original version of *Fooled by Randomness*, ISBN 978-1587990717, published by W. W. Norton and Company, is reported by Amazon.com to have been published in October 2001.

41. Hiawatha Bray, "When 'Just in Time' Isn't: Factories Return to Stockpiling as Deliveries Suffer," *The Boston Globe*, September 25, 2001.

42. Nassim Nicholas Taleb, *The Black Swan: The Impact of the Highly Improbable* (New York: Random House, 2007).

43. Paul R. Kleindorfer and Germaine H. Saad, "Managing Disruption Risks in Supply Chains," *Production and Operations Management* 14, no. 1 (2005): 53–68.

44. Léa A. Deleris and Feryal Erhun, "Quantitative Risk Assessment in Supply Chains: A Case Study Based on Engineering Risk Analysis Concepts," to appear in *Handbook of Production Planning*, ed. K. Kempf, P. Keskinocak, and R. Uzsoy, Norwell, MA: Kluwer International Series in Operations Research and Management Science, Kluwer Academic Publishers.

45. Léa A. Deleris and Feryal Erhun, "Quantitative Risk Assessment in Supply Chains: A Case Study Based on Engineering Risk Analysis Concepts," to appear in *Handbook of Production Planning*, ed. K. Kempf, P. Keskinocak, and R. Uzsoy, Norwell, MA: Kluwer International Series in Operations Research and Management Science, Kluwer Academic Publishers; Léa A. Deleris and Feryal Erhun, "Risk Management in Supply Networks Using Monte-Carlo Simulation," in *Proceedings of the 2005 Winter Simulation Conference*, ed. M. E. Kuhl, N. M. Steiger, F. B. Armstrong, and J. A. Joines (Piscataway, NJ: IEEE, 2005); Debra Elkins, Devadatta Kulkarni, and Jeffrey Tew, "Identifying and Assessing Supply Chain Risk," in *Supply Chain Risk Management*, ed. Robert B. Handfield and Kevin McCormack (New York: Auerbach Publications, Taylor & Francis Group, 2008); Robert B. Handfield and Kevin McCormack, "Case Studies," in *Supply Chain Risk Management*, ed. Robert B. Handfield and Kevin McCormack (New York: Auerbach Publications, Taylor & Francis Group, 2008), 93–103.

46. Philip E. Tetlock, *Expert Political Judgment* (Princeton, NJ: Princeton University Press, 2005).

47. Melvin J. Hinich, "Risk When Some States Are Low-Probability Events," *Macroeconomic Dynamics* 7, no. 4 (2003): 636–643.

48. Yossi Sheffi discusses how terrorists adapt their tactics on a short time scale in his *The Resilient Enterprise: Overcoming Vulnerability for Competitive Advantage* (Cambridge, MA: The MIT Press, 2005).

49. Soren Asmussen and Peter W. Glynn, *Stochastic Simulation Algorithms and Analysis* (New York: Springer, 2007); Paul Embrechts, Claudia Klüppelberg, and Thomas Mikosch, *Modelling Extremal Events* (Berlin: Springer, 1997); Sidney I. Resnick, "Heavy Tail Modeling and Teletraffic Data," *The Annals of Statistics* 25, no. 5 (1997): 1805–1849; Sidney I. Resnick, *Heavy-Tail Phenomena: Probabilistic and Statistical Modeling* (New York: Springer, 2007); Nassim Nicholas Taleb, *The Black Swan: The Impact of the Highly Improbable* (New York: Random House, 2007); Walter Willinger, David Alderson, John C. Doyle, and Lun Li, "More 'Normal' Than Normal: Scaling Distributions and Complex Systems," in *Proceeding of the 2004 Winter Simulation Conference*, ed. R. G. Ingalla, M. D. Rossetti, J. S. Smith, and B. A. Peters (Piscataway, NJ: IEEE Press, 2004), 130–141.

50. Yossi Sheffi, *The Resilient Enterprise: Overcoming Vulnerability for Competitive Advantage* (Cambridge, MA: The MIT Press, 2005).

51. Mark D. Peterson et al., Documentation for the 2008 Update of the United States National Seismic Hazard Maps, United States Geological Survey, Open-File Report 2008-1128, http://pubs.usgs.gov/of/2008/1128/.

52. Soren Asmussen and Peter W. Glynn, *Stochastic Simulation Algorithms and Analysis* (New York: Springer, 2007).

53. Soren Asmussen and Peter W. Glynn, *Stochastic Simulation Algorithms and Analysis* (New York: Springer, 2007).

CHAPTER 5

Managing the Twenty-First-Century Piracy Threat: The Somali Example

Ruwantissa Abeyratne

Waters off the Indian Ocean coast of Somalia have proved to be a dangerous area that threatens the shipping industry with the offense of piracy. Somali waters have far overtaken traditionally dangerous areas such as the Straits of Malacca in the South East Asia and the waters of Nigeria and Iraq with the recent spate of piracy off the Somali coast. The pirates carry out daring thefts of goods or food aid with the use of speedboats, frequently extending their illegal activity to impounding ships for ransom. The International Maritime Bureau has recorded that by November 2008, there had been ninety-two attacks on ships in the year, thirty-six of which ended in successful hijackings. During the same period fourteen ships were being held, along with 268 hostages.[1]

At the time of writing, the latest in the series of such acts was the impounding of a giant Saudi Arabian oil tanker 450 nautical miles (830 km) off the Kenyan coast. This was so far the largest vessel to be hijacked by Somali pirates, who are reported to have used their contacts' information and high-tech equipment such as GPS-controlled satellite phones and weapons such as AK-47s and rocket-propelled grenades.

These acts of piracy bring to bear the issue of state responsibility under the principles of public international law. Somalia,[2] although besieged by domestic strife, is nonetheless a *de jure* country with a recognized central government known as the Transitional Federal Government (TFG). The TFG is the internationally recognized government of the Somali Republic, and the republic is a member of the United Nations, which makes it an internationally recognized sovereign state. As such, all duties and responsibilities as may accrue under international law to any other member of the United Nations apply also to the Somali Republic and its government.

THE NATURE OF THE OFFENSE

There is simply no question that an act of piracy is an act of terrorism. One interpretation of terrorism given by the courts is that terrorism does not violate international law on the grounds that accusations of terrorism are often met not by a denial of the fact of responsibility but by a justification of the challenged actions.[3] This judgment clearly shows that there is no consensus among the world community that terrorism is an offense against established principles of law. It also infuses to the heart of the offense a core of legitimacy that is often considered incontrovertible, giving rise to the dichotomy that the need for a solution does not arise in the absence of a problem.[4] There is ostensibly a flavor of this attitude in Somalia, where gangs of thugs have descended to the vicinity of the hijacked oil tanker with a view to grabbing a share of the ransom demanded.

The term "terrorism" is seemingly of French origin and is believed to have been first used in 1798.[5] "Terrorism" gave connotations of criminality to one's conduct and was later explicitly identified with the "reign of terror" of the French Revolution. It is now generally considered a system of coercive intimidation[6] brought about by the infliction of terror or fear. The most frustrating obstacle to the control of terrorism is the paucity of clear definition of the offense itself. Many attempts at defining the offense have often resulted in the offense being shrouded in political or national barriers. In 1980, the Central Intelligence Agency of the United States of America adopted a definition of terrorism that read

Terrorism is the threat or use of violence for political purposes by individuals or groups, whether acting for or in opposition to established governmental authority, when such actions are intended to shock, stun or intimidate victims. Terrorism has involved groups seeking to overthrow specific regimes, to rectify perceived national or group grievances, or to undermine international order as an end in itself.[7]

This all-embracing definition underscores the misapprehension that certain groups etched in history, such as the French Resistance in Nazi-occupied France during World War II and the Contras in Nicaragua, broadly fall within the definitive parameters of terrorism. In fact, this formula labels every act of violence as being "terrorist," engulfing in its broad spectrum such diverse groups as the Seikigunha of Japan and the Mujahedeen of Afghanistan, although their aims, modus operandi, and ideologies are different.

James Adams prefers a narrower definition that reads

[A] terrorist is an individual or member of a group that wishes to achieve political ends using violent means, often at the cost of casualties to innocent civilians and with the support of only a minority of the people they claim to represent.[8]

Even this definition, although narrower than the 1980 definition cited above, is not sufficiently comprehensive to cover the terrorist who hijacks a ship or an airplane for his own personal gain.⁹ The difficulty in defining the term seems to lie in its association with political aims of the terrorist, as found in the following definition:

[Terrorism is] terror inspired by violence, containing an international element that is committed by individuals or groups against non-combatants, civilians, States or internationally protected persons or entities in order to achieve political ends.[10]

The offense of terrorism has also been defined as one caused by

any serious act of violence or threat thereof by an individual, whether acting alone or in association with other persons, which is directed against internationally protected persons, organizations, places, transportation or communication systems or against members of the general public for the purpose of intimidating such persons, causing injury to or the death of such persons, disrupting the activities of such international organizations, of causing loss, detriment or damage to such places or property, or of interfering with such transportation and communications systems in order to undermine friendly relations among States or among the nationals of different States or to extort concessions from States.[11]

It is time that terrorism be recognized as a *sui generis* offense, and one that is not always international in nature and motivated by the political aims of the perpetrator. For the moment, if terrorism were to be regarded as the use of fear, subjugation, and intimidation to disrupt the normal operations of humanity, a more specific and accurate definition could be sought, once more analysis is carried out on the subject. One must always be mindful, however, that without a proper and universally acceptable definition, international cooperation in combating terrorism would be impossible.[12]

A terrorist act is one that is *mala in se*, or evil by nature,[13] and that has been associated with the political repression of the French Revolution era where, it is said, the word *terrorism* was coined.[14] A terrorist is a *hostis humani generis*, or a common enemy of humanity.

The earliest form of terrorism against international transportation was piracy. Pirates are considered by international law as common enemies of all mankind. The world naturally has an interest in the punishment of offenders and is justified in adopting international measures for the application of universal rules regarding the control of terrorism. The common understanding between states has been that pirates should be lawfully captured on the high seas by an armed vessel of any particular state and brought within its territorial jurisdiction for trial and punishment. Lauterpacht recognized that

Before international law in the modern sense of the term was in existence, a pirate was already considered an outlaw, a *hostis humani generis*. According to the Law of Nations, the act of piracy makes the pirate lose the protection of his home State, and thereby his national character. Piracy is a so-called international crime, the pirate is considered enemy of all States and can be brought to justice anywhere.[15]

It is worthy of note that under the rules of customary international law, the international community had no difficulty in dealing with acts of terrorism consisting of sea piracy. Due to the seriousness of the offense and the serious terroristic acts involved, the offense was met with the most severe punishment available—death. The universal condemnation of the offense is reflected in the statement that

> In the former times it was said to be a customary rule of international law that after the seizure, pirates could at once be hanged or drowned by the captor.[16]

The laws dealing with the offense of piracy went through a sustained process of evolution. In 1956, while considering legal matters pertaining to the law of the sea, the International Law Association addressed the offense of piracy and recommended that the subject of piracy at sea be incorporated in the Draft Convention of the Law of the Sea. This was followed by the United Nations General Assembly Resolution No. 1105 (XI) in 1957, which called for the convening of a diplomatic conference to further evaluate the Law of the Sea. Accordingly, the Convention of the High Seas was adopted in 1958 and came into force in September 1962.

It is worthy of note that the Geneva Convention of the High Seas of 1958[17] was the first attempt at international accord to harmonize the application of rules to both piracy at sea and in air. The convention adopted authoritative legal statements on civil aviation security, as it touched on piracy over the high seas.[18]

Article 5 of the Convention inclusively defines piracy as follows:

Piracy consists of any of the following acts:

1. Any illegal acts of violence, detention or any act of depredation, committed for private ends by the crew or the passenger of a private ship or a private aircraft, and directed:
    a. on the high seas, against another ship or aircraft, or against persons or property on board such ship or aircraft;
    b. against a ship, aircraft, persons, or property in a place outside the jurisdiction of any state;
2. Any act of voluntary participation in the operation of a ship or of an aircraft with knowledge of facts making it a pirate ship or aircraft;
3. Any act of inciting or of internationally facilitating an act described in sub-paragraph 1 or sub-paragraph 2 of this article.

As provided for by Article 14 of the convention, there is incumbent on all states a general duty to cooperate to the fullest extent in the repression of piracy as defined by the convention. One commentator has observed that

> The International Law Commission in its 1956 report, however, deemed it desirable to enjoin co-operation in the repression of piracy, to define the act to include piracy by aircraft, as set forth in the repressive measures that may justifiably be taken. The United Nations conference on the Law of the Sea in Geneva in 1958 accordingly incorporated these adjustments of the law to modern times in its convention on the High Seas.[19]

Article 14 seemingly makes it a duty incumbent upon every state to take necessary measures to combat piracy by either prosecuting the pirate or extraditing him or her to a state that might be in a better position to undertake such prosecution. The convention, in Article 19, gives all states universal jurisdiction under which the person charged with the offense of aerial or sea piracy may be tried and punished by any state into whose jurisdiction he or she may come. This measure is a proactive one in that it eliminates any boundaries that a state may have that would preclude the extradition or trial in that state of an offender. Universal jurisdiction was conferred upon the states by the convention also to solve the somewhat complex problem of jurisdiction that often arose under municipal law in cases in which the crime was committed outside the territorial jurisdiction of the particular state seeking to prosecute an offender. The underlying salutary effects of universal jurisdiction in cases of piracy and hijacking that was emphasized by the convention, is discussed by Feller:

[T]he absence of universal jurisdiction in relation to a given offense, means that, if a particular State has no jurisdiction either on the basis of territoriality or protection, or on the personality principle, whether passive or active, it will not be authorized to put the offender on trial, even if he is to be found within the territorial boundaries of the State.[20]

The inclusion of the offense of "piracy" in the Convention brings to bear the glaring fact that the crime is international in nature, giving the international community the right to take appropriate measures to combat or at least control the occurrence of the offense. The General Convention by its very nature and adoption has demonstrably conveyed the message that piracy is a heinous crime that requires severe punishment. The convention also calls for solidarity and collectivity on the part of nations in combating the offense in the interests of all nations concerned.[21]

The essential features of definition of piracy as are incorporated in the Geneva Convention are as follows: (1) the pirate must be motivated by "private" as opposed to "public" ends; (2) the act of piracy involves action affecting a ship or an aircraft; (3) the acts of violence, detention, and depredation take place outside the jurisdiction of any state, meaning both territorial jurisdiction and airspace above the state; (4) acts committed on board a ship or aircraft, by the crew or passengers of such ship or aircraft and directed against the ship or aircraft itself, or against persons or property, do not constitute the offense of piracy.

PRINCIPLES OF STATE RESPONSIBILITY

The fundamental issue in the context of state responsibility, for the purposes of this article, is to consider whether a state should be considered responsible for its own failure or nonfeasance to prevent a private act of terrorism against civil aviation, or whether the conduct of the state itself can be impugned by identifying a nexus between the perpetrator's conduct and the state. One view is that an agency paradigm, which may in some circumstances impute to a state reprehensibility on the ground that a principal–agent relationship between the state and the perpetrator existed, can obfuscate the issue and preclude meaningful legal study of the state's conduct.[22]

The Theory of Complicity

At the core of the principal–agent dilemma is the theory of complicity, which attributes liability to a state complicit in a private act. Hugo Grotius (1583–1645), founder of the modern natural law theory, first formulated this theory based on state responsibility that was not absolute. Grotius theorized that although a state did not have absolute responsibility for a private offense, it could be considered complicit through the notion of *patienta* or *receptus*.[23] While the concept of *patienta* refers to a State's inability to prevent a wrongdoing, *receptus* pertains to the refusal to punish the offender.

The eighteenth-century philosopher Emerich de Vattel was of similar view to Grotius, holding that responsibility could only be attributed to the state if a sovereign refuses to repair the evil done by its subjects or to punish an offender or deliver him or her to justice, whether by subjection to local justice or by extradition.[24] This view was to be followed and extended by the British jurist Blackstone a few years later when we went on to say that a sovereign who failed to punish an offender could be considered as abetting the offense, or being an accomplice.[25]

A different view was put forward in an instance of adjudication involving a seminal instance in which the theory of complicity and the responsibility of states for private acts of violence was tested in 1925. The case[26] involved the Mexico–United States General Claims Commission that considered the claim of the United States on behalf of the family of a U.S. national who was murdered in a Mexican mining company where the deceased was working. The United States argued that the Mexican authorities had failed to exercise due care and diligence in apprehending and prosecuting the offender. The decision handed down by the Commission distinguished between complicity and the responsibility to punish, and the commission was of the view that Mexico could not be considered an accomplice in this case.

The complicity theory, particularly from a Vattellian and Blackstonian point of view, is merely assumptive unless put to the test through a judicial process of extradition. In this context, it becomes relevant to address the issue through a discussion of the remedy.

The Condonation Theory

The emergence of the condonation theory was almost concurrent with the *Jane* case[27] decided in 1925 and emerged through the opinions of scholars who belonged to a school of thought that believed that states became responsible for private acts of violence not through complicity as such as by their refusal or failure to bring offenders to justice—tantamount to ratification, or condonation, of the acts in question.[28] The theory was based on the fact that it is not illogical or arbitrary to suggest that a state must be held liable for its failure to take appropriate steps to punish persons who cause injury or harm to others for the reason that such states can be considered guilty of condoning the criminal acts and therefore become responsible for them.[29] Another reason attributed by scholars in support of the theory is that during that time, arbitral tribunals were ordering states to award pecuniary damages to claimants harmed by private offenders, on the basis that the states were being considered responsible for the offenses.[30]

The responsibility of governments in acting against offenses committed by private individuals may sometimes involve condonation or ineptitude in taking effective action against terrorist acts, in particular with regard to the financing of terrorist acts. The United Nations General Assembly, on December 9, 1999, adopted the International Convention for the Suppression of the Financing of Terrorism,[31] aimed at enhancing international cooperation among states in devising and adopting effective measures for the prevention of the financing of terrorism, as well as for the suppression of such financing through the prosecution and punishment of its perpetrators.

The convention, in Article 2, recognizes that any person who by any means, whether directly or indirectly, unlawfully or willfully, provides or collects funds with the intention that they should be used or in the knowledge that they are to be used, in full or in part, in order to carry out any act which constitutes an offense under certain named treaties, commits an offense. One of the treaties cited by the convention is the International Convention for the Suppression of Terrorist Bombings, adopted by the General Assembly of the United Nations on December 15, 1997.[32]

The Convention for the Suppression of the Financing of Terrorism also provides that, over and above the acts mentioned, providing or collecting funds toward any other act intended to cause death or serious bodily injury to a civilian, or to any other person not taking an active part in the hostilities in the situation of armed conflict, when the purpose of such act, by its nature or context, is to intimidate a population, or to compel a government or an international organization to do or to abstain from doing any act, would be deemed an offense under the convention.

The United Nations gave effect to this principle in 1970 when it proclaimed that

Every State has the duty to refrain from organizing or encouraging the organization of irregular forces or armed bands, including mercenaries, for incursion into the territory of another State. Every State has the duty to refrain from organizing, instigating, assisting or participating in acts of civil strife or terrorist acts in another State or acquiescing in organized activities within its territory directed towards the commission of such acts, when the acts referred to in the present paragraph involve a threat or use of force.[33]

Here, the words *encouraging* and *acquiescing in organized activities within its territory directed towards the commission of such acts* have a direct bearing on the concept of condonation and call for a discussion about how states could overtly or covertly encourage the commission of such acts. One commentator[34] identifies three categories of such support: *Category I* support entails protection, logistics, training, intelligence, or equipment provided terrorists as a part of national policy or strategy; *Category II* support does not back terrorism as an element of national policy but tolerates it; *Category III* support provides some terrorists a hospitable environment, growing from the presence of legal protections on privacy and freedom of movement, limits on internal surveillance and security organizations, well-developed infrastructure, and émigré communities.

Another commentator[35] discusses what he calls the *separate delict theory* in state responsibility, whereby the state incurs direct responsibility only for its own wrongful conduct in the context of private acts, and not for the private acts themselves. He also contends that indirect state responsibility is occasioned by the state's own wrongdoing in reference to the private terrorist conduct. The state is not held responsible for the act of terrorism itself, but rather for its failure to prevent or punish such acts, or for its active support for or acquiescence to terrorism.[36] Arguably the most provocative and plausible feature in this approach is the introduction by the commentator of the desirability of determining state liability on the theory of causation. He emphasizes that

The principal benefit of the causality based approach is that it avoids the automatic rejection of direct State responsibility merely because of the absence of an agency relationship. As a result, it potentially exposes the wrongdoing State to a greater range and intensity of remedies, as well as a higher degree of international attention and opprobrium for its contribution to the private terrorist activity.[37]

The causality principle is tied in with the rules of state responsibility enunciated by the International Law Commission and Article 51 of the United Nations charter, which states that nothing in the charter shall impair the inherent right of individual or collective self-defense if an armed attack occurs against a member of the United Nations, until the Security Council has taken measures necessary to maintain international peace and security. The provision goes on to say that measures taken by members in the exercise of this right of self-defense will be immediately reported to the security council and will not in any way affect the authority and responsibility of the security council under the present charter to take at any time such action as it deems necessary in order to maintain or restore international peace and security.

The International Law Commission has established that a crime against the peace and security of mankind entails individual responsibility, and is a crime of aggression.[38] A further link drawing civil aviation to the realm of international peace and security lies in the Rome Statute of the International

Criminal Court, which defines a war crime, *inter alia*, as intentionally directing attacks against civilian objects; attacking or bombarding, by whatever means, towns, villages, dwellings or buildings that are undefended and that are not military objects; and employing weapons, projectiles, material, and methods of warfare that cause injury.[39] The statute also defines as a war crime any act that is intentionally directed at buildings, material, medical units and transport, and personnel using the distinctive emblems of the Geneva Conventions in conformity with international law.[40]

The Role of Knowledge

Another method of determining state responsibility lies in the determination whether a state had actual or presumed knowledge of acts of its instrumentalities, agents, or private parties that could have alerted the state to take preventive action. International responsibility of a state cannot be denied merely on the strength of the claim of that state to sovereignty. Although the Chicago Convention in Article 1 stipulates that the contracting states recognize that every state has complete and exclusive sovereignty over the airspace above its territory, the effect of this provision cannot be extended to apply to state immunity from responsibility to other states. Professor Huber in the *Island of Palmas* case[41] was of the view that

> Sovereignty in the relations between States signifies independence. Independence in regard to a portion of the globe is the right to exercise therein, to the exclusion of any other State, the functions of a State.... Territorial sovereignty... involves the exclusive right to display the activities of a State.[42]

Professor Huber's definition, which is a simple statement of a state's rights, has been qualified by Starke as the residuum of power that a state possesses within the confines of international law.[43] Responsibility would devolve upon a state in whose territory an act of unlawful interference against civil aviation might occur, to other states that are threatened by such acts. The International Court of Justice (ICJ) recognized in the *Corfu Channel* case

> every State's obligation not to allow knowingly its territory to be used for acts contrary to the rights of other States.[44]

In this famous case, the International Court of Justice applied the subjective test and applied the fault theory. The court was of the view that

> It cannot be concluded from the mere fact of the control exercised by a State over its territory and waters that the State necessarily knew, or ought to have known, of any unlawful act perpetrated therein, nor yet that it necessarily knew, or should have known the authors. This fact, by itself and apart from other circumstances, neither involves prima facie responsibility nor shifts the burden of proof.[45]

The court, however, pointed out that exclusive control of its territory by a state had a bearing upon the methods of proof available to establish the involvement or knowledge of that state as to the events in question.

Apart from the direct attribution of responsibility to a state, particularly in instances where a state might be guilty of a breach of treaty provisions, or violate the territorial sovereignty of another state, there are instances where an act could be imputed to a state.[46] Imputability or attribution depends upon the link that exists between the state and the legal person or persons actually responsible for the act in question. The legal possibility of imposing liability upon a state wherever an official could be linked to that state encourages a state to be more cautious of its responsibility in controlling those responsible for carrying out tasks for which the state could be ultimately held responsible. In the same context, the responsibility of placing mines was attributed to Albania in the *Corfu Channel* case, since Albania was known to have knowledge of the placement of mines although it did not know who exactly carried out the act. It is arguable that in view of the responsibility imposed upon a state by the Chicago Convention on the provision of air navigation services, the principles of immutability in state responsibility could be applied to an instance of an act or omission of a public or private official providing air navigation services.

The sense of international responsibility that the United Nations ascribed to itself had reached a heady stage at this point, where the role of international law in international human conduct was perceived to be primary and above the authority of states. In its Report to the General Assembly, the International Law Commission recommended a draft provision that required

Every State has the duty to conduct its relations with other States in accordance with international law and with the principle that the sovereignty of each State is subject to the supremacy of international law.[47]

This principle, which forms a cornerstone of international conduct by states, provides the basis for strengthening international comity and regulating the conduct of states both internally (within their territories) and externally (toward other states). States are effectively precluded by this principle of pursuing their own interests untrammeled and with disregard to principles established by international law.

CONCLUSION

The above discussion leads one to conclude that the responsibility of a state for private acts of individuals that unlawfully interfere with civil aviation is determined by the quantum of proof available that could establish intent or negligence of the state, which in turn would establish complicity or condonation on the part of the state concerned. One way to determine complicity or condonation is to establish the extent to which the state adhered to the obligation imposed upon it by international law and whether it breached its duty to others. In order to exculpate itself, the state concerned will have to demonstrate that either it did not tolerate the offense or that it ensured the punishment of the offender. *Brownlie* is of the view that proof of such breach would lie in the causal connection between the private offender and the state.[48] In this context, the act or omission on the part of a state is a critical determinant, particularly if there is no specific intent.[49] Generally, it is not the intent of the offender that is the determinant, but the failure of a state to perform its legal duty in either preventing the offense (if such was within the purview of the state) or in taking necessary action with regard to punitive action or redress.[50]

Finally, there are a few principles that have to be taken into account when determining state responsibility for private acts of individuals that unlawfully interfere with civil aviation. First, there has to be either intent on the part of the state toward complicit or negligence reflected by act or omission. Second, where condonation is concerned, there has to be evidence of inaction on the part of the state in prosecuting the offender. Third, since the state as an abstract entity cannot perform an act in itself, the imputability or attribution of state responsibility for acts of its agents has to be established through a causal nexus that points the finger at the state as being responsible. For example, the International Law Commission, in Article 4 of its Articles of State Responsibility, states that the conduct of any state organ that exercises judicial, legislative, or executive functions could be considered an act of the state; this being the case, the acts of such organ or instrumentality can be construed as being imputable to the state. This principle was endorsed in 1999 by the ICJ, which said that according to well-established principles of international law, the conduct of any organ of a state must be regarded as an act of state.[51]

The law of state responsibility for private acts of individuals has evolved through the years, from being a straightforward determination of liability of the state and its agents to a rapidly widening gap between the state and non-state parties. In today's world, private entities and persons could wield power similar to that of a state, bringing to bear the compelling significance and modern relevance of the agency nexus between the state and such parties. This must indeed make states more aware of their own susceptibility.

Based on the above principles, the Somali government, however unable it might be to completely eradicate the offense of piracy committed by its nationals off its territorial waters, must at least be seen to take steps against the continuation of the offense and to prosecute and punish the offenders.

NOTES

The author is a senior official of the International Civil Aviation Organization but has written this article in his personal capacity.

1. BBC, "Q&A: Somali Piracy," January 9, 2009, http://news.bbc.co.uk/1/hi/world/africa/7734985.stm.

2. Somalia is located in the Horn of Africa and is bordered by Djibouti to the northwest, Kenya to the southwest, the Gulf of Aden with Yemen to the north, the Indian Ocean to the east, and Ethiopia to the west.

3. *Hanoch Tel Oren v. Libyan Arab Republic*, cited in Y. Alexander and S. Nanes, *Legislative Responses to Terrorism*, ed. Martinus Nijhoff, 1986, vol. 1.

4. R. I. R. Abeyratne, "The Invasion of the Maldives and International Terrorism: Definitions and Solutions," in *The 1988–89 Annual on Terrorism*, ed. Y. Alexander and H. Faxman (Lowell, MA: Kluwer, 1990), 83 at 84.

5. *Dictionnaire*, Supplement (Paris) Vol. 11 (1798), at 775.

6. Murray's *Oxford English Dictionary* defines terrorism as "[g]overnment by intimidation as directed and carried out by the party in power in France during the Revolution of 1789–1794; the system of the 'Terror.'" See James Murray, *A New Dictionary on Historical Principles* (UK: Oxford, 1919).

7. J. Adams, *The Financing of Terror* (New York: Simon & Schuster, 1989), 7.

8. J. Adams, *The Financing of Terror* (New York: Simon & Schuster, 1989), at 12.

9. See R. I. R. Abeyratne, "Skyjacker Gets Life Imprisonment in Sri Lanka," *Lloyds Aviation Law* 2, no. 24 (December 15 1983): at 4. See also generally R. I. R. Abeyratne, "The Ekanayake Hijacking Appeal in Sri Lanka: A Critical Appraisal," *Air Law* 14 (1989): 58–68.

10. H. L. Silets, "Something Special in the Air and on the Ground: The Potential for Unlimited Liability of International Air Carriers for Terrorist Attacks Under the Warsaw Convention and Its Revisions," *JALC* 53 (1987), 321 at 358.

11. Serge Nechayev, *Revolutionary Catechism*, cited in David C. Rapoport, *Assassination and Terrorism* (Toronto: Canadian Broadcasting Corporation, 1971), at 79. Another noteworthy definition was the one that was adopted at the Conference of the International Law Association in Belgrade, 1980, which states that "The definition of 'international terrorist offense' presented here is more comprehensive than the definitions which appear in the multilateral convention relating to the control of international terrorism which has been concluded in the past two decades. The term comprehends serious criminal acts, such as murder, assault, arson, kidnapping, extortion, sabotage and the use of explosives devices which are directed towards selected targets. These targets include internationally protected persons, places and international civil aircraft which are already protected under the conventional or customary international law." See R. F. Delaney, "World Terrorism Today," *California Western International Law Journal* 9 (1979): at 454. See also The Draft Convention of the International Law Association, Belgrade Conference (Committee on International Terrorism), August 1980, at 9, for definitions of terrorism proposed by the Haitian and French delegations at the conference.

12. S. Levitt, "Is Terrorism Worth Defining?" 13 *Ohio Northern University Law Review* (1986) 97.

13. See N. Kittrie, "Terrorism and Political Crimes in International Law," 67 *American Journal of International Law* (1973) 87. Also see J. J. Paust, "Some Thoughts on Preliminary Thoughts on Terrorism," 68 *American Society of International Law* (1978) 502–3.

14. See R. A. Friedlander, "The Origins of International Terrorism," *Terrorism, Interdisciplinary Perspectives*, ed. J. Alexander and S. M. Finger (London: McGraw Hill, 1977): at 31.

15. Cited in Oppenheim, *International Law* 1(8): ed. at 609.

16. Cited in Oppenheim, *International Law* 1(8): ed. at 609.

17. The Geneva Convention was opened for signature at Geneva on November 16, 1937. See Hudson, *International Legislation*, Vol. VII at 862, U.N. Doc. A/C.6/418, Annex 1, at 1.

18. League of Nations, *Official Journal*, 1934, at 1839.

19. Henry Reiff, *The United States and the Treaty Law of the Sea* (Minneapolis: University of Minnesota Press, 1959), at 86.

20. S. Z. Feller, "Comment on Criminal Jurisdiction over Aircraft Hijacking," *Israel Law Review* 7 (1972), at 212.

21. S. Z. Feller, "Comment on Criminal Jurisdiction over Aircraft Hijacking," *Israel Law Review* 7 (1972), at 212.

22. D. D. Caron, "The Basis of Responsibility: Attribution and Other Transsubstantive Rules," in ed. R. B. Lillich and D. B. Magraw, *The Iran-United States Claims Tribunal: Its Conclusions to State Responsibility* (Irvington-on-Hudson, NY: Transnational Publishers, 1998), 109, at 153–54, cited in Tal Becker, "Terrorism and the State," Hart Monographs in Transnational and International Law (Portland, Maine; Hart Publishing, 2006), at 155.

23. H. Grotius, J. B. Scott, (tr.), 2 *De Jure Belli Ac Pacis* (1646), 523–26.

24. E. De Vattel, C.G. Fenwick (tr.) 2, *The Law of Nations or, the Principles of Natural Law: Applied to the Conduct and to the Affairs of Nations and Sovereigns* (New York: Legal Classics Library, 1916), 72.

25. W. Blackstone, W. Morrison (ed.) 4 *Commentaries on the Laws of England (1765–1769)* (London: Cavendish, 2001), at 68.

26. *Laura M. B. Janes (USA) v. United Mexican States* (1925) 4 *R Intl Arb Awards* 82.

27. *Ibid.*

28. *Black's Law Dictionary* defines condonation as "pardon of offense, voluntary overlooking implied forgiveness by treating offender as if offense had not been committed."

29. Jane's case, *Supra*, note 19, at 92.

30. C. Hyde, "Concerning Damages Arising from Neglect to Prosecute" (1928), 22 *Am J Int L* 140 at 140–142.

31. International Convention for the Suppression of the Financing of Terrorism, adopted by the General Assembly of the United Nations in resolution 54/109 of December 9, 1999.

32. A/52/653, November 25, 1997.

33. Declaration on Principles of International Law Concerning Friendly Relations and Co-operation among States in Accordance with the Charter of the United Nations, UN General Assembly Resolution 2625 (XXV), October 24, 1970.

34. Steven Metz, "State Support for Terrorism, Defeating Terrorism, Strategic Issue Analysis," http://www.911investigations.net/IMG/pdf/doc-140.pdf.

35. Tal Becker, *Terrorism and the State: Rethinking the Rules of State Responsibility* (Portland, ME: Hart Publishing, 2006).

36. Tal Becker, *Terrorism and the State: Rethinking the Rules of State Responsibility* (Portland, ME: Hart Publishing, 2006), Chapter 2, 67.

37. Becker, *supra*, note 36, at 335.

38. Draft Code of Crimes against the Peace and Security of Mankind, International Law Commission Report, 1996, Chapter II, Article 2.

39. Rome Statute of the International Criminal Court, Article 8.2 (b) (ii), (V) and (XX).

40. Id. Article 8.2 (b) (XXIV).

41. The *Island of Palmas* Case (1928) 11 U.N.R. I.A.A. at 829.
42. The *Island of Palmas* Case (1928) 11 U.N.R. I.A.A. at 829.
43. J. G. Starke, *Introduction to International Law* (London: Butterworths, 1989), 10 ed. 1989 at 3.
44. International Court of Justice (1949), 1, 22.
45. The *Corfu Channel* Case, ICJ Reports, 1949, 4.
46. There are some good examples of imputability—for example, the incident in 1955 when an Israeli civil aircraft belonging to the national carrier El Al was shot down by Bulgarian fighter planes, and the consequent acceptance of liability by the USSR for death and injury caused which resulted in the payment of compensation to the victims and their families. See 91 *ILR* 287. Another example concerns the finding of the International Court of Justice that responsibility could have been imputed to the United States in the *Nicaragua* case in which mines were laid in Nicaraguan waters and attacks were perpetrated on Nicaraguan ports, oil installations, and a naval base by persons identified as agents of the United States. See *Nicaragua v. the United States*, ICJ Reports 1986, 14; also, 76 *ILR* 349. Then there was also an instance in which the Secretary General of the United Nations mediated a settlement in which a sum, *inter alia*, of $7 million was awarded to New Zealand for the violation of its sovereignty when a New Zealand vessel was destroyed by French agents in New Zealand. See the *Rainbow Warrior* case, 81 *AJIL*, 1987 at 325. Also in 74 *ILR* at 241.
47. *Report of the International Law Commission to the General Assembly on the Work of the 1st Session*, A/CN.4/13, June 9, 1949, at 21.
48. Ian Brownlie, *System of the Law of Nations: State Responsibility*, Part 1 (Oxford: Clarendon, 1983), at 39.
49. Report of the International Law Commission to the United Nations General Assembly, UNGOAR 56th Session, Supp. No. 10, *UN DOC A/56/10*, 2001 at 73.
50. E. J. de Arechaga, International Responsibility, in *Manual of Public International Law*, ed. M. Sorenson (New York: St. Martin's Press, 1968), 531 at 535.
51. *Differences Relating to Immunity from Legal Process of a Special Rapporteur*, ICJ Reports 1999, 62 at 87.

CHAPTER 6

The Global Environment and Supply Chain Security

Sean S. Costigan

> We never have 100 percent certainty. We never have it. If you wait until you have 100 percent certainty, something bad is going to happen on the battlefield.
> —General Gordon R. Sullivan, USA (Ret.), Former Chief of Staff, U.S. Army.

No aspect of the global supply chain is untouched by environmental concerns, and none more so than the security, broadly writ, of the supply chain itself. From the extraction and exploitation of natural resources to the production of goods and their movement around the world all the way to consumption, the environment impacts every link of the chain. While uncertainties[1] remain about the projected rate of sea level rise and the effects of climate change and their implications for international security, there can be no doubt that changes in the global environment will present new risks for many aspects of the global supply chain. From a practical and policy perspective, however, it is necessary to take a step back—while keeping an eye on the future—to get a better sense of where the security of the supply chain is most vulnerable and what future risks and opportunities might portend. This article will focus on reasonable expectations of what the future may resemble—as suggested by security insights and current scientific consensus—on indicators related to such concerns as sea level rise, extreme weather events, climate change, political security and overall impacts on the supply chain.

SEA LEVEL RISE

Nearly any rise in sea levels will bring complex challenges to the supply chain, particularly in vulnerable areas at sea level, like ports, and in areas already subject to coastal flooding and erosion. Without the establishment of extensive and expensive defenses, the entire transit system for materials and products to and from ports would also be extremely vulnerable to sea level rise and weather events that would increase damage from flooding. In 2007 the Intergovernmental Panel on Climate Change (IPCC) predicted that over the next century sea levels would rise by up to 23 inches, a number that many scientists now consider to be a conservative estimate and that others perceive as the gold standard. Current estimates project that the population of the 136 large port cities that are exposed to coastal flooding will treble over the next century, to 150 million.[2] An OECD study published in July 2008 forecast that the value of flood-exposed economic assets in these port cities in the form of buildings, transport networks, utilities, and other infrastructure could grow even more dramatically than population exposure, reaching $35 trillion by the 2070s, or approximately 9 percent of projected global gross domestic product, up from 5 percent in 2005. The same OECD report found that fifteen of the top twenty port cities, ranked in terms of population, exposed to coastal flooding from climate-linked storm surge and rises in sea level in the 2070s would be in Asia, with four of them in China—Guangzhou, Shanghai, Tianjin and Ningbo. The vulnerable population of these four cities is projected to be nearly 23 million.[3]

Sea level rise will also present unique challenges throughout the world. Some particular and notable challenges are addressed below.

In March 2009, an article in *Nature Geoscience* estimated that the melting of Greenland's ice would directly impact northeastern North America with an additional increase of 8 inches; making matters seem more dire, a newer report in *Nature Geoscience* has now suggested that if melting continues at current rates, New York, Boston, and other northeastern coastal cities will face a sea level rise of twice as much as other parts of the continent.[4] Taking into consideration other factors such as paleoclimatic evidence and weaknesses in current simulations has caused some in the policy world to consider the effects of even more rapid sea level rise.[5]

The Port of New York and New Jersey is America's third largest port and its largest container complex, serving some 20 million people in the immediate vicinity and millions more throughout the Northeast. As of 2006, eighty percent of U.S. imports were received through the port and the transport network serves 40 percent of the nation.[6] The surrounding territory would be greatly affected by a sea level rise of much less than predicted by the IPCC or by more recent estimates.

Indeed, much of the eastern coast of North America is vulnerable. For example, in 2008, a U.S. multi-agency report produced in collaboration with agencies that included the U.S. Geological Survey, the National Oceanographic and

Atmospheric Administration, and the Department of Transportation, suggested that 70 percent of the Port of Wilmington, Delaware, would be adversely affected by a sea level rise of less than two feet.[7] According to yet another recent report by the National Academies of Science, 60,000 miles of coastal highways are already subject to periodic flooding and are thus especially vulnerable to increased sea levels.[8] These coastal highways are critical to the movement of goods to and from ports.

While there is uncertainty and much remains unknown about ice melt, a further concern relating to the melting Greenland ice is the effect the freshwater will have on the Gulf Stream. Models suggest that a massive infusion of freshwater, such as that which would come from the Greenland ice, would have the effect of significantly altering the Atlantic's water temperatures, thereby affecting the ocean conveyor belt that drives the Gulf Stream, which might in turn cause a greater sea level rise on the northeastern side of the continent and alter weather patterns throughout the region.

With consideration to the western coast of the United States, in March 2009 the Pacific Institute, a nonpartisan research institute based in Oakland, published an in-depth report on the potential effects of sea level rise on California ports, including those of Los Angeles–Long Beach and Oakland. The report notes that together these ports are central to the economy of California, the nation, and the world. The Port of Los Angeles–Long Beach handles 45–50 percent of the containers shipped into the United States. Of these containers, 77 percent leave the state, half by train and half by truck.[9] Noting that the 2002 work slowdown at West Coast ports cost the nation an estimated $1–2 billion per day, the effects of sea level rise on ports without adaptation would cause certain and extensive damage to global economies

Whatever the amount, sea level rise will also cause changes in navigation and will make movement under bridges and other existing infrastructure more difficult if not impossible. Companies should examine the potential for disruption in their transportation network and consider the development of flexible strategies to increase their resilience.[10] Rising waters may also exacerbate political tensions in unstable areas, where transport is already vulnerable to piracy and terrorism, if not throughout the globe.

EXTREME WEATHER EVENTS

While uncertainty remains regarding variability in weather and the links of global warming, climate change and extreme weather events, as well as the nonlinear tipping points, there is increasing concern that the weather will cause greater systemic damage than previously estimated.[11] National and international agencies, including the U.S. Environmental Protection Agency and the World Meteorological Organization, have also linked increasing extreme weather events to global warming, and the science behind the links is a topic of in-depth study. In two widely cited articles in the journal *Science*,

Hoyos et al. state that their result "show that the increasing trend in number of category 4 and 5 hurricanes for the period 1970–2004 is directly linked to the trend in surface sea temperature."[12] Webster et al. also reported similar results, stating that "[t]his trend is not inconsistent with recent climate model simulations that a doubling of CO_2 may increase the frequency of the most intense cyclones."[13]

On the economic side of the equation, studies have examined the potential financial losses associated with more extreme weather. For example, a noteworthy study developed for the International Scientific Congress on climate change at the University of Copenhagen shows that "while it will cost up to 128 billion yen (1 billion euro) to secure Japanese harbors against stronger winds and more frequent storms, failure to do so could result in the loss of 1.5 to 3.4 percent of Japan's GDP by 2085 (Japanese GDP in 2007 was 3.41 trillion euro). This is due to an increased number of days where harbors will be forced to close."[14] According to Miguel Esteban, at the United Nations University Institute of Advanced Studies, "Port planners should factor this in when designing port capacities. Their designs must be able to prevent delays and increased downtime due to winds and rain. Similarly, they must plan for sea defenses that can limit damage caused by waves. Failure to do so could lead to bottlenecks in the shipments of products and constrain Japanese economic growth."[15]

CLIMATE CHANGE

Climate change is altering weather patterns and also threatens to change many nodes in the supply chain, including where and when materials and products are sourced, logistics for moving products and components, and myriad other concerns leading all the way up to changes in company policies, the regulatory environment and even the global economy and political landscape.

The effects of globalization have already provided a number of indicators to consider, many of which will be amplified by climate change. For example, it is widely accepted that trade has increased the spread of invasive species, for which ports are both the primary point of entry and the first line of defense.[16] According to the U.S. Environmental Protection Agency, ballast water taken on by ships at port and released at other ports is a major source for introducing nonnative species into aquatic ecosystems where they would not otherwise be present.[17] One of the best known examples is the zebra mussel, which apparently traveled in ballast water from a freshwater European port to a Canada in 1988. Zebra mussels reproduce rapidly, deplete freshwater of nutrients, and clog vents and machinery, resulting in required costly removal efforts for drinking water industrial and power plants, averaging hundreds of thousands of dollars per year. The resulting destruction of native ecosystems and the economic costs of cleanup or management of aquatic invasive species is difficult to calculate, but by one measure the costs exceed $9 billion annually.[18]

Packing material has also served to increase the spread of damaging species. Native to China, the Asian longhorned beetle is thought to have come to New York City in the 1980s, probably in wood pallets from a plumbing supplies company. The beetle lives on hardwood trees, which it kills, and the associated costs to the lumber and tourism industries could costs billions. Eradication in Chicago took 10 years and cost $70 million.[19]

Emerging and reemerging disease is also likely to spread, and there is particular concern that increased extreme weather events related to climate change might unleash a so-called perfect storm of infection and epidemic.[20] Again, ports, whether air or sea, will serve as one of the first lines of defense against potential catastrophe. Awareness of pathogens affecting the supply chain should also be taken into consideration, as many may grow in prevalence. Companies should be focused on the risks of climate-driven environmental changes to disease patterns, such as the spread of tropical diseases to non-endemic regions, and of the links of the supply chain in the transmittal of pathogens.[21]

McKinsey & Company has reported that their 2008 survey of 2,000 global executives identified climate change as a top supply chain concern. Nonetheless, less than one-quarter of respondents noted that their companies "always or frequently take climate change into consideration in these areas. Among high technology and other manufacturing executives, 54 percent and 56 percent of respondents, respectively, say climate change is important in purchasing, yet these executives were no more likely than average to say it was considered in practice."[22] According to McKinsey & Company's analysis, these companies may be missing an opportunity: "for consumer goods makers, high-tech players, and other manufacturers, between 40 and 60 percent of a company's carbon footprint resides upstream in its supply chain—from raw materials, transport, and packaging to the energy consumed in manufacturing processes. For retailers, the figure can be 80 percent."[23]

While many uncertainties remain about climate change, regulations to curb carbon dioxide emissions are likely to have profound near-term impacts on corporations and climate change will increase pressure on the trade in commodities, to mention but two business-side concerns regarding the supply chain. A particularly in-depth study by the Carbon Disclosure Project echoes that much of corporate greenhouse gas emissions reside in supply chain activities, many of which are outside of the control of any single company in the chain.[24] The study surveyed hundreds of executives from companies around the globe, affording unique insight into the challenges perceived by companies and indications on planning to mitigate risks.

Considering the current economic crises and the need for companies to grow and make a return on investment, effective analysis of costs associated with climate change and the associated changes to supply chain are critical. The field is developing rapidly to meet the needs for effective business planning. According to research conducted by PricewaterhouseCoopers in 2008, 48 percent of CEOs were responding to climate change by altering their supply chain, and 66 percent were making a return on investment. Undoubtedly, expertise on the effects of climate change on the supply chain will be of critical importance to companies worldwide.

THE INTERNATIONAL SYSTEM AND GLOBAL SECURITY

Throughout human history, changes to the environment have played a decisive role. Today the environment is a point of concern and prospective conflict. According to Thomas Fingar, then chairman of the U.S. National Intelligence Council, "The United States depends on a smooth-functioning international system ensuring the flow of trade and market access to critical raw materials, such as oil and gas, and security for its allies and partners. Climate change and climate change policies could affect all of these with significant geopolitical consequences."[25] Of course, it is not only the United States that depends on a smoothly functioning system, but—to a greater or lesser extent—all the countries of the world share in the same need for stability, security and access to resources.

Though concerns about the environment and national security have been around for decades, and many of the same questions remain that were articulated by Kenneth Keller in his 1996 article about the locus of government involvement in environmental and security concerns.[26] "National Intelligence Assessment on the National Security Implications of Global Climate Change to 2030," which brought much of the current concerns on climate change to the minds of national security experts and politicians, was widely criticized for being a classified document that should have received wider readership, scrutiny, and debate. In an earlier thirty-five-page 2007 study, the CNA Corporation detailed many of the same risks, suggesting that climate change acts as a "threat multiplier for instability in some of the most volatile regions of the world" and that "climate change, national security and energy dependence are a related set of global challenges."[27] While the CNA study examines energy dependence, it also goes steps further and advocates that the United States engage in proactive efforts to minimize and stabilize climate change and assist developing countries in their efforts to mitigate and adapt.

Precipitation patterns and groundwater levels are also changing, with results that will undoubtedly affect agricultural production, nourishment, and human health and that will likely lead to migration, environmental refugees, and, potentially, conflict. Semi-arid and arid regions may be the hardest hit.[28] Already, countries that are short on arable land but long on cash reserves are securing growing rights elsewhere. China and South Korea have procured expanses of territory in Asia and Africa. One of the largest recent deals is between South Korea's Daewoo Logistics and the country of Madagascar, which will result in investment about $6 billion dollars to develop 3.2 million acres (1.3 million hectares)—a swathe of land almost half the size of Belgium.[29]

THE EFFECTS ON SUPPLY CHAIN SECURITY

As we have seen, while uncertainty remains regarding the effects of climate change, there can be no doubt that supply chain security will require substantial investments in the form of study, energy, and development of resilient and flexible plans to counter new risks. Resiliency in the supply chain will pay dividends in other ways, too. According to Stephen Flynn of Council on Foreign Relations, supply chain resiliency also creates a deterrent against terrorists, who are likely to look elsewhere if the net effect of their attacks won't be seen as catastrophic.

Companies should consider the realities of their current sourcing plans, taking into account the effects of political and economic instability, climate change, sea level rise, and extreme weather events, among other global concerns. Environmental changes may bring about substantial setbacks and cause disruptions to the supply chain, so long-term business plans must take these changes and risks into account. Undoubtedly, climate change will alter the supply chain—it's less a question of when but of how, and of what is to be done about it.

Advances in computer simulations and better indicators[30] and data on emissions and long-term data regarding historical trends are critical tools for modeling the environment effects on supply chain security. Without modeling the effects of such elements on the supply chain, access to commodities and key supplies will be more apt to lead to costly adjustments and last-minute defenses, with negative effects throughout the supply chain and for companies all along the way. Consumers are also becoming more aware of supply chain concerns and the environment through such tools as GoodGuide;[31] undoubtedly, more Web services will be created to help consumers examine their environmental choices in greater detail, with concomitant effects on corporations and their supply chains.

Radical changes to the supply chain may also alter the political landscape. Because of this, the interconnectedness of decisions made at the local, national, and international levels must be taken into account to help retain a measure of stability in an uncertain world.

NOTES

1. For a useful breakdown of uncertainties as they apply to this paper, see New York City Panel on Climate Change. "Climate Risk Information," February 17, 2009, p. 7, http://www.nyc.gov/html/om/pdf/2009/NPCC_CRI.pdf.
2. Michael Richardson, "Facing a Rise in Sea Level," *The Japan Times Online* (2008), http://search.japantimes.co.jp/cgi-bin/eo20080924a1.html.
3. Michael Richardson, "Facing a Rise in Sea Level," *The Japan Times Online* (2008), http://search.japantimes.co.jp/cgi-bin/eo20080924a1.html.

4. Richard A. Lovett, "New York Seas to Rise Twice as Much as Rest of U.S.," *National Geographic News* (2009), http://news.nationalgeographic.com/news/2009/03/090315-new-york-sea-level.html.

5. New York City Panel on Climate Change, "Climate Risk Information," February 17, 2009, http://www.nyc.gov/html/om/pdf/2009/NPCC_CRI.pdf.

6. "Facts and Figures of the Port of New York and New Jersey," July 11, 2007, www.njmsc.org/education/ahod/pdf/FactsandFiguresof%20the%20PortofNYandNJ.pdf.

7. "Coastal Elevations and Sensitivity to Sea Level Rise," April 10, 2008, http://climatescience.gov/Library/sap/sap4-1/public-review-draft/.

8. Cornelia, Dean, "Government Reports Warn Planners on Sea-Rise Threat to U.S. Coasts," *New York Times* (2008), http://www.nytimes.com/2008/03/12/science/12coast.html?_r=1.

9. Matthew Heberger, et al., "The Impacts of Sea-Level Rise on the California Coast," March 1, 2009, www.pacinst.org/reports/sea_level_rise/report.pdf.

10. Hal, Feuchtwanger, "Managing Supply Chain Disruption with Continuous Design," http://www.i2.com/supplychainleader/best_practices/managing-supply-chain-disruption.cfm.

11. P. Vellinga and W. J. van Verseveld, "Climate Change and Extreme Weather Events," September 1, 2000, http://assets.panda.org/downloads/xweather.pdf.

12. Carlos D. Hoyos et al., "Deconvolution of the Factors Contributing to the Increase in Global Hurricane Intensity," March 16, 2006, http://www.sciencemag.org/cgi/content/abstract/1123560v1.

13. P. J. Webster et al., "Changes in Tropical Cyclone Number, Duration, and Intensity in a Warming Environment," September 16, 2005, http://www.sciencemag.org/cgi/content/full/309/5742/1844.

14. "Fighting Global Warming Offers Growth and Development Opportunities, Leading Economist Proposes," *ScienceDaily* (2009), http://www.sciencedaily.com/releases/2009/03/090312093918.htm.

15. "Fighting Global Warming Offers Growth and Development Opportunities," March 12, 2009, http://climatecongress.ku.dk/newsroom/mitigation_growth_development/.

16. Alex Steffen, "How to Prepare Ports and Waterfronts for Climate Change?" March 17, 2009, http://www.worldchanging.com/archives//009592.html.

17. "Factsheet: Ballast Water and Aquatic Invasive Species," http://www.epa.gov/owow/invasive_species/factsheet.html.

18. D. Pimentel, "Economic and Ecological Costs Associated with Aquatic Invasive Species," Cornell University, Proceedings of the Aquatic Invaders of the Delaware Estuary Symposium, Malvern, Pennsylvania, May 20, 2003, pp. 3–5, http://sgnis.org/publicat/proceed/aide/pime2003.htm.

19. Murray Carpenter, "The Return of the Asian Longhorned Beetle," February 21, 2009, http://www.npr.org/templates/story/story.php?storyId=100961303.

20. "Extreme Weather Events Can Unleash a 'Perfect Storm' of Infectious Diseases, Research Study Says," *ScienceDaily* (2008), http://www.sciencedaily.com/releases/2008/06/080625073804.htm.

21. For an examination of these issues, see "Environmental Health and Disease," http://globaleese.org/static/future_scenarios/post/12.

22. Chris Brickman and Drew Ungerman, "Climate Change and Supply Chain Management," July 1, 2008, http://www.mckinseyquarterly.com/Climate_change_and_supply-chain_management_2175.

23. Chris Brickman and Drew Ungerman, "Climate Change and Supply Chain Management," July 1, 2008, http://www.mckinseyquarterly.com/Climate_change_and_supply-chain_management_2175.

24. "Carbon Disclosure Project Supply Chain Report 2009," March 5, 2009, http://www.cdproject.net/download.asp?file=65_329_201_CDP-Supply-Chain-Report_2009.pdf.

25. "Global Warming Could Increase Terrorism, Official Says," *CNN* (2008), http://www.cnn.com/2008/POLITICS/06/25/climate.change.security/index.html.

26. Kenneth H. Keller, "Unpackaging the Environment," *World Policy Journal* (1996), pp. 5–14, www.wilsoncenter.org/topics/pubs/ACF14A8.pdf.

27. CNA Corporation, "National Security and the Threat of Climate Change," 2007, http://securityandclimate.cna.org/report/.

28. David Chandler, "Water Supplies Could Be Strongly Affected by Climate Change," December 18, 2008, http://web.mit.edu/newsoffice/2008/agu-groundwater-1218.html.

29. Bonnie Malkin, "Rising Sea Levels 'Could Spark Conflict over Energy and Food Reserves'," Telegraph.co.uk (2009), http://www.telegraph.co.uk/earth/environment/climatechange/4161206/Rising-sea-levels-could-spark-conflict-over-energy-and-food-reserves.html.

30. For an examination of some key indicators, see "Climate Change: Treaties, Indicators, and National Responses," http://sedac.ciesin.org/entri/guides/sec3-climate.html.

31. Cf. http://www.goodguide.com/.

CHAPTER 7

Barbary Coast Revisited: International Maritime Law and Modern Piracy

Charles Bumstead

In the old days it was the fantasy of society to attribute piracy to bearded, one-eyed, peg-legged cutthroats, and during the time when old-time piracy was in its prime, that was nearly always so. But lately there has arisen a new kind of pirate—one who is armed with the latest in weapons, one who cruises along side a vessel in a small speedy boat and rakes it with gunfire from a variety of very modern weapons, including automatic rifles, submachine guns, and rocket-propelled grenades. The ultimate goal of the new pirate is to board ship and to take control, either for refitting or for ransom. Ransom demands are nearly always conducted via computer interface and through well-dressed mediators who act on behalf of the pirates.

Piracy is a crime with ancient origins. As long as there have been ships at sea, there have been pirates. International laws against piracy have ancient origins too, but U.S. law developed chiefly in the eighteenth and nineteenth centuries. The power to criminalize piracy originated in the U.S. Constitution, which was followed by the first federal law in 1790 and several crucial revisions over the next six decades. The United States and other states cooperated to combat piracy in the twentieth century, which has helped give rise to the commonly held view that piracy can be punished by any nation. The U.S. Constitution addresses piracy in Article 1, Section 8, giving the Congress "the Power . . . To define and punish Piracies and Felonies committed on the high Seas, and Offenses against the Law of Nations."

Pirates exist today, even though most think of them as myths and legends of the past. Nevertheless, they are real, and they have a history of violence about them. Pirates today are much like the ones of old: they prey on weak, unarmed, and unescorted commercial vessels. There has been a steady increase in the number of attacks by pirates since the early 1980s. The number of attacks in the 1990s increased threefold, while the increase in the 2000s has more than tripled again, with 200 attacks having been reported in the first half of 2004. States have experienced difficulty in arresting the modern-day pirate for many shared reasons: the lack of specific authority to attack, apprehend, and take into custody pirates caught in the act. Many states do not have an existing policy to treat with acts of piracy, and other states do not have to naval power to escort or to otherwise prevent acts of piracy on their flag vessels.

The types of attack have varied from those of the distant past and have become a great deal more sophisticated. The modern pirates use the same old tricks of the old ones; they often disguise themselves behind the flags of the state they choose, or the state to which they actually belong. In the case of Somalia, where the vast majority of pirates operate from, it is recognized that the state cannot prevent the pirates from using Somalia as a sanctuary and a base of operations. The government of Somalia has been in turmoil fighting for its own existence against Muslim extremists. As a result, many of the pirates have simply moved in and taken over entire towns, often with the support of the townspeople. The money that is brought into the towns by the pirates through their ransom efforts has proven to be a positive incentive for the citizens to simply overlook the criminal aspect of the operation, and the welcome mat stays out. The political situation in the area precludes states like the United States from taking direct action against the sanctuary towns in Somalia, which are located inland. The United States and other concerned nations cannot blockade ports in Somalia, which would be an act of war against a sovereign nation. The preventive measures are limited due to obedience to international maritime law. Existing laws need to be examined and new laws promulgated to meet with this most contentious of issues.[1]

What is it that has inspired these latest piratical acts, which have increased in number and kind, and which affect world commerce, posing an unacceptable burden to international shipping on the high seas? Some analysts say that two relatively new trends have led to this rise in piracy: the increase in numbers of international vessels plying the high seas and the lack of protection or vulnerability of the vessels.

International commerce, particularly on the world's oceans, continues the trend of expanding the global market. Rather than nations maintaining the bulk of their trade with near neighbors and operating in localized areas of commerce, they have increased international ocean traffic to the point where a full 95 percent of the foreign trade of one nation, the United States, is conducted on the high seas, according to the U.S. Maritime Administration. Many nations in other parts of the world have enjoyed a similar increase in their foreign trade using international sea commerce. As the traffic continues to increase, so does the vulnerability of those vessels to the possibility of international piracy.

Flag carriers on the high seas are easy prey to those pirates who operate in and along the coasts of states that lack the armed forces and other necessary resources to secure their shores. Security specialists say that the waters off Somalia, Nigeria, Bangladesh, Philippines, and Kenya are especially volatile areas of high risk to oceangoing travel. These waters have seen a phenomenal increase in violence in the 1990s, and even more so in this century. Add to that the inability, at least to this point, of states sponsoring flag carriers to protect them while they are traveling in these troubled waters.

The pirates have enjoyed a modicum of success while engaged in seaborne criminal activity. They have succeeded in accomplishing their goal of capture in approximately 75 percent of cases. In some cases, the boarded ships are sailed to a safe port, where cargo is unloaded and the ship's registration and appearance changed; the vessel subsequently reappears in some other area of the world. In other cases, the crew or passengers are held ransom by the pirates.

The important thing about this critical situation is that to date, little or nothing has been done to protect the vessels—or to hunt down the perpetrators after the fact. The international community cannot continue to allow pirates to operate with impunity and without fear of redress. There must be a concerted international effort to treat with this situation, as these acts have approached a critical point in the evolution of modern-day piracy.

The pirates operating out of Somalia have been provided safe haven and protected ports in and along the coast by the citizens of some communities. The money that the pirates bring to these communities is considerable. This situation allows the citizens of the "safe haven" cities a heretofore unparalleled level of financial abundance.

The central government of Somalia has been very busy attempting to maintain some semblance of a viable government while struggling against the incursion of Islamic extremists who have taken over a large portion of Somali territory. The central government has been unable to deny pirates access to the safe havens or to police its territorial waters. The existence of safe ports and sanctuaries in a state like Somalia add to the problems facing forces attempting to prevent such attacks. If the pirates are able to escape to the territorial waters of a state like Somalia, the pursuing vessels, because they lack jurisdiction in Somali waters, cannot enter into the protected seas to continue pursuit of the pirate vessel. The safe harbors and sanctuaries cannot be attacked, nor the ports blockaded, in accordance with international maritime law.

The UN acted upon the request by many governments to assist in providing a force in Somalia capable of protecting the state from its internal struggles against Islamic extremists while maintaining the integrity of a central government.[2] The requirement would necessitate large numbers of ground troops to stabilize the country. Even though many states requested that assistance be provided, no state has volunteered forces to accomplish that task. This situation has offered a rare look at the inner workings of an international body whose member states loudly proclaim the need for action but fail to support their own issues when put to the test.

The United States joined in the call for ground troops from affected states but offered only logistical support and training, not "boots on the ground."[3] UN Secretary General Ban Ki-moon complained that the organization (UN) had "limited options" to deal with a very dangerous and volatile situation in Somalia because of the lack of resources and troops for an effective peacekeeping operation there. On Tuesday, December 16, 2008, the United Nations approved and authorized land and air operations against pirate positions on the land areas of Somalia.[4] It must be stated here that operations against pirates on the high seas are authorized by the UN Convention on Maritime Law. The question is what kind of action—and by whom, and to what end? These questions need to be answered before concerted action is taken against the inland or coastal havens, in Somalia or any state, that are operated by pirates.

What action can be taken to punish, imprison, or otherwise prevent the pirates from repeating their acts of piracy? Can they be jailed? executed? Is there *any* action that can be taken against them? Some states will not allow their forces to take into custody or detain pirates if captured, in order to avoid an international incident. What purpose is served by releasing pirates after being captured, only to see them again in another, perhaps more violent, episode?

It is recognized that active pursuit of and punishment of the pirate organizations is of immediate and critical importance, for pirates are growing more and more aggressive in their attacks. There have been scattered efforts by several states to interfere with the operations of the pirates, with some success, but there needs to be a very different approach to the problem. The concerned states cannot continue to throw resources piecemeal at a very determined enemy. There must be a concerted effort by many, if not all, of the capable states that are operating flag carriers in the area.

One of the primary problems facing any force that attempts to prevent or interfere with the pirates is the common practice of many of the states: paying ransoms without notification to any international organization—in some cases the incident is not even reported. The rationale is that if the international body has no knowledge of the incident, insurance rates will not go up, and their crews may be safe from an attack in the future.

The current strategies for fighting piracy are not very well thought out, and in some cases they have totally opposite results from that expected. There have been some concerted efforts by a significant naval force in the Red Sea and the Gulf of Aden, but the results have been less than satisfactory because of the reluctance of participating states to use significant and effective force. This restraint is blamed on the real or imagined legal constraints. Recently it is reported that British Foreign Office warned the Royal Navy not to detain any captured pirates, lest it violate their human rights and provoke a claim for asylum in Great Britain.[6] This demonstration of the lack of political will demonstrates the deep problems associated with this entire scenario.

The British are not alone in their efforts to effectively coddle the pirates; recently a German force intercepted an attempted attack on a vessel and sent a helicopter to "scare away" the pirates, because the German rules of engagement did not allow for fighting pirates.[7] This keynotes the need for an effective central force with the authority and authorization to attack the pirates wherever they are and wherever they go, to seek and destroy the capabilities of the pirates to field an effective attacking force. Anything less is an exercise in futility.

Given the current situation, it becomes clear that all of the efforts expended by the various states are not working. There must be a new approach to the problem.

EFFECT OF INTERNATIONAL PIRACY

The possibility of a major interruption or interference with international trade, together with the recognition of the critical nature and vulnerability of the global supply chain, is a situation that sends shockwaves rippling through the various economic centers throughout the world.

Recently two cargo ships were hijacked in the Gulf of Aden by modern-day pirates.[9] The fact that there are pirates operating in several places in the world is only one of the issues, but the fact that the pirates operate with total disdain for international authority is an important issue. One of the pirated ships had on board Russian-made T-34 tanks and arms and ammunition of an unknown quantity.[10] The crews of the ships were overwhelmed by pirates in small boats who boarded the vessels under a curtain of gunfire and swarmed the vessels' crews. The incident only highlights the vulnerability of a state's international commerce traveling the high seas. There appears to be little that can be accomplished in the area of protection of vessels on the high seas. States are attempting to ensure safe passage of vessels sailing under the aegis of their national flag, but they are meeting with limited success. There just aren't enough resources and manpower to police the many active areas in which piracy abounds.

The international community, until now, had little or no knowledge of the magnitude or the seriousness of the threat of international piracy and its effect on the global community. Approximately 60 percent of the world's international commerce is conducted on the high seas, making the sea lanes of the utmost importance to international trade. If nations are inhibited from moving goods from one country to another via the sea, the impact would be horrendous.

As an example, the amount of sea traffic using the Red Sea route and the most direct route to the European markets through the Suez Canal is extremely heavy, and there are hundreds of vessels plying that route at all hours of the day and night. It is estimated that as many as 21,000 vessels travel the Gulf of Aden each year. The route is one of the most, if not the most, traveled sea routes in the world. The recent attacks by pirates, particularly those operating from Somalia, and other states in the area, has centered international attention on the Red Sea and the Gulf of Aden. The critical nature of the problem has been brought to the attention of the international community and has resulted in demands that the United Nations, other international bodies, and the affected states step up to the plate and offer concrete assistance in combating the problem.

The problem impacts international trade organizations and shipping companies, which affects not only the state of registry of the individual vessel, but each of that nation's trade partners in the international community. As a result, the necessary steps to secure such activity fall to the operating organization or the flag under which the vessels operate. The various state military organizations that are tasked with the protection of their state interests have not been able to provide the necessary ships and arms to protect all the shipping traffic.

International trade organizations need to understand the extent of trade security initiatives implemented by the United States and other nations, and they need to develop a strategy and a comprehensive plan to ensure the highest level of security. The involved states must also assess the costs of such added procedures and apply risk management principles to ensure the safety and security of their supply chain. It is also necessary to consider the likely necessity of reassessing their international trade agreements and to meld with the security procedures of other states, perhaps even to the point of a major reconsideration of current trade security regulations.

All affected and otherwise involved states should assess their responsible role in helping shape regulations affecting trade security, and in implementing such procedures so as to ensure the stability of the global trading system. The recent rash of incidents occurring in and near the Gulf of Aden has emphasized the necessity of international cooperation among the states sponsoring the various flag carriers operating in the gulf.

International insurance companies are hesitating to insure ships operating in the affected areas or are increasing their rates so much that some states, rather than risk the loss of a vessel, will consider a reroute of the vessel. Recently, insurance rates have escalated because of the threat, and they will only continue to do so if the threat level is maintained or increased. The escalating insurance rates and the threat of piracy has already caused many nations to direct their vessels to sail the far less direct routes to Europe by traveling around the southern tip of Africa. These states are experiencing rapidly rising operating costs because of the increased mileage necessary for safe passage of their flag vessels. They are very aware of the ever-present threat of piracy.

It would be remiss to fail to mention that the problem of piracy on the high seas is not restricted to the Red Sea and the coasts of bordering states, but is increasing in other areas as well. Among those areas of the world where most of the piratical incidents occur are the Malacca Straits, the areas off the coast of the Philippines, the area around Brazil, coastal areas adjacent to

Bangladesh, in and around Nicaragua, and in diverse coastal areas throughout the world.

It can be speculated that the major reason for the current increase in the illegal taking of vessels on the high seas is the inability of the major world powers to agree on a mutually agreeable course of action, coupled with the fact that the United States, a major player on the international scene, is in the throes of an economic crisis of epidemic proportions. Added to the problem of the United States, it must be understood that the economic crisis has international implications and plays an important role in determining the "lack of action" by any of the major power players on the international scene. The pirates are taking advantage of the economic unrest and the instability of several of the "world powers."

Articles 101 through 107 of the United Nations Convention of Maritime Law provide for the definition and interpretation of permissible actions that govern countermeasures that can be taken on the high seas when piratical action is detected. The following items contained in the convention may be of some help in understanding the perplexity of the problems facing states that have flag carriers plying the affected waters.

United Nations Convention on Maritime Law

Article 101
Definition of piracy
Piracy consists of any of the following acts:
  (a) any illegal acts of violence or detention, or any act of depredation, committed for private ends by the crew or the passengers of a private ship or a private aircraft, and directed:
      (i) on the high seas, against another ship or aircraft, or against persons or property on board such ship or aircraft;
      (ii) against a ship, aircraft, persons or property in a place outside the jurisdiction of any State;
  (b) any act of voluntary participation in the operation of a ship or of an aircraft with knowledge of facts making it a pirate ship or aircraft;
  (c) any act of inciting or of intentionally facilitating an act described in subparagraph (a) or (b).

Article 102
Piracy by a warship, government ship or government aircraft whose crew has mutinied
The acts of piracy, as defined in Article 101, committed by a warship, government ship, or government aircraft whose crew has mutinied and taken control of the ship or aircraft are assimilated to acts committed by a private ship or aircraft.

Article 103
Definition of a pirate ship or aircraft
A ship or aircraft is considered a pirate ship or aircraft if it is intended by the persons in dominant control to be used for the purpose of committing one of the acts referred to in Article 101. The same applies if the ship or aircraft has been used to commit any such act, so long as it remains under the control of the persons guilty of that act.

Article 104
Retention or loss of the nationality of a pirate ship or aircraft
A ship or aircraft may retain its nationality although it has become a pirate ship or aircraft. The retention or loss of nationality is determined by the law of the State from which such nationality was derived.

Article 105
Seizure of a pirate ship or aircraft
On the high seas, or in any other place outside the jurisdiction of any State, every State may seize a pirate ship or aircraft, or a ship or aircraft taken by piracy and under the control of pirates, and arrest the persons and seize the property on board. The courts of the State which carried out the seizure may decide upon the penalties to be imposed, and may also determine the action to be taken with regard to the ships, aircraft or property, subject to the rights of third parties acting in good faith.

Article 106
Liability for seizure without adequate grounds
Where the seizure of a ship or aircraft on suspicion of piracy has been effected without adequate grounds, the State making the seizure shall be liable to the State the nationality of which is possessed by the ship or aircraft for any loss or damage caused by the seizure.

Article 107
Ships and aircraft which are entitled to seize on account of piracy
A seizure on account of piracy may be carried out only by warships or military aircraft, or other ships or aircraft clearly marked and identifiable as being on government service and authorized to that effect.

It should be noted that Article 103 notes a specific problem in the current events in the Gulf of Aden. According to Article 103, a ship that has been captured by pirates and is used by the pirates in further piratical action, that ship is considered a "pirate ship" as long as it remains under the control of the pirates. Consider the consequences if the pirates, under duress, abandon the ship while being fired upon by a friendly force, and the pirates make good their escape, but in the subsequent action, the ship is heavily damaged or sunk; the friendly force may be held accountable for the cost of the ship and cargo if maritime law is strictly followed. The operative phrase in Article 103 is, "so long as it remains under the control of the persons guilty of that act." In the example cited, a case could be made that as soon as the pirates commenced abandoning the ship, they effectively relinquished control, making the operative phrase very important.

An additional problem arises when it becomes necessary to apply UN Convention of Maritime Law to any incident occurring on the high seas. It will be necessary to determine which of the hundreds of laws concerning operations and responsibilities of vessels operating on the high seas are applicable.

It is necessary to understand the many, many different conventions, agreements, and memorandums that exist when dealing with law on the high seas.

The concept of maritime law includes as a first definition national law, international public law, and international private law. (For further reading on the legal provisions for integrated coastal zone management and other international maritime laws, please visit http://www.globelaw.com/LawSea/lsconts.htm.)

What's wrong with any universal statement concerning the actions allowable on the high seas when piratical action is detected is that old bugaboo: nationalism. What if a Turkish vessel were being attacked by pirates, and a warship from Great Britain engaged the pirates and the vessel being attacked by the pirates were damaged or sunk? Where does the responsibility lie for recompense to the Turkish government? Maritime law is vague, except to imply that the British government could be held liable for civil action by the Turkish government. It is unlikely that a warship of any state would engage a pirate on behalf of any state's vessel but its own.

It appears that there exists a need for international cooperation between all participating states operating military vessels in affected waters. There must be a consistent policy between all states whose vessels ply the affected areas, covering the rules of engagement when interdicting pirates in action on the high seas. There must be preventive measures developed and put into place that are agreeable to all of the states. It is important and necessary to examine the several actions deemed essential to effectively counter the threat of seizure and ransoming of vessels by pirates on the high seas.

OPTIONS FOR THE MINIMIZING OF THE EFFECT OF PIRACY

There are several options open to the owners and operators of flag carriers that ply the seas in the Gulf of Aden and the area around the Red Sea.

Blockade of Ports That Harbor Pirates

The strategy would be an effective one if it could be promulgated, with all friendly craft able to pursue the pirate craft within the territorial limits of a nation such as Somalia. Thus is not the case. International law precludes any state from interfering in another sovereign state's affairs within its territory, which includes the twelve-mile territorial limits provided by maritime law on the high seas. The state in which the pirates have sanctuary must approve any actions in their territorial limits, and that includes interference with free access to all ports on the states coastline. To attack "pirate" vessels or to invade a state with the purpose of attacking the "haven" cities/ports that harbor the pirates would be an act of war. Somalia, for instance, does not have a stable government capable of offering assistance to states pursuing pirates. Somalia cannot maintain control over its own territory; yet neither can it take unilateral action to combat piracy in its country.

Pursuit/Capture of Pirates

Pursuit or capture of pirates is not a clearly defined issue. Since most of the vessels are operating "on the high seas" as defined in maritime law, the law itself must govern all of the activities of all the vessels that operate in the milieu. The term "high seas" means all parts of the seas that are not included in the territorial waters or the internal waters of a sovereign state. The high seas being open to all nations, no state may validly subject any part of them to its individual sovereignty. As long as the rogue ships can flee to the territorial waters of a sovereign state (Somalia) they are safe, for there can be no pursuit into those protected waters. The capture of pirates offers a completely new set of problems. What will the capturing forces do with the captives? Will they transport them to a neutral country for incarceration, and possibly trial? Will they transport the captives to their own states and incarcerate them? Will they bring them to trial? Under what law will they be prosecuted? What penalties can be assessed? And finally the big question: what are the political repercussions of any of the above actions? Is it known that any of the military forces presently providing protection to international shipping have an international agreement with all of the states' operating ships in the area? Can they, in fact, intercept piratical activity and be ensured that the state that has ownership of the vessel being attacked will support their actions, or will they hold the military vessels liable for damage to such ships? Does current international law provide for viable options to deal with piracy as it is being exercised currently? The answer to most of the questions is a resounding no.

Convoy

There are so many problems associated with convoy operations that it will suffice to say that it is not a viable option for operations in the Gulf of Aden area. Some of the problems are coordination, delays due to shipping times (which are variable), providing appropriate protection, arriving at a number of ships that can be provided protection; states laws against such operations, the sheer magnitude of the problem associated with the numbers of vessels plying the seas of the Gulf of Aden—among many other obstacles.

Paying Ransom or Tribute

If the truth be known, ransom has been paid many times unbeknownst to the states or the United Nations. Many operators choose to pay the ransom quietly and hope to build some kind of relationship with the pirates so as not to be attacked again. As a viable option, however, paying ransom or tribute is never productive in the long haul. The more successful operations the pirates enjoy, the more pirates join the criminal groups in order to partake of the "booty" collected. The more ransom paid, the more pirates there will be—and the more illegal activity there will be. The pirates have no moral compunction about reattacking a previously ransomed vessel. The ransom option, unfortunately, will be exercised many times in the future, as it is the only one that has produced the freeing of a captured vessel.

Execution of the Pirates "En Scene"

There must be effective repercussions to an act of piracy. There must be some punishment administered to those offenders that are captured in the act of piracy. In the recent past, and—as far as can be determined—even currently, the pirates are disarmed and then released. A cogent question is, "What motivation does the pirate have to cease his criminal actions?" The answer, of course, is none. Immediate execution of pirates apprehended in the act of committing an act of piracy should be considered. The pirate should pay the ultimate penalty, and pay it immediately. It is an option that must be considered. Execution would have to be sanctioned by the international community in a separate law of the sea specifically designed to treat with acts of piracy, and would have to be agreed to by the international community. This is an option that will probably never be agreed to by the United Nations, for some of the member states of the United Nations are sponsors of international terror and have direct ties with the rogue states and organizations currently participating in the piracy.

So what *can* be done to protect ships operating on the high seas from pirates?

INTERNATIONAL AGREEMENTS AND COOPERATION

As a beginning, it is absolutely essential that states that have flag carriers operating in affected areas all be on the same page when it comes to dealing with pirates. There are many states that have a vital stake in the outcome of the struggle with the pirates. Because of the possibility of international sea trade being seriously diminished or even stopped entirely, an immediate plan of action must be implemented by the free and affected states. It goes without saying that the current level of incidents concerning attacks on vessels in the Gulf of Aden cannot be allowed to continue. The most important step, and one that must be taken immediately, is the joining together of all of the affected states that have vessels operating on the high seas. These states must gather together in a coalition of states and agree to work closely together to combat piracy. A common set of outcomes must be agreed upon by all of the coalition forces, and authority sought under the auspices of the United Nations to develop a strategic policy to eliminate the threat of piracy wherever it may be found.

There are many approaches to deal with this situation, but there must be one approach that will be used by all coalition forces. There can be no state operating independently of the coalition plan that is put into effect.

The plan must be preceded by mutual agreement of all states participating in the action. This would entail and require a written plan delineating purpose and responsibility. The resources to be provided by each state would be specifically defined. A single organization, perhaps made up of members of several of the coalition states, would be required, whose responsibility would be to coordinate all efforts by members of the coalition forces.

One of the most important of the items to be defined by the controlling organization would be the rules of engagement (ROE). It is of the utmost importance that the purpose of the ROE be clearly stated and directed toward clearance of the sea lanes of pirates, and the ROE must reflect that concept. Since the coalition would be acting on the high seas, it is necessary that the organization and the subsequent rules of engagement be approved and authorized by the United Nations. The track record of the United Nations on issues such as this has been less than sterling, so it must be clearly stated by the United Nations that the coalition is acting under its aegis, and that it has the sanction and full authority to conduct operations against the pirates under the rules of engagement promulgated by the coalition forces.

There must be binding agreements between *all* participating states, and the agreement must include the dedication of adequate resources to meet any situation that may occur. Included in the agreements there must be a single controlling organization, hereinafter called the "coalition," constituted from among the member states. Finally, there must be a total agreement on the rules of engagement to be employed by the coalition forces.

The coalition must have as its membership all states that have flag carriers operating in the affected area. This is essential to the conduct of military operations against an enemy that intends to deprive the various states of ships, cargo, and crews. The purpose of the enemy actions may be to take over or hijack a vessel to be held for ransom, to threaten to attack a vessel, or even to destroy a vessel. The coalition forces must have contingency plans to meet any and all possible exigencies. This will require a crisis management team to assess the vulnerabilities of the flag carriers and assess the possible risk factors for every vessel that plies the gulf. Protection would be provided to operating vessels commensurate with the crisis management team's assessment of threat and vulnerability. How could this be accomplished?

1. A command post would be established where all shipping and shipping schedules would be coordinated.
2. Personnel manning the command post would be of those states capable of providing some measure of protection to shipping on the high seas and currently signatory to the international agreement promulgating the command post and associated operations supporting protection of vessels operating in the affected area.
3. Sufficient resources must be made available to the coalition forces so that protection can be afforded commensurate with the threat level.
4. Surveillance of the entire Gulf of Aden and surrounding areas must be provided, whether by stationary satellite, ships operating in the area, or unmanned aircraft capable of providing surveillance of the area.

5. All vessels plying the high seas would be provided with an operating IFF and would be assigned appropriate codes to use when operating normally and when an emergency or hijacking is taking place or is anticipated. This procedure would allow appropriate responses from protective forces. Upon receipt of an emergency signal from a vessel in distress, help would be rushed to the area.
6. The rules of engagement must also include instructions of treatment of captured pirates. This should include the authority to "shoot to kill" during rescue operations, (perhaps) authority to incarcerate the pirates in a "jail" provided by international law, and the subsequent trial of the pirates by the International Court in The Hague.
7. As a minimum, the rules of engagement must include total authority to the on-scene commander to take such action, as deemed necessary, to effectively counter any actions taken by the pirates.
8. The rules of engagement must include provisions to "not hold liable" the on-scene commander of coalition forces for any damage to ships that have been captured by pirates and subsequently used as a "mother ship" or a launching platform for piratical activities. The rules of engagement must place that responsibility on the pirates.
9. The rules of engagement must include in its provisions authority to use air-to-sea missiles launched from manned or unmanned aircraft and surface-to-surface missiles launched from a coalition vessel at sea.

Organization of Operations Control

The command post would offer threat assessment and apply risk management principles in ascertaining the vulnerabilities of the shipping for which it holds responsibility. It would advise the operating states of the threat as assessed by the risk management team. The command post would assign forces and resources to the operating arm of the coalition to send ships or aircraft to areas where they are deemed necessary, with specific instructions and rules of engagement that are realistic and that reflect the assessed threat.

Actions Required

Essential to any antipiracy activity by friendly forces must be the dedication of sufficient resources and forces capable of meeting any challenge presented by the pirates. It must be understood that pirates are terrorists and criminals preying on peaceful vessels in the operation of their duties on the high seas. It is equally essential that the activities of the pirates must not be underestimated, for their goal is to bring the entire Gulf of Aden, if not large areas of the high seas, totally under their control. State payments of ransom and tribute to these criminals will only lead to increased criminal activity on the part of these terrorists. It must be remembered that at one time in the not-too-distant past, "looting" was an offense that was punishable by "shoot to kill" authority. Times have changed, and since the advent of the United Nations and other international bodies that have come under the influence and control of states that condone such activities, looting is now tolerated. Such a state of affairs must not be extended to piracy on the high seas.

Comments

The current situation in the Gulf of Aden is extremely sensitive and critical. Action must be taken immediately, and it must be concise and direct in its application. Force must be used—if necessary, "deadly force"—to minimize the threats in the area. It is, unfortunate however, that such positive action probably will not be taken, that token forces will continue to "pick at the issue." There is no political will among the governments of the West to take any kind of definitive action as described above. The politically correct age is upon us, and affected states would rather be "admired" than "feared." What keeps nations from attacking the United States? Great Britain? Australia? Fear of repercussions. It is possible that in the near future, because of the ineffective steps taken by the international community, pirates will openly defy the United States and other of the great powers, because they know that the international community will simply stand by helplessly and observe rather than be proactive in the war against piracy. Anarchy is upon us. Is there no one state willing to stand up for the rule of law?

NOTES

1. BAN Africa News, "Countries want peace in Somalia, but no major offer of troops," December 17, 2008, http://www.monstersandcritics.com/news/africa/news/article_1449039.php.

2. London Telegraph, "Indian Ocean Rife with Pirates" Janaury 10, 2009, http://www.telegraph.co.uk/news/worldnews/africaandindianocean/somalia3814571/Somalia.

3. StrategyPage.com, "Somali Pirates" March 12, 2009, http://www.strategypage.com/htamph/articles/20090312.aspx.

4. India Times, "Anti-piracy operation approved in Somalia" March 19, 2009, http://www.economictimes.indiatimes.com/PoliticsNation/Anti-piracy_operations_approved_in_Somalia/articleshow/3851317.cms.

5. AGI News, "Somalia and the New Pirates," February 17, 2009, http://www.agi.it/world/news/200902171619-cro-ren0035-art.html.

6. Ilke Rademaker "Modern Piracy and the Global Supply Chain," *Washington Times*, March 1, 2009, http://www.ModernPiracy.com/GlobalSupplyChainPaper/globalsupplychainsecurity/PiracyPaper/washingtontimes-ILKE-RADEMAKER/o.htm.

7. Ilke Rademaker "Modern Piracy and the Global Supply Chain," *Washington Times*, March 1, 2009, http://www.ModernPiracy.com/GlobalSupplyChainPaper/globalsupplychainsecurity/PiracyPaper/washingtontimes-ILKE-RADEMAKER/o.htm.

9. Swiss Institute of Technology Zurich "Security Watch: Modern Piracy" February 10, 2009, http://www.isn.ethz.ch/isn/layout/set/print/content/view/full/73?id=97585&lng=en&ots591=4.

10. Swiss Institute of Technology Zurich "Security Watch: Modern Piracy" February 10, 2009, http://www.isn.ethz.ch/isn/layout/set/print/content/view/full/73?id=97585&lng=en&ots591=4.

CHAPTER 8

Supply Chain Security in a Developing Economy: India

Dr. Mohd. Nishat Faisal

New opportunities for a global marketplace made available by the ubiquitous Internet have brought with them challenges for supply chain security. Supply chains can be disrupted due to security breaches and may prove fatal for the partnering firms in a supply chain. For example, in cases of terrorist attack it is very common to seal ports and border crossings for certain amounts of time—in many cases, doing so has a huge effect on overall supply chain profitability and, ultimately, viability. The December 2008 terrorist attacks in Mumbai had a huge impact in terms of increased security checks, and, in some cases, even termination of trade from neighboring countries. In case of supply chain disruption, experts find it difficult to quantify the related costs, which in many cases may also include loss of customers and erosion of brand image.[1] Supply chain security–related practices have been transformed tremendously after September 11, 2001. Although earlier the focus was on controlling theft, illegal immigration, and drugs, after 9/11, supply chain security efforts are more directed toward improving security from possible terrorist attacks.[2] New standards emerged in many countries for secure transportation of goods across nations. As most of the efforts were focused on enhancing air transportation security, many experts suggested putting in place an overall comprehensive strategy for managing supply chain disruptions that would include carrier modes other than air transportation. But an all-inclusive framework for securing supply chains is still in its nascent stages.[3]

As geographical boundaries blur with the expansion of businesses, supporting supply chains become even more vulnerable to security threats. There are efforts by collaborating partners in supply chains to improve security, but the imminent threat of possible terrorist attacks that may cripple the international transportation system always remains high. In recent days, however, awareness about security concerns related to supply chains and possible disruption risks is high on the agenda of the businesses around the globe.[4] In a survey by the A. T. Kearney[5] security company, such concerns were ranked as more important by supply chain executives than traditional supply chain issues such as lead time reduction, inventory management, and minimizing stock-outs.

Several cases of disruptions to the flow of materials in supply chains feeding assembly plants have resulted as consequences of the September 11, 2001, terrorist attacks. For example, Ford had several stoppages in its assembly lines waiting for material that got delayed at the Canadian and Mexican borders. Toyota, known for its just-in-time (JIT) production systems, also faced problems due to the nonavailability of steering sensors shipped by air from Germany, due to the disruption in air traffic, and barely managed to keep running the production line at its Sequoia SUV plant in Indiana.[6] Though the advantages of just-in-time inventory have been widely publicized, vulnerability is a less-advertised side effect. JIT dictates the keeping of very low inventory—sometimes even only hours' worth—and depends on frequent deliveries of supplies, making the system under threat from supply chain disruption. Supply chains that operate across national boundaries are subject to growing concern about the safe transportation of goods across national borders in the aftermath of terrorist attacks worldwide. Due to increased stress on security, today these trading boundaries are being visualized as "security" boundaries.[7] Furthermore, supply chain disruptions not only impact the organizations that are part of the supply chain, but also may ripple into the regions where these supply chains conduct business.[8]

"Supply chain security is the application of policies, procedures, and technology to protect assets, product, facilities, equipment, information, and personnel from theft, damage, or terrorism and to prevent the introduction of unauthorized contraband, people, or weapons of mass destruction."[9]

In the wake of new threats emerging for supply chains, firms involved in handling physical goods face four distinct challenges:[10]

- Proactive planning involves simulating events that might disrupt the supply chain and developing suitable strategies in case a disruptive event took place. These risk mitigation strategies should take into account the vulnerabilities of all the partners in the supply chain.
- Supply chain planning under uncertainty acknowledges that increased security procedures also tend to create bottlenecks, adding to uncertainty in lead times. Firms need to find ways to schedule their operations and delivery times accordingly to meet customer requirements effectively.
- Partnering with the government helps ensure supply chain security as firms realign their relationships with various governmental agencies. This cooperation transcends geographical boundaries in the same way that supply chains have done.

- Managing in the new era creates a balance between cost and the requirements of security, one of the most vital—and challenging—tasks in this new era, when security is of prime importance. New metrics have to be developed to help management make more informed decisions.

To improve supply chain security, parallels can be drawn with the quality movement. The total quality management (TQM) philosophy, which focuses on process control and a continuous improvement cycle rather than on end product inspection and error detection, can be of particular help in this regard. A novel study entitled "Innovators in Supply Chain Security" carried out by the Stanford University Graduate School of Business in collaboration with the Manufacturing Institute (the research and education arm of the National Association of Manufacturers), tried to make more apparent the business value of supply chain security investments. Participants, mostly manufacturers, reported the following benefits of investments in the security initiatives:

- Enhanced product safety
- Better inventory management
- Transparency across the supply chains
- Reduction in product damages
- Process improvements
- Delivery time improvements
- Improvement of supply chain resilience
- Efficient cross border movement of goods
- Higher levels of customer satisfaction

There has been a lot written on supply chain vulnerability during crises or disasters such as the 9/11 terrorist attack in 2001 or natural disasters such as Hurricane Katrina, but not much attention has been paid to day-to-day supply chain security. As supply chains reach around the globe, potential security concerns are present every day.[11] Security initiatives like CSI (Container Security Initiative), C-TPAT (Customs-Trade Partnership Against Terrorism), and 24-Hour Manifest Ruling can be considered new to companies, particularly in developing economies, and this has led to serious problems for supply chains importing from these countries. In one instance, a clothing importer incurred huge costs finding an alternative source of supply because its original supplier from Pakistan was not able to meet the requirements of information details as required by new homeland security regulations.[12]

In today's economic slump, all eyes are focused on economies such as those of China and India. Although there are signs of economic slowdown in India, they are not as severe as in Western economies. Because the scale of operations in India is quite large in terms of volume, supply chains operations are quite complex. The following section discusses security concerns very specific to India that should nevertheless also be taken into consideration by Western companies attempting to secure their supply chain operations.

COMMUNAL RIOTS

Though India is emerging as a major economic power in the world, it unfortunately could not wipe out the threat of communalism. Although communal discords appeared even before independence, independence and the subsequent formation of Pakistan have led to further polarization of the society and have escalated these sorts of incidences. It can be said that the communal disharmony reached its zenith in 1992, and again in 2002. Steve I. Wikinson, in his book *Votes and Violence*, argues that "politicians both cause [such incidences] and, more importantly, have the power to prevent them, through their control of the state governments responsible for law and order." Some other recent research also considers certain specific town level factors as key to explaining the occurrence and, in many cases, reoccurrence of communal riots in that area. Paul Brass,[13] for instance, has focused on the importance of "institutional riot systems." According to this theory, there exist certain situational factors that oftentimes aid in starting such riots, particularly in those areas where they are already quite widespread. Ashutosh Varshney[14] contends that "state and national-level politics are less important than town level civic organizations and networks: where a town's civic organizations are interethnic and associational." Communal riots as witnessed in Gujarat, Mumbai, or in many parts of India in the aftermath of the Babri mosque demolition create unprecedented disruptions for supply chains. As these issues are very unpredictable—and, more important, companies' operations in developed economies have rarely witnessed such sort of supply chain disruptions—there are in fact no well developed strategies to meet the contingencies in such situations.

CASTE-BASED AGITATIONS

Caste-based agitations and clashes are a scourge for India, because society has been divided among a number of castes for thousands of years. In the year 2007, Gujjar community's demand to be included in the list of Scheduled Tribes for more government benefits degenerated into bloodshed and lawlessness. The national highway (NH11) from Jaipur to Agra became the focal point of the May 2007 agitation, which started with roadblocks and ultimately resulted in the loss of twenty-six lives in clashes with police forces. The railway route passing through the area of agitation was also heavily affected, resulting in large-scale diversions, cancelation, or short-termination of trains. This resulted not only in monetary loss to the public exchequer, but also in immense inconvenience to the populace. The impact of such flareups on supply chains are tremendous; for many days, a whole network is disrupted. Many parts are totally cut off during such tensions, and supply chains are left wanting because of the unavailability of materials from suppliers, or the inability of such materials to reach customers.

NAXALITE MOVEMENT

In general, Naxalites are identified as antiestablishment forces who take their name from Naxalbari, a village in the state of West Bengal, India, where the naxal movement took roots in late sixties. Today, the region that is most affected by naxal violence is called the "red corridor"; it stretches from the border of Nepal through almost half of India's twenty-eight states. The naxal rule runs through the thick jungles of central India, and the movement garners support and depends on recruits from the region's deprived population. The states most affected by naxal activity are Andhra Pradesh, Bihar, West Bengal, Jharkhand, and Orissa, but for Chhattisgarh the year 2006 was particularly bad as large-scale naxal violence resulted in the loss of more 300 human lives. Because of the extent of its spread, and also because of the local support that the naxal movement garners in many regions, it is more difficult to control than terrorist attacks. In areas where the naxal movement is flourishing, many logistics companies are not ready to operate for fear of losing property—and even human lives. Thus companies are puzzled over to how to effectively meet such supply chain security risks.

SUPPLY CHAIN SECURITY ENABLERS

In the present scenario, supply chain security has emerged as an essential, central part of supply chain planning. There is an urgent need for all partners to develop skills and strategies to deal with new security demands. Supply chain security has four dimensions:[11]

- Security of the product or service
- Security of information flow
- Security of money flow
- Security of logistics systems

To improve upon the above dimensions, the dynamics among the various enablers of supply chain security must be understood. Some of these are discussed in the following section.

Supplier Relationships

In a globalized economy, where supply chains transcend geographical boundaries, logistics and supply chain managers find it difficult to determine exactly where to start the process of managing and controlling the security of supply chains. In this context, it is accepted by all that it is neither economically feasible—nor in fact even viable—for the smooth flow of goods in a supply chain to be accomplished by 100 percent inspection of containers. But lately, governmental agencies have become stricter in their controls, particularly because of new threats, and through mandatory guidelines set up in wake of such threats. Thus, the success of the supply chain now rests to a large extent in the judicious selection of partners who meet tough criteria in such key activities as selecting carriers that are cognizant of security needs, depending on secure ports, using ways of packaging that enhance security, and also continually updating employee databases.[15]

In the extant supply chain literature, supplier relationships can be analyzed on the basis of their position on a continuum. At one end of the continuum are those relationships that are generally based on cost minimization, low trust, little commitment to the relationship, and very little contact—often depending greatly on the Internet. On the other end are long-term symbiotic relationships based on commitment and trust. These relationships try to optimize overall supply chain efficiency rather than individual parts. Logistics and supply chain managers are required to understand the current position on the continuum and then to ascertain the most effective security strategy for the type of relationship.

One of the major advantages that accrues because of long-term relationships is supply assured by suppliers even in cases of disruption. This is a certainty because the supplier is also assured of purchases by the customer, giving it good reason to value the relationship and show commitment to it. Although in recent times many of the manufacturing firms in the United States and Europe shifted their manufacturing base to low-cost countries to take advantage of cheap labor, they have lately realized that although offshore suppliers can deliver goods in lesser cost, in general, because of the distances involved in transportation of goods, lead times are longer, making supply chains more prone to disruption. Local suppliers may be more expensive, but their proximity makes supply chains more responsive to contingent situations. Experts are now advising sourcing from both local and offshore suppliers, with the bulk of material supplied from low-cost offshore destinations and smaller quantities provided by local suppliers. During a disruption, a company may rely wholly on the local supplier without major stoppage, for the local supplier already has the know-how required to produce what the company needs. This way, the high cost paid to the local supplier acts as the premium paid to ensure that supply chain keeps on serving the markets even during disruptive events.[10]

In addition to collaborating within the supply chain, businesses must share their experiences and best practices related to supply chain security across industry groups. From a supply chain perspective, there is a growing realization that the success of a firm is dependent not only on its suppliers but also, in many cases, its customers, and even, sometimes, its competitors. Thus it is now incumbent upon organizations to choose supply chain partners who keep on updating their skills to take on supply chain security challenges and who can integrate with the response strategies of the partnering firms.[16]

Supply Chain Security Strategy

"You need to focus on supply chain security at the strategic level to make it work across all business units," explains John Mascaritolo, director global logistics with financial electronics company NCR Corp. "If you only look at security at the local level, you'll have different approaches throughout the company."[17] A supply chain security workshop conducted at Michigan State University underscored the need to understand the strategic nature of supply chain security. The participants underlined the need of moving from a single-firm focus to all-inclusive strategies to improve overall security in a supply chain. To secure a supply chain, all the stakeholders of a supply chain that may be involved in all the activities required for the delivery of goods to the ultimate consumer must be brought together. This is a major requirement, for a supply chain is considered to be only as secure as its weakest link. Further, because supply chain partners may be from different parts of the globe, it requires an understanding of the procedures, laws, and regulations of the countries where the supply chain operates.

To be successful, supply chain security initiatives require top management support. This is critical, for security implementation requires a huge change in employees' behavior, a transformation only possible when top management lends support to security policies. Changes in attitude toward security concerns requires an understanding that processes are not going to run smoothly all the time, and that planning for only very specific types of disasters won't ensure supply chain security by itself. It is been observed that in general, organizations plan for those risks that have a high probability of occurrence but less impact; supply chain risks that have a low probability of occurrence but a huge impact are generally ignored. To ensure supply chain security, process performance must be tracked, and companies must ensure that they are in compliance with supply chain security measures. This would then ensure that organizations would get early warning about possible supply chain security problems.[18] Security initiatives requires investments, and with the absence of metrics to exhibit that supply chain performance improves with increase attention on security, it is extremely difficult to convince senior management of possible benefits, and to ensure its support. This is even more difficult because many of supply chains have not yet encountered such disruption, making it difficult for management to conceptualize it in the future.[19]

Third-Party Logistics (3PL) Partners

Third-party logistics providers (3PLs) have a major role to play in supply chain security initiatives, because today it is 3PLs who, in the majority of cases, manages issues like carrier selection and procurement, warehouse management, management of drivers and vehicles, freight brokerage, and, above all, supply chain visibility. Because customer demands are quite varied, it is imperative that 3PL companies understand security requirements, procedures, and protocols and devise strategies accordingly. In addition to this, businesses should develop security criteria for their 3PL partners. This would not only help to reduce congestion at borders but would also minimize the impact of disruption on supply chains. These criteria should be well documented and widely accepted to ensure the existence of another level of protection against disruptions in supply chains.

3PL providers can be instrumental in reducing security concerns for supply chains. For example, at Mallory Alexander, there is a constant flow of information through the maintenance of regular contacts with other security professionals and law enforcement officials. This helps in understanding and devising methods to reduce cargo theft and deter loss. But all this is only possible when companies have a limited number of 3PL partners with whom they share long-term relationships or agreements. Long-term agreements would motivate 3PLs to constantly upgrade their security systems in order to satisfy the growing security needs of their clients.

Supply Chain Resilience

One of the major results of all the efforts of securing supply chain is resilience—the capability of a supply chain to quickly bounce back after a disruption. "A resilient supply chain is one that can reduce costs and improve customer satisfaction and customer relations under normal supply chain operations, while sustaining supply chain operations during major disruptions."[20] Supply chain resilience can be improved by strategies like postponement, build-to-order, multiple suppliers, maintaining strategic stock, using a mix of transportation modes, and dynamic assortment planning. Using a mix of these strategies, companies like Dell, Nokia, and HP are very successful in satisfying their customers.

Supply chain resilience is a function of flexibility or change and the speed by which the change can be brought about. Flexibility not only helps supply chains quickly adapt to changing scenarios in case of disruption, but it helps effectively meet customer requirements. Transforming supply chains into flexible entities also ensures resilience, and vice versa.[6] For example, most of Toyota's suppliers are based in North America, which ensures a high degree of supply chain resilience when compared with that of automobile manufacturers like GM or Ford, who outsource the majority of their components from low-cost offshore suppliers.

Security-Dedicated Communications and Technology

Technology can play a major role in securing supply chains. Unfortunately, although companies understand this, they are not able to employ technology solutions to effectively manage the security of their supply chains. But many currently available technologies, like biometrics for access control, tracking software and GPS systems, and sensors to detect tampering during transit, can be very useful to improve supply chain security.[18] Development and operating security–dedicated communications channels coupled with cutting-edge technology for improving security are major contributors to overall supply chain security at the organizational level.[16] Many of the technological solutions available today help facilitate the exchange of risk-related data and communication in real time to enhance supply chain security. For example, to improve communications with government departments that are particularly involved in ensuring security, Prokop[21] suggests that "shippers and carriers [ ] start using electronic tracking, accounting, and reporting systems that are connected to government-run electronic checkpoints ensuring faster customs clearance." In case of a supply chain disruptive event occurring, quick rerouting of shipments can be done if there is a fast transfer of information to supply chain partners using satellite communications coupled with RFID.[22]

Further, visibility software and real-time information transfer are also important components to mitigate security related risks as they improve the overall visibility in a supply chain. Because of the impact that disruptive events can have on a supply chain, the development of software tools and data systems that can support disaster response planning and simulate events are being accorded high priority by a number of software companies.[23] In addition to this, electronic data processing and integrating latest technology solutions such as RFID, GPS, and transportation management systems with supply chain management software would be useful in detecting gaps in overall supply chain security.[16] As a technology manager noted: "We should be tracking our shipments with GPS devices, examining shipments electronically for both safety and accuracy of item picked, and generally watching out for suspicious events using real-time (technology)."

Participation in initiatives like Safe and Secure Tradelanes (SST) aims to improve the physical security and ensure improved tracking of the containers throughout the supply chain. This is the reason that companies like IBM, Sun Microsystems, and Qualcom are using SST for transporting goods in their supply chains. In SST, real-time cargo tracking works as an audit system which ensures quick adaptation to changed scenarios. In addition to RFID, GPS, tracking, and management software is also the use of anti-intrusion sensor systems and automated video surveillance. Around fifteen ports are now using the tradelanes baseline network, making it much easier to track sensor-deployed containers arriving in the United States.[24] Techniques like data mining, which was earlier employed by businesses to improve their market share and understand their customers, are now being used by customs to have prior information about each shipment, along with information about the past activities of the same shipper, and about similar consignments. This allows government agencies to conduct screening, and to become more alert for consignments that falls under the category of "higher" risks.

Contractual Agreements and Sharing Risks and Rewards with Partners

Formal contractual agreements among supply chain partners facilitates the establishment of common security goals.[16] To ensure suppliers' compliance with supply chain security, it is necessary to identify specific security-related actions expected from the key partners and then detail them explicitly in contractual agreements. A supply chain security mechanism defined formally through a contract would certainly improve the overall trust in the security procedures adopted by various partners in a supply chain.

To ensure adherence and compliance with security agreements, there should be joint sharing of risks and rewards among supply chain partners. Partners should be responsible for minimizing security breaches and improving the overall supply chain's ability to meet contingencies along, and provision should be made for sharing revenues when the supply chain works smoothly and satisfies customers.

Knowledge and Process Backup

Supply chain continuity planning has emerged as a major topic of research in the area of supply chain risk management. The business continuity plan can be very useful for supply and purchasing professionals to mitigate risks in a supply chain. In general this plan consists of four major steps: awareness creation, prevention, remediation, and knowledge management.[25] The most vital assets that require backup are the knowledge base, processes, and relationships. For many organizations, the information and communication technology backbone is so vital for survival that they have established backup or mirror sites for their critical hardware, software applications, and databases. The importance of backups can be understood in cases of terrorist attacks like 9/11, or even in natural disasters like Hurricane Katrina. Solomon Smith Barney, a financial services firm, was operational again within twelve of 9/11—it maintained a backup site.

But even when faced with so many threats, very few companies maintain backup emergency business processes. These emergency measures should consist of all the procedures and protocols to be followed when a disruptive event has occurred. An organization's human resources are its most important assets, so efforts should be made to document critical processes. In this context, techniques employed in knowledge management are of particular importance, as are inculcating multitasking capabilities in employees. The success of maintaining backups is dependent on keeping the backups up to date; otherwise, backups are out of date and of little use.

In addition to business processes, relationships that a company creates over a period of time are also critical for its survival. Customer relationship management software offers opportunities for documenting, and later deriving advantage from, such relationships. This can be of immense help in cases of supply chain disruption; supply chains can easier return to normalcy when the extent of relationships both downstream and upstream side can be identified and recollected. Similarly, standardizing various business processes across supply chains positively affect the capability of the supply chain to regain quickly from a disaster. Thus, incompatible and nonscalable information systems across a supply chain make it more vulnerable to disruptions than does operating standardized seamlessly integrated information systems across supply chains.

Sharing Information

Information sharing is categorically important for mitigating risks in a supply chain,[26] but firms don't like to share information with their supply chain partners, fearing that such information could be passed to competitors. To address this concern, Secure Supply Chain Collaboration protocols are being developed to facilitate supply chain partners' developing collaborative plans safely.

There is an increased stress in both governmental agencies and businesses to create more confidence in supply chain security. This would require several new initiatives that would facilitate information exchange among trading partners.[1]

Security Certifications (ISO 28000:2007)

To establish a framework for supply chain security, the International Standards Organization (ISO) has developed its ISO 28000:2007 standards, which define procedures, policies, and mechanisms for managing vulnerabilities in the supply chain and establishing preventative action plans. The ISO 28000 series focuses on the overall security of an organization's supply chain, acting as an umbrella standard that incorporates the requirements of all major international supply chain security initiatives. It integrates both the process-based approach of ISO's management systems and the "plan–do–check–act" model. Its characteristic features include

- Risk-based approach aligned with ISO 14001
- Foundation in the ISO 9001 and ISO 14001 management systems
- Compliance with the ISO 28000 series, verifiable by internal or external audits
- Use of best practice risk assessment tools
- Requirements for a supply chain security management system specified

ISO 28000:2007 can be implemented in organizations of all types and sizes that are involved in the production of goods, manufacturing, services, storage, or transportation at any stage of the products' development or movement in the supply chain. It provides a systems approach for any organization to manage its security program and can be the foundation for a variety of international security initiatives, including the International Maritime Organization's International Ship and Port Facility (ISPS) Code, the National Customs Department's Authorized Economic Operator (AEO) program (based on the World Custom Organization's Framework of Standards to Secure and Facilitate Global Trade by Operator program); the EC's Regulation for Enhancing Supply Chain Security AEO program, and the U.S. Customs and Border Protection initiative, the Customs-Trade Partnership Against Terrorism (C-TPAT).

Companies using ISO 28000 will implement a protective security program based on the identification of risks. ISO 28000 is emerging as the international benchmark for managing security programs in different countries while simultaneously applying a globally consistent standard of operations. In India, Mumbai's Nhava Sheva port terminal became the country's first security-certified port terminal after achieving ISO 28000:2007 series certification from the Dutch firm DNV. This certification assures a user about the processes followed to ensure port security and integrity of the chain. More ports will adopt this method as such certification becomes the baseline for securing world maritime trade.

Public–Private Partnership

Although security is mainly considered a domain of government agencies, it is now widely accepted that government cannot do it alone. Thus there is need for businesses to partner with the government at federal and local levels to improve security across the supply chain. Partnerships between businesses and government, including firms' collaboration with customs and trade agencies, are particularly good at minimizing tampering with and damage to shipments.[21] Further, government partnerships can also be extended to include the sharing of responsibility for securing supply chains by the governments where the firms are located.[22] Although certain private–public crisis management systems exist, there is still much scope for improving collaboration and integrating plans across jurisdictions.[23] Regardless of the methodology employed for actual implementation, building partnerships is a key element of effective supply chain security program. Some possible areas of collaborating with the government include the following:

- Government agencies involved in security come across various security threats; their knowledge base may be extremely useful to businesses devising supply chain security strategies. Likewise, supply chains that encounter disruption from various security threats must share relevant information with the agencies involved in enforcing procedures related to security.
- Today, in general, supply chains operate across nations; thus, in many cases, information available from their own offices in other countries or from their partners can be of importance to them.

For supply chain security programs to be successful, collaborative efforts between public and private sectors are needed. Also, government agencies should take the lead in formulating and enforcing security-related guidelines. In this regard, an organization with transnational character including personnel both from government as well as from businesses can work to create comprehensive set of regulations from the point of view of all security concerns with a consideration of the impact of the regulatory framework on businesses.[27]

Investments and Cost Savings

Security initiatives in a supply chain, though implemented with the major objective of avoiding and minimizing impact due to disruptions, can also result in potential cost savings. This may accrue because of improved visibility of material and information flow across supply chain resulting in the visibility of real-time information and lesser errors in shipments.[28] In general businesses like to adopt and implement those activities for which return on investment is evident (particularly in the short run). But because the value added due to the investment on security initiatives is difficult to measure, particularly in the short term, maintaining investments according to a changing security scenario is hard to do.[10] Recent studies suggest that there are also business benefits that may accrue from security strategies. There may be a reduction in transit times and inventories due to improvements in visibility achieved through the availability of real-time information, as suggested by a study conducted by Stanford University and released through the Manufacturing Institute, the research arm of the National Association of Manufacturers. The Dow Chemical Company, one of the companies participating in the study, reported improvements in both transfer of materials across borders and reduction in overall inventories.[29] The increased visibility of containers and their movement across the supply chain, as well as information regarding container contents and expected arrival, results in inventory reduction, reduced lead time variance, increased manufacturing uptime, fewer out-of-stocks situations, minimization of theft, better service for the importer, and better relations with customers and suppliers.[5, 6, 30]

SUPPLY CHAIN SECURITY: AN ANALYSIS OF INTERACTIONS AMONG THE ENABLERS

Based on a review of the literature, and using a modified Delphi technique[31] to identify the enablers of supply chain security, this study employed a decision-making group comprising seven experts. Identified enablers for secure supply chains are

1. Contractual agreements
2. Information sharing

3. Regulatory framework
4. Supply chain security policy and strategy
5. Top management commitment
6. Public–private partnerships
7. Security-dedicated communications and technology
8. Investments in supply chain security initiatives
9. Collaborative planning
10. Improved supply chain resilience
11. Knowledge backup
12. Trust based long-term relationships
13. Third-party logistics providers
14. Improvements in customer service
15. Employee training

Figure 8.1

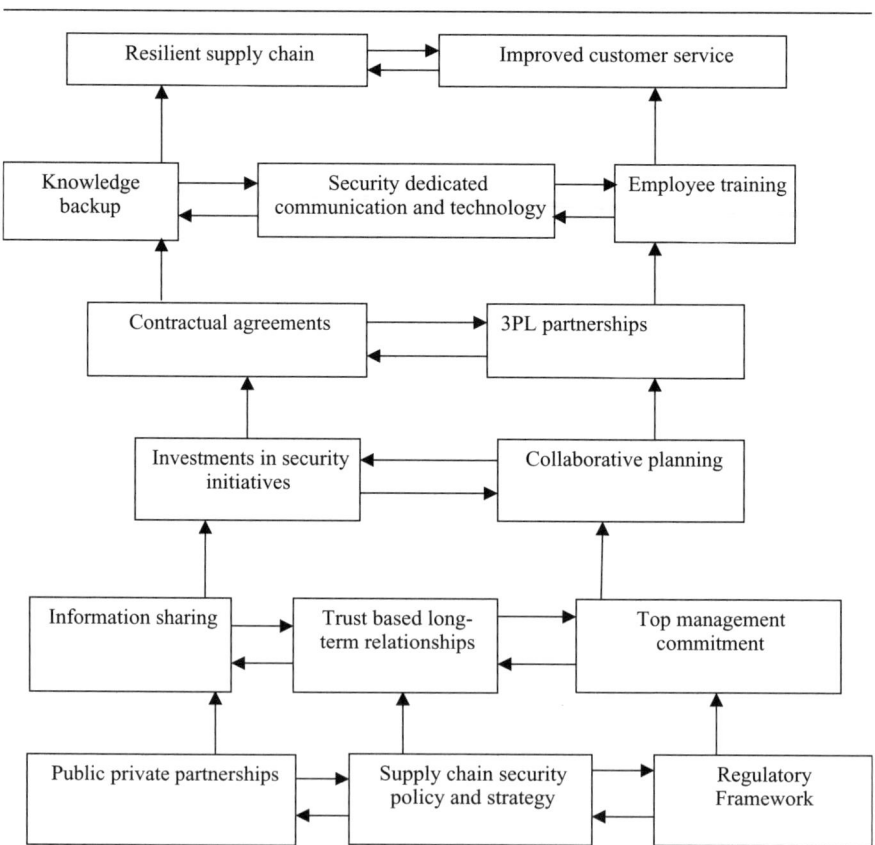

CONCLUSION AND DISCUSSION

This chapter provides an understanding of supply chain security concerns from the perspective of a developing economy. The chapter outlines some of threats that specific to supply chains operating in a country like India. Furthermore, it approaches supply chain security from the perspective of variables that can be effective in transforming supply chains into secure entities. Many of these variables are familiar to the supply chain experts, but what is important is their mutual relationships in context of supply chain security. The chapter also proposes an interpretive structural model to understand the relative importance among these variables.

Today, rapid proliferation of Internet and its wide acceptance has provided opportunities to select suppliers without the limitation of geographical boundaries. These supply chain partners work under different regulatory frameworks and cultural environments. As supply chains expand around the globe and firms know less about their suppliers, and have less contact with them, firms must be aware of the dimensions of supply security and devise ways of managing them. In addition to minimizing the possibility and impact of disruptions, better security measures improve supply chain responsiveness and can also help reduce risks of contraband, theft, embezzlement, and loss of intellectual property. Implementing a security framework across the supply chain improves relationships with partners in the supply chain and also provides impetus to the work of standard-setting organizations. Since 9/11, supply chain managers around the world have become more vigilant, resulting in an increased impetus to integrate compliance and security procedures into international supply chains. The resulting supply chain structures have better capabilities to rebound from security mishaps, and at the same time, they have the potential to create ever more comprehensive, efficient, and well managed supply chains.

REFERENCES

1. H. L. Lee and S. Whang, "Higher Supply Chain Security with Lower Cost: Lessons from Total Quality Management," *International Journal of Production Economics* 96 (2005): 289–300.

2. H. L. Lee and M. Wolfe, "Supply Chain Security without Tears," *Supply Chain Management Review*, January/February 2003, 12–20.

3. D. Closs, C. Speir, J. Whipple, and M. D. Voss, "A Framework for Protecting Your Supply Chain: Recent Terrorist Threats and Security Incidents Have Heightened Awareness Regarding Supply Chain Security," *Supply Chain Management Review* 12, no. 2 (2008): 38–44.

4. B. Anderson, "Strengthening Global Supply Chain Security," *Security* 45, no. 6 (2008): 86–89.

5. A. T. Kearney, *Smart Boxes* (Chicago: Sage, 2005).

6. Y. Sheffi and J. B. Rice Jr., "A Supply Chain View of the Resilient Enterprise," *MIT Sloan Management Review* 47, no. 1 (2005): 41.

7. J. L. S. de. Vivero and J. C. R. Mateos, "New Factors in Ocean Governance: From Economic to Security-Based Boundaries," *Marine Policy* 28 (2004): 185–188.

8. P. Barnes and R. Oloruntoba, "Assurance of Security in Maritime Supply Chains: Conceptual Issues of Vulnerability and Crisis Management," *Journal of International Management* 11 (2005): 519–540.

9. D. J. Bowersox, D. J. Closs, and M. B. Cooper, *Supply Chain Logistics Management*, 2nd ed. (Irwin, NY: McGraw-Hill, 2007).

10. Y. Sheffi, "Supply Chain Management under the Threat of International Terrorism," *International Journal of Logistics Management* 12, no. 2 (2001): 1–11.

11. J. A. Pope, "Dimensions of Supply Chain Security," *Southern Business Review*, Summer 2008: 21–27.

12. T. A. Cook, "A New Security Mandate," *Supply Chain Management Review*, 7, no. 5 (2003): 11–12.

13. R. P. Brass, *The Production of Hindu-Muslim Violence in Contemporary India* (Oxford, : Oxford University Press, 2003).

14. A. Varshney, *Ethnic Conflict and Civic Life: Hindus and Muslims in India* (New Haven, CT: Yale University Press, 2002).

15. L. M. Rinehart, M. B. Myers, and J. A. Eckert, "Supplier Relationships: The Impact on Security," *Supply Chain Management Review* 8, no. 6 (2004): 52–59.

16. C. W. Autry and L. M. Bobbitt, "Supply Chain Security Orientation: Conceptual Development and a Proposed Framework," *International Journal of Logistics Management* 19, no. 1 (2008): 42.

17. H. L. Richardson, "Think Supply Chain Security—Think Strategy," *Logistics Today* 46, no. 9 (2005): 17–19.

18. N. Radjou, "Securing the Supply Chain: Constructive Paranoia," *Network Computing* 14, no. 19 (2003), 0–2.

19. N. Shister, "Recalibrating the Risk/Return Ratio of a Secure Supply Chain," *World Trade* 21, no. 1 (2008): 7–8.

20. C. S. Tang, "Robust Strategies for Mitigating Supply Chain Disruptions," *International Journal of Logistics: Research and Applications* 9, no. 1 (2006): 33–45.

21. D. Prokop, "Smart and Safe Borders: The Logistics of Inbound Cargo Security," *International Journal of Logistics Management* 15, no. 2 (2004): 65–75.

22. D. M. Russell and J. P. Saldanha, "Five Tenets of Security-Aware Logistics and Supply Chain Operations," *Transportation Journal* 42, no. 2 (2003): 44–54.

23. O. K. Helferich and R. L. Cook, *Securing the Supply Chain* (Oak Brook, IL: Council of Logistics Management, 2002).

24. B. Jorgensen, "Remedies for an Insecure Supply Chain," *Electronic Business* 29, no. 14 (2003): 37.

25. G. A. Zsidisin, S. A. Melnyk, and G. L. Ragatz, "An Institutional Theory of Business Continuity Planning for Purchasing and Supply Chain Management," *International Journal of Production Research* 43, no. 16 (2005): 3401–3420.

26. M. N. Faisal, D. K. Banwet, R. Shankar, "Supply Chain Risk Mitigation: Modeling the Enablers," *Business Process Management Journal* 12, no. 4 (2006): 535–552.

27. S. Kumar, H. Jensen, and H. Menge, "Analyzing Mitigation of Container Security Risks using Six Sigma DMAIC Approach in Supply Chain Design," *Transportation Journal* 47, no. 2 (2008): 54–67.

28. R. Sarathy, "Security and the Global Supply Chain," *Transportation Journal* 45, no. 4 (2006): 28–51.

29. R. Michel, "Profit from Secure Supply Chains," *Manufacturing Business Technology* 24, no. 11 (2006): 29–36.

30. R. Bhatnagar and S. Vishwanathan, "Re-engineering Global Supply Chains," *International Journal of Physical Distribution and Logistics* 30, no. 1 (2000): 13–34.

31. A. L. Delbecq, A. H. Van de Ven, and D. H. Gustafason, *Group Techniques for Program Planning* (Chicago: Scott, Foresman and Company, 1975).

32. J. W. Warfield, "Developing Interconnected Matrices in Structural Modeling," *IEEE Transactions on Systems and Cybernetics* 4, no. 1 (1974): 51–81.

33. A. P. Sage, *Interpretive Structural Modeling: Methodology for Large-Scale Systems* (New York: McGraw-Hill, 1977), 91–164.

34. A. Mandal and S. G. Deshmukh, "Vendor Selection Using Interpretive Structural Modeling (ISM)," *International Journal of Operations and Production Management* 14, no. 6 (1994): 52–59.

35. J. P. Saxena, M. Sushil, and P. Vrat, "Scenario Building: A Critical Study of Energy Conservation in the Indian Cement Industry," *Technological Forecasting and Social Change* 41 (1992): 121–146.

36. M. N. Faisal, D. K. Banwet, R. Shankar, "Supply Chain Risk Management in SMEs: Analyzing the Barriers," *International Journal of Management and Enterprise Development* 4, no. 5 (2007): 588–607.

37. R. Bolanos, E. Fontela, A. Nenclares, and P. Paster, "Using Interpretive Structural Modeling in Strategic Decision Making Groups," *Management Decision* 43, no. 6 (2005): 877–895.

38. M. N. Faisal and Z. Rahman, "e-Government in India: Modelling the Barriers to Its Adoption and Diffusion," *Electronic Government, An International Journal* 5, no. 2 (2008): 181–202.

CHAPTER 9

The Human Element of Supply Chain Security: Mobilizing a Workforce After an Emergency

Frank T. Mongioi Jr., Lisa Moraiya McNally, and Ryan Elizabeth Thompson

In order to avoid supply chain disruption, the business community must be prepared for a variety of emergencies, ranging from simple incidents such as electricity outages to emergencies such as natural disasters or terrorist attacks. Services and goods markets need to consider a variety of factors to minimize supply chain disruption. Supply chain security aims to maintain the smooth transaction of a product or service—including the resource systems needed to facilitate goods movement—from supplier to customer. This being the case, strategies focused on the deployment of resources immediately after an emergency is a necessary logistical element in the overall protection of resource transport. A critical element to maintaining the flow of goods after an emergency is ensuring employee mobility. This chapter focuses on the human element of supply chain security and identifies best practices and lessons learned aimed at ensuring workforce mobilization after an emergency.

BEST PRACTICES IN MOBILIZING A WORKFORCE AFTER AN EMERGENCY

This section summarizes best practices and procedures for resuming business as usual as it relates to employee mobility in the business community in order to avoid stagnation of goods and services. The lessons learned and presented in this chapter are categorized under the following topics: planning and partnerships, institutional communications, and technology. Each section identifies effective approaches to developing plans to support business continuity during and after an emergency.

Because emergency management must be considered by both private and public sectors, both sectors have much to provide in way of best practices and lessons learned that specifically illuminate strategies that also address supply chain security. The best practices and lessons learned reflected in this chapter were collected from a series of interviews with transportation planners, emergency management coordinators, and transit providers across the United States, as well as with members of the private sector.[1] This chapter also summarizes secondary research culled from online webinars, government documents, and telecommuting and transportation clearinghouses.

PLANNING AND PARTNERSHIPS

Both public and private entities have a role to play in ensuring employee mobility after an emergency. Public entities, including county and local planning departments, can be an important resource in workforce mobilization and are in a strong position to facilitate and promote partnerships that will improve and solidify planning efforts for responding to any emergency that disrupts travel options for a workforce. These best practices in developing partnerships, sharing resources, and leading emergency preparedness exercises can help supply chain security companies develop an employee mobilization plan.

RESOURCE SHARING

Businesses need to understand what services will be available to their business and their employees to get their workforce home and back to work. In addition, they need to be aware of limited services and assistance to avoid supply chain disruptions. Both public and private organizations have potential resources to share to assist with maintaining supply chain security, including rolling stock, staging areas, and technology. Formalizing these resource agreements can better solidify public–private relationships and increase the likelihood of cooperation and corroboration during an incident that may disrupt the supply chain. These public–private relationships can further benefit from formal evacuation exercises and drills that encourage regular communication between organizations, thereby increasing awareness of resource availability across sectors. Some examples of the strategies are included below.

Both public and private entities are taking steps to identify overlapping resources available in an emergency, and ensuring that agreements are in place to effectively access those assets in an emergency. An example of a public–private partnership promoting resource sharing across sectors is illustrated by a large West Coast corporation's use of agreements with local taxi companies to establish priority access to some of the service fleet in the event of an emergency. Such an agreement would ensure that many of the company's employees could get to and from work if there were an emergency. Additionally, the company has established agreements with private charter bus companies to have access to a defined amount of buses for preidentified occasions. Preestablished agreements can also be used in an emergency, lending a certain structure to the transaction of resource sharing.

After the Northridge earthquake in January 1994, this same firm worked with the city of Burbank to ensure that commute shuttles would be made available to employees to get home or to connect to other transit. While the company had the shuttles after the event about one year, the TMA and the city of Burbank received grants to keep the clean natural gas shuttles in service. Although a memorandum of understanding (MOU) was not in place that would allow access to shuttles, the firm does have an MOU in place with the city of Burbank for Emergency Ride Home services in case of an emergency.

Likewise, regional government agencies in Denver facilitated the development of an MOU with local hotels and transit providers to help with service continuity for regional hospitals, a vital facility whose demand for services would inevitably increase following an emergency. The MOU allows for hospital staff to stay in hotels close to the hospital after an emergency in the event that transit into and out of the city is unavailable. If travel disruptions (such as those resulting from frequent snowstorms in the area) were to limit hospital employee access to the facility, there is also an MOU to allow for plow trucks to pick up critical staff or executives and transport them to the hospital. This best practice provides a framework that can be adapted by goods and services sectors to ensure employee mobility and maintain supply chain security. These types of MOUs help stabilize business operations despite limited travel options or travel disruptions related to an emergency, and would assist with supply chain security.

Similarly, the Washington, D.C., Emergency Management Agency has mutual aid agreements in place with the local school districts and the local transit agency, Metro, to have access to buses in the event of an emergency. Earlier this year, the city utilized its mutual aid agreement with Metro after a major apartment fire in Mount Pleasant displaced 200 residents. Buses were used to keep residents warm until further shelter could be provided.

Genentech, a biotechnology company employing more than 8,500 employees in south San Francisco, is reaching out to private and public sector transportation service providers. A current challenge to developing agreements with these service providers is that there is no guarantee that the resources be tagged for Genentech's use will not be commandeered by government authorities for other uses in the event of an emergency. Nonetheless, Genentech is working with the Water Emergency Transportation Authority, a public agency, to develop a contingency plan to transport employees in the event of an emergency. Businesses have found though that even if resources were made available, there needs to be greater assurance that public (or private) asset entities would be able to ensure that staff would be available to manage and operate the resource.

As an alternative to these public partnerships, Genentech has also been exploring agreements with private vessel operators to develop a water transit evacuation plan. A similar challenge arises in that complete assurance cannot be provided to Genentech given that these private resources could also be coopted for other users.

In addition to creating formal MOUs, some cities are beginning to develop resource inventories to track public and private assets that may be available in an emergency. For example, New York City created a Private Asset and Logistics Management System (PALMS), a database of private assets and resources collected by the New York City Office of Emergency Management (OEM). The purpose of the database is to identify potential resource-sharing opportunities for the community during an emergency. Businesses can enroll to become members of PALMS and list goods and services available for use by the city in an emergency. The advantage of this tool is that it further formalizes resource sharing between public and private entities so that networks are in place in the event of an emergency to ensure employee mobility with the intent of maintaining smooth business operations. Businesses may consider participating in similar resource inventories or developing their own in order to prepare for an emergency.

The city of Denver has a system similar to the PALMS system described above, but the focus is less on resources and more on skill sets. The regional and local government agencies in Denver developed an inventory of people with specific skill sets that can be reached or accessed during an emergency. Similar inventory systems can be developed and utilized on a smaller or larger scale for businesses interested in logging existing vanpools or rideshare arrangements that can be accessed during an emergency.

An important step for businesses interested in protecting supply chains may be to work with regional stakeholders to develop a schematic that identifies the private and public networks and relationships that can facilitate commuting and enable business continuity in the event of an emergency. Businesses can also host annual meetings/conferences with companies interested in being part of an emergency preparedness network to find out about their own strategies and to identify areas in which travel coordination is necessary and viable. Businesses can even develop a database system to register both public and private transit inventory and assets that may be utilized during an emergency. New York City's Private Asset and Logistics Management System (PALMS) provides an example of this system. Businesses can also develop templates for memorandums of understanding (MOUs) that can be used by public and private organizations interested in formalizing their transportation resource agreements.

EXERCISES AND DRILLS

Public and private organizations engaged in resource sharing are also looking for ways to increase awareness of existing resources and to evaluate their state of preparedness for an emergency. Seattle's local government has formally extended its evacuation procedures and meetings to include private companies, many of which have now become a major part of the conversation regarding resource sharing. Bringing private and public partners together can be critical to fostering a stronger linkage between supply chain security, emergency preparedness, and business continuity. Businesses are identifying strategies for maintaining business continuity as it pertains to employee mobility, including finding ways to remain actively involved in the decisions made at the county level about how to access local transit resources for emergencies. For government, bringing private companies into the conversation through forums and seminars can be critical to determining a region's state of preparedness. Some examples of emergency preparedness drills are included below.

The Washington, D.C., region has formalized public–private relationships in order to test and evaluate the region's emergency preparedness in the area. For example, the hotel industry meets annually with the D.C. Emergency Management Agency (EMA) to run through potential emergency scenarios and discuss ways to improve the evacuation process and continuity of operations. The D.C. Emergency Management Agency holds similar exercises for the public with its Community Emergency Management exercises. The D.C. EMA invites chambers and businesses to run through an exercise once a year to identify how the community would respond in the event of a major emergency, whether manmade or natural. The D.C. EMA reaches out to businesses by leveraging associations, such as the board of trade and the D.C. Chamber of Commerce. This example, although facilitated by the government, illuminates an important strategy focused on ensuring mobility after an emergency.

Capital Metro, the transit provider in Austin, Texas, organizes tabletop drills to respond to potential emergency scenarios, hiring a consultant annually to evaluate its plans and strategies. Capital Metro relies on the city of Austin to determine whether or not an evacuation is required. If a travel disruption is anticipated while the buses are in service—for example, due to an approaching major storm—Capital Metro would plan to shut down its operations and only run emergency shuttles, which would be accessible to the public for trips into and out of the city. If a travel disruption would be declared for the following day—for example, in preparation for large protests such as Austin experienced last year—Capital Metro would begin providing services earlier than normal and would operate express routes. The purpose of the emergency drills is for Capital Metro to run through a scenario and ensure that all of the networks are in place to operate the contingency plans. Based on Metro's approach, the business community could consider developing emergency drills in order to assess its preparedness for a disruption to services.

One of the larger instances of emergency evacuation drills is Seattle's Soundshake 2008, a regional earthquake preparedness exercise planned by city, county, and state officials. Soundshake 2008 includes seminars, drills, and tabletop exercises that either have already or will take place throughout the year. Counties, cities, businesses, hospitals, tribes, and schools were invited to take part in the activities to test the state of preparedness in the community. Public information dissemination and resource allocation are two topics evaluated during the exercises. An after action conference was held after the series of events to discuss ways to improve the state of preparedness. The exercise offered practical training, templates, and improvement plans for participants. These types of exercises are vital to preparing communities and businesses for how to respond in an emergency. The exercises integrate the business community into emergency planning and allow for discussions on resource sharing and contingency planning.

Businesses can promote emergency drills that require city, county, transit, and private business participation. Integrated emergency drills would solidify the networks that need to be in place during a real emergency, evaluate the state of preparedness of the business community, and enhance cooperation with business community initiatives. Businesses can also host workshops bringing together private and public sectors to discuss the commuting and travel issues that could result from a natural or manmade emergency and the preparedness efforts each participating entity has made.

INSTITUTIONAL COMMUNICATIONS

Prior to and during an emergency, the exchange of information between and within the public and private sectors can be paramount to mitigating impacts on the flow of goods and services. Best practices for facilitating this information demonstrate that networks and systems of institutional communications must be in place prior to an emergency event to allow for businesses to learn about transportation options available to their employees immediately following an emergency. Research has evidenced that "effective coordination and communication among the many different operating agencies in a region and across the nation is absolutely essential. In the aftermath of emergencies, the focus has been on funding better communication strategies that can be used for coordinated response to future incidents."[2] This section explores best practices related to communications networks, including company hotlines, to highlight specific strategies to support to enhance supply chain security through the mobilization of a workforce after an emergency.

INTERNAL COMMUNICATIONS AT BUSINESSES

Resumption of employee mobility after an emergency can be dependent on the preexisting communications network of an agency. For example, a large West Coast service firm provides an internal staff hotline to all employees. Staff may call the hotline to access information about emergency events and the types of travel options available to them. Companies without internal hotlines may consider contracting with a communications vendor to provide mass communications to employees in the event of an emergency. Such a service could be used to distribute e-mails with available transportation options during an emergency to support the smooth flow of employee movement and to mitigate the firm's service disruption.

This same company promotes an internal ride match program that encourages employees to sign up for the "emergency only" portion of the company's ride match program. Employees who normally do not use a ride share program could still take advantage of a ride matching option in an emergency. Ride match would provide them with a type of "safety first" buddy who would be available, for example, to walk home with in the event of an emergency. All staff are entered into the "emergency only" section of the ride match program, regardless of their involvement in the larger ride match program (but employees may opt out at any time at their own discretion).

It is critical that businesses have a plan in place to communicate emergency plans for employees to get home after an emergency. Genentech's first steps in responding to an emergency during businesses hours would be to triage its campus community needs and organize employees into groups to make use of buses to facilitate trips home for employees who either do not have cars on campus (because they accessed the site using an alternative commute mode) or who may have personal vehicles on campus (but cannot make use of them due to corridor closures or not having enough gas to drive alternative routes back home). Further contingency planning could help prepare for various scenarios. Shelter in place is a part of Genentech's overall strategy for recovery and business operations continuity, one of the reasons being that they likely will not have sufficient transportation resources to provide evacuation services to all staff during the first day's daylight hours. Furthermore, some of the work that is done on campus needs to be supervised by technicians, and it might be necessary and preferable to house these key personnel at or near the facility.

Another approach to leveraging internal communications as a tool for supporting employee mobility after an emergency is demonstrated by the Louisiana Small Business Development Center (LSBDC). The LSBDC encourages small businesses to identify a peer company when considering their continuity plan. This would encourage likeminded businesses, whether in close geographic proximity or not, to communicate with one another in the development of business continuity plans, think through hypothetical responses to disasters in order to maintain daily operations, and determine if there are resources that can be shared, or what type of professional networks could be relied upon in the event of an emergency.

Such examples show how businesses can identify and arrange for the most appropriate and expedient means to provide critical information to employees in the event of an emergency (e.g., organize workshops/panels comprised of private and public constituents to share case studies and lessons learned).

REGIONAL COMMUNICATIONS

Cities and counties creating emergency preparedness plans are developing or participating in regional communication networks that allow for information dissemination and coordination of messages. The strengthening of regional communications helps ensure that the public and business community is aware of transport options in real time. For example, Seattle's King County developed a Regional Public Information Network (RPIN) designed to facilitate communication across government and nongovernment lines. The network includes 200 members representing seventy-five public and private entities. Member agencies and companies include transportation, utility, emergency response, law enforcement, and hospital services. The network is set up to provide coordinated messages and information quickly to the public in the event of an emergency. For example, coordinated messages may be distributed regarding alternative transit routes in the event that roads are closed after an emergency.

The RPIN is especially important for business continuity because it allows for uniform information to be passed along to private companies that want to know how their employees can get home from and back to work. The RPIN site also includes mapping capabilities to provide directions and routes to employees who do not usually commute.

Businesses can also establish their own regional communications frameworks, as illustrated by a large service firm based in southern California that has encountered several emergency situations. The company's proactive planning, resource sharing, and integrated involvement with local and regional government allowed it to mitigate the disruptive effects of these potentially catastrophic emergencies. For example, immediately after an early-morning commuter train derailment, the company worked with its leasing company to make use of additional vanpool vans to help shuttle employees to and from work. The company communicated with local transportation management associations (TMAs) to exchange communication about the event as the company received direct updates from Caltrans, Metrolink (schedules), and the California Highway Patrol. The company also provided signage for shuttles. In this event, the company became a key information source for the general area. This event underscored the critical need to build relationships and a communication framework with external agencies *early*, to be able to quickly respond to mobility needs of their large workforce in an event, whether the event is big or small.

DEVELOPMENT AND PROMOTION OF TELECOMMUTING SYSTEM

Telecommuting can be an important strategy for maintaining business continuity, especially when transit options are limited. Increasingly since the 1990s, businesses and governments have integrated telecommuting systems into their operations. A telecommuting system offers employees the ability to work remotely via computer (Internet), phone, and fax, providing employee flexibility. Some more robust systems allow employees to access e-mail and files from any location. Increasingly, telecommuting systems are being used by the business community to ensure service continuity in the event of disruption. The sections below include examples that businesses may consider in developing plans for business continuity.

The State of Colorado has set guidelines for businesses to use telecommuting in the event of an emergency, as part of its Pandemic Emergency Guidelines. The state, with support from the Denver Regional Council of Governments and the Downtown Denver Partnership, encourages businesses to proceed with telecommuting guidance for regular operations so that the systems are in place for non-emergencies and to ensure that systems run smoothly should an emergency occur. Telecommuting pilots were planned for the state and national Democratic conventions. Likewise, the Department of Labor has implemented a continuity of operations plan that establishes telecommuting as a key function of business continuity. The department tests networks, staff, and management processes regularly to improve the agency's preparedness for an emergency.[3]

Another federal agency, the Internal Revenue Service (IRS), also implemented a telecommuting policy in response to severe flooding. After a storm in Washington, D.C., in June 2006, the subbasement of the IRS building was filled with twenty feet of water, and the basement above was filled with four additional feet of water. Located in one of the lowest points of D.C., the IRS building was surrounded by five feet of water, resulting in the displacement of many of the 2,400 employees in the building. Although many of the computers were lost in the flood, the data centers were located outside of the city. The IRS used a telecommuting system to allow employees to continue working as the building was renovated. To facilitate the communication of plans and changes, all employees were given access to an emergency hotline to be apprised of updates.[4]

The public and private sector rely on various approaches to promote its use within their organizations. For example, AT&T established an "Employee Telework Initiative" that provides corporate-wide information and support to all staff and management interested in part- or full-time telecommuting. AT&T has developed a telecommuting Internet portal that can provide a guide for other companies interested in telecommuting.[5] Federal and state government agencies are progressively promoting telecommuting programs, and not just for the flexible benefits it provides employees. For example, the Office of Personnel Management (OPM) recognizes the natural link between telecommuting and emergency preparedness. It is committed to assisting agencies meet their goals by providing technical support and assistance for supporting broader insertion of telecommuting into mainstream culture of federal organizations.[6]

In some cases, the greater adoption of telecommuting is being promoted through the use of incentives. For example, the Louisiana Small Business

Development Center (LSBDC) provides regional small business owners telecommuting vendor information so that they can explore the available options and identify those that fit best with the structure and goals of their business. To promote its use as an effort to make businesses more resilient to disasters, the LSBDC intends to develop and implement a certificate program offering small business owners with training in how to implement a telecommuting system while also providing hands-on-training in how to develop a tailored business continuity plan. As an incentive, the certificate would then act as quality assurance for businesses applying for funding with the state. Businesses can pursue telecommuting as a viable business strategy that provides multiple benefits and that can play a major role in supporting short- and long-term business continuity after an emergency.

TECHNOLOGY

Businesses dependent on supply chain security are identifying technologies that can assist in the quick mobilization of employees when there is an emergency, in order to ensure the smooth transaction of goods and services. Often these technologies facilitate communication of emergency plans. Other types of technology include emergency access to buildings that may be locked due to security measures, and the use of GIS to identify important travel routes for employees to support the resumption of the workforce.

EMERGENCY NOTIFICATION SYSTEMS

Much like institutional communication networks described above, emergency notification systems have the potential to provide employers critical information about what transit options are available. More specifically, 511 services provide an opportunity to share information during an emergency and many businesses may also consider linking to existing 511 emergency systems. Many states either have or are developing 511 systems. A 511 system is usually a Web site or telephone number that provides up-to-date travel information for a region. Some programs, such as Sacramento's 511 system, also act as one-stop sources for ridesharing, transit, and traffic information that could be useful to employees finding out how to get to and from work after an emergency. Areas that do not have 511 programs have developed emergency notification systems to disseminate information to the public rather than waiting for the public to contact them. For example, Washington, D.C., which does not have a 511 number, has a Citizen Emergency Notification System known as Alert D.C. Residents and business travelers are encouraged by the city to subscribe to these real-time emergency updates. Subscribers can receive the alerts by e-mail or text message. The city also encourages associations—for example, a consortium of ten local universities—to sign up for the alerts so that their communities can be informed when there is an emergency. When an emergency occurs, alerts are distributed with instructions about evacuation procedures and information about availability of transit options.

New York State instituted a 511 system (telephone line and Web site) in November 2008 for use in the New York metro region. Businesses in New York City can also sign up through the New York City Office of Emergency Management (NYC OEM) Corp Net program to be specifically contacted when emergencies in the area may require businesses to respond. NYC OEM recognizes that many small businesses do not have the emergency planning resources that larger companies have (e.g., an onsite disaster recovery staff member) and has thus prepared an Emergency Resource Guide for small businesses highlighting details of how to prepare a continuity of operations plan, as well as additional guidance on responding to an emergency.[7]

For some states with 511 systems, like Washington, emergency preparation information is not accessible regularly, but is only provided after an emergency has occurred. For example, Washington State's 511 system has the ability to handle floodgate messages, a capability that is used in emergencies for critical information. The up-front message is the first thing heard by all callers when they access the system. It is used for significant detours, major closures, and other events that have a potential to impact many people or that have statewide or large regional significance. Businesses may want to consider linking their emergency hotline numbers to 511 numbers and 511 Web sites that may help displaced employees may find out what transit options are available to them.

CORPORATE EMERGENCY ACCESS

New York City OEM's Corporate Emergency Access System (CEAS) aids in business continuity by providing certification to essential employees that are part of CEAS's member organizations. This system allows employees access to their businesses in areas that may be restricted due to an emergency. In this case, previously identified critical staff needed for business continuity would be able to access buildings that may otherwise be restricted to the general public after an emergency. Additionally, some private companies in California, such as Genentech, have developed a special arrangement with local government to allow preidentified employees to access restricted areas in order to maintain critical business functions. For example, designated personnel have been assigned a pass that would allow them to travel beyond restricted areas and curfew limits to access the business site immediately following an event.

USE OF GEOGRAPHIC INFORMATION SYSTEMS IN PLANNING AND PREPAREDNESS

Both the public and private sectors are using geographic information systems (GIS) mapping (e.g., developing population density maps, identifying fixed transit routes) to better determine immediate disaster impacts on employee travel options. These data will help companies make more informed decisions about how to effcctively and quickly meet the mobility needs of employees. The public sector is also employing GIS to develop models to assist recovery across its region. For example, the Southern California Association of Governments is working with local agencies to collect regional geographic data in a common format and offer a regional repository to synthesized geographic data for emergency planning, training, and response.[8] Businesses can use regional geographic data for map development to identify areas most in need of available rideshare resources relative to available commute options and home/employment locations.

SUMMARY

Identifying plans to maintain business as usual is a critical aspect of ensuring supply chain security. Among a variety of other factors, employee mobility must be considered a major part of avoiding supply chain disruption. Both the public and private sector are proactively thinking about maintaining employee mobility. Specifically, this chapter provides examples of strategies that could be adapted by the business community with the intent of ensuring goods and service continuity through the maintenance of employee mobility. To avoid supply chain disruption and ensure goods and service continuity, businesses can learn from others about how to develop partnerships, institute communications protocol, and pursue a variety of technologies that can facilitate the mobilization of a workforce after an emergency.

NOTES

This chapter was presented at the 88th Annual Meeting of the Transportation Research Board, Washington, D.C., January 2009, and is scheduled for publication in *The Transportation Research Record: Journal of the Transportation Research Board*, Transportation Research Board of the National Academies, Washington, D.C., 2009.

1. Private-sector interview participants were selected from the Association for Commuter Transportation member directory.

2. M. Meyer, *The Role of MPO in Preparing for Security Incident and Transportation System Response*, Georgia Institute of Technology, http://www.planning.dot.gov/Documents/Securitypaper.htm.

3. "Telework as a Continuity of Operations Strategy" [webinar], http://www.teleworkexchange.com/coopwebcast/.

4. Patrick Thibodeau, "IRS Flood Spurs Telecommuting," *Computerworld: Government*, http://www.computerworld.com/action/article.do?command=viewArticleBasic&taxonomyName=it_in_government&articleId=9001560&taxonomyId=69.

5. For more information and a detailed case study, see http://www.toolsofchange.com/English/CaseStudies/default.asp?ID=129.

6. The Status of Telework in the Federal Government, 2005. http://www.telework.gov/Reports_and_Studies/tw_rpt05/status-director.aspx.

7. The emergency resource guide is available at http://nyc.gov/html/oem/html/ready/biz_guide.shtml.

8. Southern California Association of Governments, *Transportation Security Report*, draft, 2007.

BIBLIOGRAPHY

American Public Transportation Association, *America under Threat: Transit Responds to Terrorism*. 2003. http://www.apta.com/services/security/documents/911.pdf.

Lindell, Michael K., and Ronald W. Perry. *Emergency Planning: Improve Community Preparedness*. 2007. http://www.govtech.com/em/261418.

Meyer, M. *The Role of MPO in Preparing for Security Incident and Transportation System Response*. Georgia Institute of Technology, 2008. http://www.planning.dot.gov/Documents/Securitypaper.htm.

National TDM and Telework Clearinghouse. http://www.nctr.usf.edu/clearinghouse.

Southern California Association of Governments. *Transportation Security Report*. Draft. 2007.

Special Report. "Telework and Continuity of Operations." *Homeland Defense Journal*, 2006. http://www.homelanddefensejournal.com.

"Telework as a Continuity of Operations Strategy" [webinar]. 2008. http://www.teleworkexchange.com/coopwebcast/.

The Testimony of William Mularie, Chief Executive Officer, Telework Consortium Inc., Herndon, Virginia to Committee on Government Reform, Subcommittee on Federal Workforce and Agency Organization, U.S. Congress, July 18, 2006.

Thibodeau, Patrick. "IRS Flood Spurs Telecommuting." *Computerworld: Government*. 2004. http://www.computerworld.com/action/article.do?command=viewArticleBasic&taxonomyName=it_in_government&articleId=9001560&taxonomyId=69.

Transportation Planning Activities for the Centennial Games: An After Action Report, Atlanta Regional Conference, December 1996.

U.S. Department of Transportation, Federal Highway Administration. *Managing Demand through Travel Information Services*. 2006. http://ops.fhwa.dot.gov/publications/manag_demand_tis/travelinfo.htm.

U.S. Department of Transportation, ITS Joint Program Office. *Effects of Catastrophic Events on Transportation System Management and Operations: Cross-Cutting Study*. 2003. http://www.itsdocs.fhwa.dot.gov/JPODOCS/REPTS_TE/13780.html.

CHAPTER 10

International Aviation Security Practices Relating to the Global Supply Chain

Moses A. Alemán

The global economy depends heavily on the movement of valuable materials, goods, and manufacturing components. Air cargo provides the means by which the world is able to receive the benefits from the worldwide movement of all the essential items needed by mankind. Naturally, the cost involved is a major priority, and the safe transportation of these goods is of utmost importance as well.

Air freight thrives when economies are growing and the international trade market is booming. In short, air cargo can be considered as extremely valuable to the global economy. The economy can certainly cause a slowdown in the global supply chain, but this should not be expected to be of major significance insofar as global air freight traffic is concerned. Traffic figures for air cargo tend to fluctuate. The latter part of the year is usually up for air freight because of the Christmas season in December, but that is not always the case. When the economy goes up, the movement of goods by air increases as well.

There are other factors that affect the movement of air cargo. For example, Japan enjoys a good economy—just like the United States—and in Japan the air cargo business depends heavily on the automobile and electronic industries. Even in China, to whom the world turns for manufacturing, there has been excellent growth in the air freight business. As an example, semiconductor sales are a leading indicator for air cargo traffic because of the rapid movement of microelectronic parts and equipment in order to keep the supply chain operating.

In summary, when FedEx, UPS, DHL, and European express operator TNT see rises in the global economy, this translates into an upsurge in the air freight movement of materials and goods. When an economic slowdown spreads to all parts of the world, air cargo growth tends to slow to a standstill. The 2007 and 2008 global air traffic numbers show a potential flat growth prediction for 2009. But how safe is the movement of air freight throughout the world in these times of world tensions caused by the ever-increasing threat of international terrorism, and with air cargo becoming a viable target for acts of unlawful interference against international civil aviation?

ICAO INTERNATIONAL STANDARDS AND RECOMMENDED PRACTICES ON AIR CARGO SECURITY MEASURES

The International Civil Aviation Organization (ICAO), a specialized agency of the United Nations, adopts and publishes guidance and directives for all 189 ICAO member states for the purpose of achieving safe and secure air flights and air navigation. Specifically, the Council of ICAO adopts international standards and recommended practices that are published in annexes to the Convention on International Civil Aviation. Annex 17 to the Convention on International Civil Aviation, entitled "Security—Safeguarding International Civil Aviation Against Acts of Unlawful Interference," contains international standards and recommended practices relating to measures and procedures intended to prevent unlawful acts against civil aviation. The member nations of ICAO are required to implement all international standards, but the recommended practices are merely advisable procedures.

The eighth edition of Annex 17 dated April 2006 is the current ICAO edition, and in paragraph 4.6, entitled "Measures relating to cargo, mail and other goods," it contains the following specifications dealing specifically with the protection of air cargo and mail:

Standard 4.6.1: "Each Contracting State shall ensure that security controls are applied to cargo and mail, prior to their being loaded onto an aircraft engaged in passenger commercial air transport operations."

The first concern in the above standard is to define "security controls." ICAO considers all member nations as sovereign and able to develop and implement their own aviation security programs, but if the countries have different definitions for "security control," the results of security measures for air cargo may vary widely throughout the world. Although the widespread implementation of aviation security measures regarding passengers and their baggage has become more effective, it must be pointed out that this has made air cargo a more attractive option for terrorists attempting to carry out an act of unlawful interference. ICAO defines "security control" as "a means by which the introduction of weapons, explosives or other dangerous devices, articles or substances which may be used to commit an act of unlawful interference can be prevented."

The large volume of air cargo carried continues to increase, and the cargo system is well known, thereby making it easy for perpetrators to target specific flights. Cargo consignments can be difficult to screen, and it is impractical to screen 100 percent of air cargo. Also, the personal risk to the perpetrator is very low. Just what is considered "air cargo"? This is a very good question, and one that needs to be specifically answered in each nation's national civil aviation security program (NCASP). For purposes of civil aviation security, the term "air cargo" can refer to items that include normal freight, consolidations, transshipments, unaccompanied courier items, and even unaccompanied baggage that has been shipped as freight on a passenger-carrying aircraft. ICAO's definition of air cargo is "Any property carried on an aircraft other than mail, stores and accompanied or mishandled baggage." Some transportation security specialists have intimated that the airlines should not carry air cargo on passenger flights. These individuals do not realize that the revenue derived by the carriers from carrying air cargo far exceeds the revenue received from passenger travel. It has even been said that many airlines would go bankrupt if they ceased to carry air cargo.

ICAO contracting states are urged to screen or examine all mail destined to be carried on aircraft engaged on passenger-carrying flight operations. In view of the legalities affecting mail and possible operational or technological constraints on individual postal administrations, the appropriate authority should work closely with the designated postal authority security section to make sure there is a coordinated application of necessary security measures on a national basis. Security measures for mail should follow the guidelines described by ICAO for the security of air cargo.

Standard 4.6.2: "Each Contracting State shall ensure that cargo and mail to be carried on a passenger commercial aircraft are protected from unauthorized interference from the point security controls are applied until departure of the aircraft."

The intent of the ICAO Council and the ICAO Aviation Security Panel, of which the writer was a participating member in the U.S. delegation for five years, was to ensure that all ICAO member states developed and maintained airport security programs that provide for an overall security protected area that denies access of unauthorized persons to the vulnerable areas of the airport—especially areas between the application of security controls and the parked aircraft. In order to counter the threat to air cargo, some specific security procedures and principles have been developed that represent a cost-effective and pragmatic approach. This approach consists of three core principles:

- Aircraft carrying air cargo must operate from within a secure environment.
- All air cargo must be subject to some degree of security control before being placed on board a passenger-carrying aircraft, with the devotion of maximum

effort to the screening of air cargo consignments whose security cannot be readily determined.
- A consignment of air cargo, once security-cleared, must be protected from interference.

The security clearance of air cargo can consist of active procedures to detect devices that may have been already placed into air cargo or preventive security measures in order to stop devices from being placed onto an air cargo when it is initially packed, and at all stages thereafter in its handling prior to its being loaded onto an aircraft. The active procedures utilized can include the use of conventional X-ray equipment, explosive detection systems, explosive trace detection equipment, hand searches, simulation chambers, and explosive detection dogs. The preventive security measures are based on the rationale that if the consignment is packed securely initially, and then kept secure thereafter, the requirement for screening or searching is reduced.

The use of well-trained explosive detection dogs should be highlighted because it is believed that the trained canine is far more effective than any detection machine. Through the years, the industry has seen the research and development of explosive detection systems that have become more sophisticated and efficient in the detection of some but not all existing explosives. Aviation security explosives detection specialists have stated that the appropriate type of canine can be properly trained to detect all types of explosives, and such dogs with handlers (both trained together) have been around for more than thirty-five years. It should also be pointed out that the explosive detection dog and the narcotics detection dog are two differently trained canines; the same dog should not be cross-trained for both functions.

Standard 4.6.3: "Each Contracting State shall establish a process for approval of regulated agents, if such agents are involved in implementing security controls."

Annex 17 provides for the establishment of the concept of a regulated agent. This is defined in Annex 17 as "[a]n agent, freight forwarder or any other entity who conducts business with an operator and provides security controls that are accepted or required by the appropriate authority in respect of cargo, courier and express parcels or mail."

The guidance provided by ICAO on this concept is that aircraft operators (airlines), freight forwarders, postal authorities, and courier companies should be made specifically accountable for the security of all consignments of air cargo, mail, and other goods by implementing the following conditions:

- A program of specific operating procedures defining the role and responsibilities of regulated agents should be detailed in the state's national civil aviation security program, and regulated agents should be approved and inspected by the appropriate authority for civil aviation security.

- All buildings, premises, transport facilities, and vehicles involved with the processing or movement of air cargo must be secure at all times.
- A security training program should be established, including refresher training at specified intervals, for staff involved in the handling of air cargo. The program contents should be defined and should be approved by the appropriate authority for civil aviation security.

Regulated agents should be inspected regularly by the appropriate government authority and should be required to develop and implement their own written cargo security program as well as training programs to maintain an efficient and up-to-date workforce. The government authority responsible for the civil aviation security program should establish a system of regulations and inspections to ensure the correct application of the required operating procedures and security measures for all air cargo that is to be carried in aircraft engaged on passenger flights. ICAO guidance offers states the option to delegate the inspection of regulated agents to the police, airport authorities, or airlines; or states may have different methods for vetting consignors. Individual states to decide on their own how they will comply with the standard, but the procedures should be adequately described in the state's national civil aviation security program. The aim is for the airline to have confidence in the integrity of security declarations made by regulated agents.

Standard 4.6.4: "Each Contracting State shall ensure that operators do not accept cargo or mail for carriage on an aircraft engaged in passenger commercial air transport operations unless the application of security controls is confirmed and accounted for by a regulated agent, or such consignments are subjected to appropriate security controls."

The above paragraphs pertaining to the regulated agent concept contain all of the information needed for compliance; if that is accomplished, Standard 4.6.4 is fully complied with.

Standard 4.6.5: "Each Contracting State shall ensure that catering, stores and supplies intended for carriage on passenger commercial flights are subjected to appropriate security controls and thereafter protected until loaded onto the aircraft."

This standard of ICAO covers the catering items, company stores, and supplies carried on the aircraft just as Standard 4.6.1 covered the air cargo and mail items. Catering supplies and airline stores and supplies intended for carriage on passenger flights are considered vulnerable items because they provide a means for introducing weapons, explosive devices, or substances intended for use by a perpetrator of an act of unlawful interference. The protection against these acts then requires careful consideration and planning by all organizations, security agencies, and aircraft operators involved. One key issue is the application of security measures to the operation and buildings used for the preparation and storage of catering supplies and stores. These measures should be detailed in a security program approved by the nation's designated appropriate authority responsible for aviation security. The contents of this security program should be based on the requirements contained in the country's national civil aviation security program. The intention of the security measures applied to any catering supplies or stores should be to prevent any articles able to be used to carry out an act of sabotage from being taken on board an aircraft concealed within catering supplies or stores. This can be achieved by abiding by the following general principles:

- Security measures must be applied in buildings where catering supplies and stores are prepared, stored, and dispatched to ensure that no device or weapon is introduced into consignments.
- Security measures must be applied during the transportation and delivery of catering supplies and stores to the relevant aircraft to ensure that the consignment remains secure.
- Security measures must be applied by the airline operator on receipt of catering consignments to ensure that all catering supplies or stores loaded on the aircraft are correctly assigned for that flight and have not been tampered with.

Sometimes the aircraft operator owns its own catering operation, but more often, the catering is operated by independent contracted companies that provide catering services for several airlines. In both cases, the caterer must have a written security program approved by the state's relevant authority responsible for aviation security. The caterer's program should be based on the state's national civil aviation security program and should be prepared in a short narrative form outlining how the organization meets both the national aviation security requirements and the relevant airline's requirements at all catering operation locations from which catering supplies and stores are prepared and dispatched. The caterer should also have an individual responsible for the implementation of the aviation security requirements. This person should be a suitably qualified and trained individual formally appointed with the overall responsibility to ensure that all the security requirements are enforced. In cases in which caterers are operating at more than one location, such as at different airports, they should be required to formally appoint a person with the same responsibility at each location. All staff employed in the preparation and delivery of catering supplies and stores should undergo a preemployment background check to establish identity and previous experience, including any criminal history. The standard of this background check should be equal to that required as part of the assessment of the individual's suitability for unescorted access to a security restricted area. These persons shall also be provided with sufficient security awareness training to enable them to understand and carry out their security responsibilities. This training must be carried out before they are allowed access to any supplies or stores that are to be dispatched to an aircraft as "known stores."

Standard 4.6.6: *"Each Contracting State should ensure that security controls to be applied to cargo and mail for transportation on all-cargo aircraft are determined on the basis of a security risk assessment carried out by the relevant national authorities."*

When the ICAO Council, composed of representatives of thirty-six member nations of ICAO, discussed the recommendations of the Aviation Security Panel of experts in regard to the International Standards pertaining to the security of air cargo, it was assumed that only passenger-carrying flights would be considered for the required security measures, obviously because of the danger posed to the passengers and crew aboard the aircraft. During their discussions, some council representatives brought up the matter of cargo security for all-cargo aircraft. This drew the attention of the International Air Transport Association (IATA), because so many IATA member airlines have cargo aircraft, and their safety is also at risk. IATA and courier companies such as FedEx, DHL, and UPS lobbied the council, expressing their concerns, and so did pilots' associations—although no passengers would be aboard those aircraft, the lives of the crew on cargo aircraft could be exposed to imminent danger. Because the required security equipment and measures represent tremendous cost to airlines and governments, the council decided that the measures should be required of aircraft with passengers but not aircraft with only a crew. But when this angered the pilots of all-cargo aircraft, the council reconsidered and agreed to adopt a recommended practice for all-cargo aircraft as stated in specification 4.6.6, adding that the need for such security should be determined on the basis of risk assessment surveys carried out by state authorities. Since this specification is only a recommended practice, it is left up to individual states to perform security risk assessments in order to make the decision of implementing security measures for all-cargo aircraft or whether to merely apply reduced security measures in those cases. As is usually the case, an act of unlawful interference against an all-cargo aircraft would immediately attract the attention of aviation security officials of any country to make the proper adjustments to their national civil aviation security program (NCASP).

RESPONSIBILITY OF THE TRANSPORTATION SECURITY ADMINISTRATION OF THE UNITED STATES ON AIR CARGO SECURITY

The Transportation Security Administration (TSA) of the United States has the same obligations as all member nations of ICAO, since the United States is not only a contracting state of ICAO but also the leading nation of the world in aviation, with more airlines, airports, air passengers, airline operations, and air cargo miles flown than any other state. Aviation regulations in the United States, which are enforced by the Federal Aviation Administration (FAA) (for safety regulations) and by the TSA (for security regulations), contain, for the most part, stricter requirements than those adopted by ICAO. Therefore, when U.S. carriers and airports comply with FAA and TSA requirements, they automatically comply with ICAO International Standards. Only on rare occasions has the ICAO Council adopted security measures that exceed United States aviation regulations. One such instance was in 1992, when Annex 17 was amended by the Council of ICAO with the eighth amendment to this document, resulting in the fifth edition of the annex. This amendment included the introduction of important new provisions in relation to the comprehensive security screening of checked baggage and security control over cargo, courier, and express parcels and mail. The incident that precipitated the council's concern of checked baggage was the destruction of Pan American World Airways (PAWA) Flight 103, a Boeing 747 ripped apart by a bomb in a suitcase while at 31,000 feet over Lockerbie, Scotland, on December 21, 1988, killing 259 passengers and crew in addition to 11 persons on the ground. The suitcase containing the bomb was located in a ULD-3 container in the forward cargo hold immediately forward of the wing on the left side of the aircraft. The important issue in this case was that the suitcase containing the bomb was unaccompanied baggage—no passenger was connected to the checked bag. At that time FAA regulations required 100 percent preboard screening of passengers and their carry-on baggage but only cursory examination of checked baggage. When ICAO adopted the International Standard requiring 100 percent screening of hold baggage on all international flights, this caught the United States off-guard. With about 135 international airports in the United States at that time, the checking of all checked baggage on all the international flights in this country posed a monumental task that could not be complied with overnight. Many ICAO member states have anywhere from one or two—up to perhaps somewhat less than fifty—international airports, but none matches the United States. Consequently, a major effort began in the United States to comply with that international standard. Of interest to the subject of this document is the fact that the same amendment change to Annex 17 included the addition of security controls over cargo, courier, and express parcels and mail.

The evolution of air cargo security checks in the form of screening for security purposes has been long in development in the United States because of the need to take care of the screening of checked baggage first, but a cargo security program has existed in this country for some time; however, as the role of air cargo grows in the global supply chain, so does the task of being able to adequately screen all cargo in the United States. In February 2009 the TSA informed air cargo shippers that 2009 will be a year of accountability, but many are questioning how the U.S. government will implement new security initiatives dealing with air cargo security. The freight forwarders wholeheartedly embrace the cargo screening initiatives of the TSA but would like to have it implemented in an organized, measured manner. Meanwhile, the TSA is moving ahead with high-tech systems designed to inspect cargo loaded aboard passenger airlines. The TSA was mandated to screen at least half of all cargo by February 2009, and 100 percent in August 2010 as part of the Department of Homeland Security (DHS) mission to provide a level of security for cargo equal to that for passenger baggage. It is unclear whether or not the February 2009 deadline was met. These deadlines were congressionally imposed, and not subject to change. A government report released in March 2009 specifies a plan to check every package of business cargo for explosives before it is loaded onto passenger airplanes faces major obstacles. The report by Congress' Accountability Office said that the TSA may not have enough inspectors, nor adequate equipment to guarantee that all cargo is checked for bombs.

Passenger aircraft carry about 7.6 billion pounds of cargo per year in the United States, including electronics, auto parts, clothes, fresh produce, and medical supplies. The cargo is placed alongside luggage in the aircraft's belly. Although carry-on and checked baggage has been screened in the United States for many years, air cargo has been subject to much looser inspection requirements, raising concerns that terrorists could slip a bomb into a package. Along with problems of research and development of new technologies is always the additional issue of sufficient staff properly trained to accomplish all the added tasks. This, therefore, highlights the major problem existing in the United States when coping with the security of air cargo. Screening of all air cargo in the United States is considered an almost impossible task. There is simply just too much air cargo, and no matter how many machines, canines, and staff are utilized, the work task is insurmountable. For this reason, the threat of a terrorist attack on civil aviation by means of a bomb contained in air cargo remains a serious threat.

BIBLIOGRAPHY

AVSEC, Inc. 2009, Training Files, McKinney, Texas.
Aaron Karp, "Air Cargo Flattens Out," *Air Transport World, the Magazine of Global Airline Management*, January 2009.
International Air Transport Association (IATA) Security and Facilitation Headlines, February 16–23, 2009, and March 18, 2009.
International Civil Aviation Organization Annex 17 to the Convention on International Civil Aviation, 8th edition. Montreal: ICAO Publications, April 2006.
Security Manual for Safeguarding Civil Aviation Against Acts of Unlawful Interference, 6th edition. ICAO Document 8973. 2002.

CHAPTER 11

Customs-Trade Partnership Against Terrorism: A Step Toward Supply Chain Security

John O'Connell

In November 2001, the U.S. Customs and Border Protection unit of the U.S. Department of Homeland Security began to implement C-TPAT (Customs-Trade Partnership Against Terrorism). C-TPAT is a very successful example of a voluntary public–private partnership specifically designed to improve the security of U.S. borders.[1] The implementation of C-TPAT was a direct result of the September 11, 2001 (9/11), terrorist attack on the World Trade Center and the Pentagon.

One of the major concerns of both government and private sectors was the possibility that terrorists might use cargo containers or other transportation means to carry weapons of mass destruction (WMDs)[2] into the United States. The 9/11 commercial aircraft attacks on U.S. properties proved that terrorist strikes could be successfully carried out against targets within the country. Although the attacks on the World Trade Center and the Pentagon were the most destructive of any single terrorist incident in history, one can only speculate as to the death and destruction that might have occurred had WMDs been present on one of the aircraft.

PROTECTING THE BORDERS OF THE UNITED STATES: T-CPAT

Protection of U.S. borders is a very difficult task. It requires the coordinated efforts of many governmental agencies and nongovernmental organizations. This is not a newly discovered need. In fact, since the formation of the United States over 200 years ago, various governmental agencies have been in charge of securing the borders against smugglers, pirates and many other sources of illegal activity or national security threats. In the early stages of the country's development, there was little concern over the risks of trade with other nations, because it was not of any significant size, and the threats to people and property seemed to be controllable.

The expansion of and reliance on international trade during the nineteenth and twentieth centuries has made the United States susceptible to attack because it is virtually impossible to assure that all goods and persons entering the country are free from hazards. Another problem associated with the expansion of world trade is that it requires the input and cooperation of large numbers of people and organizations to reduce interruptions in the trade process and to make the process more efficient. A recent study of 362 transportation carriers indicated that each used an average of 37 service providers, including cargo-handling facilities, terminal operators, vendors, and other contractors.[3] Supply chains involving sometimes hundreds of organizations, both domestic and foreign, developed as trade increased. After 9/11 it became apparent that the only realistic approach to securing national borders was to enlist not only organizations involved in trade within the United States but their partners in the trading process as well as governments worldwide.

The U.S. government sought to develop a program that would be implemented by the various supply chains servicing American industry and consumers. The program also had to have the cooperation and input of governments throughout the world in order to be successful. This nearly impossible task was able to be accomplished due to the importance of the United States in world trade and because the threat of terrorism knows no national boundaries.

The C-TPAT program was developed with the above obstacles in mind. In 2005, CBP Commissioner Robert C. Bonner characterized the program as follows:

The Customs-Trade Partnership Against Terrorism (C-TPAT) is, beyond question, the largest and most successful government-private sector partnership to emerge from the ashes of 9/11. T-CPAT was launched in November 2001, with just seven companies—seven major importers. Today, over 7,400 companies are enrolled, and these companies—critical players in the global supply chain—include United States importers, customs brokers, terminal operators, carriers and foreign manufacturers.[4]

PRIOR TO SEPTEMBER 11, 2001

The general feeling of citizens of the United States prior to 9/11 was that if they just stayed home, they would not be subjected to terrorism's many horrors. This same feeling was held by most businesspeople and even governmental units whose job it was to deal with risks faced by the United States and its citizens. Prior to 9/11, the United States was in what could be called an "ignorance-is-bliss" mindset regarding terrorism and its impact on the country. Even major governmental police and security agencies did not classify (at least for public distribution) situations such as bombings of abortion clinics or environmentalist attacks on building developments encroaching on undeveloped land as terrorist activities, when in fact these actions were.

Most agree that the major reason for the above feelings was that the United States had never been the site of a major foreign-based terrorist attack, with the exception of the 1993 bombing of the World Trade Center. A feeling of safety and, eventually, complacency descended upon the country. There was talk about being concerned with terrorism and how it might impact U.S. citizens traveling abroad or international organizations with employees in some countries or those dependent upon raw materials or supplies from outside the United States. Except for a few regulations related to certain technologies, war materials, and other items identified by the U.S. government, goods, services, people, and ideas flowed with relative ease across the borders of the United States.

From a business management point of view, in all but a few industries there was no pressing need for a board of directors to ensure that the organization had a contingency plan to address terrorist acts either within or outside U.S. borders. There were few attempts to monitor information flowing in or out of the organization and the foreign port through which imports flowed (although a few countries were looked upon as somewhat more dangerous than others); even employee and service provider background checks usually only existed to verify information on an employment application or service contract rather than acting as security measures. Things have changed a great deal since the attack on the World Trade Center in 2001.

FORESEEABLE HARM AND THE DUTY OF REASONABLE CARE

Today's business owners and managers must realize that since 9/11 their responsibility to protect the public and their various constituencies against injury or damage wrought by terrorists has expanded. Because of 9/11 two important legal concepts took on new meaning with respect to business action related to terrorism: "foreseeable harm" and "the duty of reasonable care." With respect to terrorism,

> What September 11 did do . . . was to make everyone pay greater attention to all types of risks. In this way, even non-terrorist attacks may be considered more foreseeable than they were before September 11. With more and more property owners and possessors performing risk assessments of their properties, it is increasingly difficult for them to hide behind a lack-of-forseeability defense.[5]

One of the important impacts of 9/11 was that it placed everyone on notice that terrorism was a real and continuing threat to the United States and its citizens. Statements made by terrorist groups targeting U.S. interests regardless of where located in the world continue to this day to reinforce the foreseeability of actions to cause injury, death, or damage. The U.S. legal climate is such that "[t]oday, corporations are on notice that they can be liable for not exercising due care by having adequate safeguards in place to mitigate direct damage suffered by potential plaintiffs due to another terrorist attack."[6]

In short, there is no longer any excuse for a business not being prepared for a terrorist attack or not taking reasonable care to assure that its supply chain (sources of information, raw materials, port security, etc.) is as secure as possible. There has been ample warning of foreseeable harm, as well as a continuous stream of regulations and suggestions from government and industry itself concerning the types of damages to expect and possible risk assessment and management steps to take.[7]

THE CUSTOMS-TRADE PARTNERSHIP AGAINST TERRORISM (C-TPAT)[8]

Since 9/11, the government of the United States of America has approved laws and regulations to allow the Department of Homeland Security to either (1) require international businesses to comply with rules defined by those regulations or (2) allow international businesses to voluntarily comply in return for benefits as provided in the regulations. Every business involved in or contributing to U.S. trade is affected in some way by Homeland Security regulations.

At first glance, there appear to be three inevitable and negative outcomes of Homeland Security legislation: (1) it will be more expensive to conduct international business; (2) it will take longer for trade transactions to take place, thereby indirectly increasing the cost of transactions; (3) international business firms will have greater liability for action/inaction related to compliance with Homeland Security legislation. However, upon further review, there are also a number of positive effects, including potentially quicker movement of goods for those meeting security requirements, a new source of competition between organizations based upon levels of security being provided, and a general sense of contributing to the common good by decreasing the chance of terrorist attacks.

In order to function appropriately, many Homeland Security provisions require cooperation and compliance of governments of other countries and organizations throughout the world. Former Secretary of Homeland Security Tom Ridge stated that "[h]omeland [s]ecurity can't stop at a nation's border. The same threats are present for all of us and we must work together to meet them."[9] Homeland security requires the sharing of information between countries on such diverse topics as trade and the movement of people across the many borders of the world. Thus, businesses and others from throughout the world are being called upon to contribute their efforts to joining with the United States in its fight against terrorism. One of the major problems with this approach is that if foreign governments and business organizations do not contribute security efforts, this can impact the delivery of goods and services to U.S. firms. On the other hand, foreign governments and organizations that do support security efforts may be rewarded with preferential treatment in the transportation and clearing of goods at the U.S. border. Fortunately, the actual experience for most governments and members of C-TPAT has been positive, as is indicated by the increasing numbers of participating supply chain partners.

WHY JOIN C-TPAT?

When C-TPAT was introduced, it promised several potential benefits to those who were accepted to the program and who maintained compliance with its requirements. The CBP offers the following description of C-TPAT benefits:

C-TPAT offers trade-related businesses an opportunity to play an active role in the war against terrorism. By participating in this first worldwide supply chain security initiative, companies will ensure a more secure and expeditious supply chain for their employees, suppliers and customers. Beyond these essential security benefits, CBP will offer benefits to certain certified C-TPAT member categories, including:

- A reduced number of CBP inspections (reduced border delay times).
- Priority processing for CBP inspections. (Front of the Line processing for inspections when possible.)
- Assignment of a C-TPAT Supply Chain Security Specialist (SCSS) who will work with the company to validate and enhance security throughout the company's international supply chain.
- Potential eligibility for CBP Importer Self-Assessment program (ISA) with an emphasis on self-policing, not CBP audits.
- Eligibility to attend C-TPAT supply chain security training seminars.[10]

Note that the benefits are indicated as being "potential" or being offered to "certain certified C-TPAT member categories." The CBP may grant some or all of the benefits, depending upon the degree of compliance of the importer member and the firm's supply chain partners. There is also the possibility that the import firm will be audited at a later date to test for compliance under the C-TPAT agreement. Member benefits may be reduced or expanded, depending upon the outcome of the CBP "validation" (the CBP term for the audit).

A recent cost–benefit survey by the University of Virginia provides insight into the reasons organizations join the C-TPAT. The list of importer for joining C-TPAT is provided below.[11, 12] Note that the items in the survey were supplied by the researchers, which is one of the reasons for their high ratings (on a 4-point scale).

- Maintain CPB inspection rate
- Maintain lead time
- Increase supply chain

- Visibility
- Improve ability to monitor and track orders
- Improve predictability of lead time
- Reduce lead time
- Reduce CPB inspection rate

Although the actual University of Virginia survey contains more detailed information for a variety of industry types (importers, carriers, service providers, and manufacturers) the importer category was selected for review as an example of the types of businesses who may be members of C-TPAT.

It is not surprising that the highest-rated reason for importers is to "reduce disruptions to the supply chain." The ability to adequately estimate the timing of deliveries from overseas decreases the lead time for orders as well as the amount of capital and facilities devoted to setting aside inventory for unexpected disruptions and other unforeseen events. It should also be noted that another major reason for eventually "voluntarily" joining the program is to mimic what competitors have done, as well as respond to other supply chain partners who require that all other partners join the program. Thus, the C-TPAT program may be voluntary from the standpoint of the United States government, but practical considerations of supply chain partners are placing additional pressure to join.

THE REQUIREMENTS OF THE IMPORTER PROGRAM

The C-TPAT program is meant to provide added security to a firm's entire supply chain, so an importer must not only inform its partners of the program requirements but also establish a means for auditing partner compliance. The entire supply chain must be willing and able to comply with the program requirements, or the CBP authorities will not allow all of the potential benefits to accrue to the member organization. The old analogy of a chain being as strong as its weakest link is appropriate to the theory behind C-TPAT. In fact, once implemented, CBP felt that as large numbers of importers increased their own security measures, also dealing only with supply chain partners who also subscribe to increased security, the ultimate goal of C-TPAT would be achieved.

Of course the real problem from the outset was that few importers actually have such control over their entire supply chain that they can dictate security measures to their partners. It is also true that many large importers can and do exert such control over their partners and have been very successful in spreading the word about complying with C-TPAT requirements. Major business organizations and associations have also made it a part of their role on behalf of their membership to explain, recommend, or require C-TPAT compliance.[13]

There are eight categories of security criteria that apply to an importer who voluntarily seeks membership in the C-TPAT for importers. Each of the categories includes a set of security requirements or suggestions which must be met by the importer in order to maintain continued membership in C-TPAT. Each criterion will be discussed in turn to better determine its potential impact.

The criteria take on even greater importance when taken in the context of the legal environment of the United States, as discussed earlier. The importer security criteria explicitly provide for certain activities to be carried out and certain requirements to be imposed upon supply chain partners. Thus, the foreseeability of terrorist actions arising from a deficiency in one or more of the criteria is clear, thereby imposing upon the importer a duty of reasonable care. However, the reasonable care must now be taken not only by meeting the importer's own requirements but also by ensuring that trade partners also meet theirs on a continuing basis. C-TPAT's validation system (to periodically audit supply chains) to ensure continued compliance of supply chain partners can have a disastrous impact on members' operations if it finds even a single partner who fails to carry out its part of the program.

C-TPAT IMPORTER SECURITY CRITERIA[14]

1. Business partner requirement
2. Container security
3. Container inspection
4. Physical access controls
5. Personnel security
6. Procedural security
7. Security training and threat awareness
8. Information technology security

Business Partner Requirement

Importers must have written and verifiable processes for the selection of business partners including manufacturers, product suppliers and vendors.[15]

Within this criteria are three major subsections: First, the importer must have documentation that its trade or supply chain partners are providing the security that is required under C-TPAT. Partners can certify their compliance with C-TPAT by actually becoming a member, if eligible, or by supplying the importer with written proof of compliance. Compliance by the partner is required for the member to maintain full compliance itself. The partner must also allow the importer to independently verify the extent of security of the partner's operations, and that it meets all C-TPAT requirements.

One of the major problems with the first criteria is that the ability of the importer to convince their supply chain partners that compliance with U.S. Homeland Security regulations is a requirement to continue the supply chain relationship. Although as more importers subscribe to C-TPAT, the simpler this problem will become, it will be a great challenge during the formative years of this program.

The greater the intricacy of the supply chain, the more daunting the task of ensuring partner compliance. A large importing business could afford to establish a department to deal with compliance concerns, but most businesses cannot afford this luxury.

Many of the C-TPAT security activities (e.g., employee background checks, information technology security) are part of sound management principles and are probably practiced, to one extent or another, by most managers. But when the criteria are used to determine reasonable care on the part of an importer, as reviewed "after a terrorist attack," the security measures take on entirely new meaning. An importer as a member of C-TPAT could no longer shift the blame of ineffective security to its foreign trade partners, but instead signs an agreement with C-TPAT that it will verify and then monitor its partner's security efforts.

The second subsection of the business partner requirement requires that importers see their partners meet C-TPAT at the point of origin of the shipments made to the importer. Thus, the importer must verify the security of the manufacturer, the processor, the shipping company, and others at their home locations. Normally this is accomplished by securing written certifications from the partner's governments, independent security consultants, or business associations who may provide certification for member firms. Depending upon the country of origin, verification and or certification may be difficult because of the lack of certification bureaus and so forth (in developing countries, for example).[16] The importer and the partner must either be able to meet C-TPAT criteria, drop out of the C-TPAT program, or sever their relationship. Failure to do so places the importer at the mercy (and little would probably be forthcoming) of the U.S. legal system should a terrorist event occur.

Another subsection of the Business Partner Requirement deals with the actual selection of business partners. Importers must have a written and verifiable process that describes the procedures used to select partners. Partners must provide to the importer a statement of the partner as to its willingness and ability to meet security requirements, as well as to self-monitor and correct any security deficiencies. The fact that selection criteria must be subject to verification means that importers can be assured that if a terrorist event occurs and involves the importer or its partners, the criteria "will" be verified—again, probably through the U.S. legal system, not just by the CBP.

Container Security

Container integrity must be maintained to protect against the introduction of unauthorized material and/or persons. At point of stuffing, procedures must be in place to properly seal and maintain the integrity of the shipping containers. A high security seal must be affixed to all loaded containers bound for the U.S.[17]

Although not normally a part of an importer's job, container security is a very important part of Homeland Security regulations.[18] It is through the introduction of contamination, explosives, and other foreign objects into means of shipment of goods that terrorists seek to inflict injury or damage at later dates. It now becomes the responsibility of the importer to determine the security procedures in place when its imports are transported, stuffed into containers, and eventually shipped and unloaded for the importer.

Container Inspection

Procedures must be in place to verify the physical integrity of the container structure prior to stuffing, including the reliability of the locking mechanism of the door. A seven point inspection process is recommended for all containers.[19]

Although a separate security criteria, container inspection is but another step in the chain of security measures necessary to assure the safety of the goods being shipped. Prior to 9/11, most shippers made a rather cursory inspection of a container, mainly to see if the doors closed correctly and to look for any obvious damage. Today, a complete inspection of the container must be performed. CBP suggests that the container be inspected on all outside surfaces (including underneath) and the door-locking mechanism be certified as being reliable. It is the responsibility of the importer to develop procedures that will allow verification of such an inspection by the importer or others. It seems today that a written inspection program would comply with this criterion if attested to by partners who would stuff and haul containers as long as the system was capable of verification and monitoring over time.

Written procedures must also be developed to deal with the storage of containers in secure areas and "for reporting and neutralizing unauthorized entry into containers or container storage areas."[20] This criterion is reference to on-the-ground physical security capable of counteracting trespassers or other unauthorized visitors to any area holding or storing containers at any point in the supply chain. For the importer, this is a particularly dangerous criterion. The methods by which trespassers or other unauthorized visitors are dealt with in various countries varies greatly as do the types of security officers, their training, and the way uninvited visitors are treated. Lawsuits in foreign countries because of overzealous security guards, or attempts to bring such lawsuits in the United States, may well be a possibility.

A failure of any partner to follow inspection procedures or complete the inspection forms (if used) will place the importer at risk of personal public liability and penalties imposed by the CBP for noncompliance. It is important that importers make certain that as their business activity increases over time, supply chain partners (existing and new) are continually reminded of their roles in the Homeland Security process.

Physical Access Controls

Access controls prevent unauthorized entry to facilities, maintain control of employees and visitors and protect company assets. Access controls must include the positive identification of all employees, visitors, and vendors at all points of entry.[21]

Whereas the criteria above was general in nature and applied only to container security, this criterion is more specific and applies to any unauthorized entry to the premises for any purpose. There are four categories of persons in need of control:

1. Employees
2. Visitors
3. Deliveries (including mail)
4. Unauthorized persons

As with other security measures, access control procedures should be in written form, subject to inspection and verification. Such measures also have to be adopted by the importer's supply chain partners.

Security in this area revolves around identification systems for employees, visitors, and vendors, as well as appropriate protection against entry at all plant perimeters and access points (doors, windows, air shafts, etc.). Access to the importer's or supply chain partner's premises is granted only to those having acceptable identification—and care must be taken to protect the plant from trespassers or any other unauthorized visitor.

Normally, employee identification will easily identify the person (e.g., photo, name, employee ID number), allow entrance only to areas authorized for the employee's job with the importer (restricted access via keys, cards, etc.), and be able to be carefully controlled (canceled upon leaving the firm, changeable in case of promoted or demotion, etc.). Explicit measures must be in place to control the issuance of identification cards/tags and the retrieval of these items when they are no longer needed. Visitors and deliverypersons will be screened by requiring that they carry positive identification of their own and receive temporary ID badges when entering the premises. Temporary badges will restrict areas of access and be collected upon leaving the premises. It is possible to issue more permanent ID to vendors who frequent the premises, but restriction of movement is important in these cases to limit access to portions of the premises. Temporary badges must also be carefully issued and redeemed to afford proper control of visitors.

This criterion is one that has additional payoffs to the importer, because it also lowers the threat of theft, vandalism, slipping and falling, and other similar problems facing a business in the everyday operation of plant sites, storage areas, and other premises. Allowing only authorized personnel on premises is not only good terrorism risk management, it is also good business practice. However, when the importer's responsibility for verification and monitoring of security is extended to supply chain partners, the same problems with public liability and penalties from the CBP arise as with the other criteria.

The importer must also have procedures for challenging and denying access to unauthorized persons. The greatest difficulty in this area is treating everyone the same. Everyone is required to have appropriate identification. Everyone is subject to challenge by security guards or other means, and no one gains access or remains on site until identification procedures are met. This applies to *all* employees, whether visitors, owners, or other persons with need to be on the premises. Failure to implement such a broad-based identification system throughout the supply chain exposes the importer to penalties under C-TPAT.

Personnel Security

Processes must be in place to screen prospective employees and to periodically check current employees.[22]

This is one of the most important of all security criteria for any international business organization. It is people who carry out terrorist activities. People can participate in carrying out terrorist activities in one of two ways: (1) as a terrorist or coconspirator with the intention to cause injury or damage, or (2) as an employee of a trade partner who acts unintentionally because of lack of problem awareness or training in important aspects of the security field.

Personnel security is probably one of the most accepted and applied security measures in business firms. This is because international businesses have long attempted to avoid employee theft, industrial espionage, employees with backgrounds different than that given on their applications, and numerous other problems associated with employee dishonesty during or after employment. To meet this criteria, the importer (and supply chain partners) must institute procedures for conducting background checks and verifications before employment and continued monitoring during employment for those employees who may be privy to sensitive information. Procedures must also address terminated employees and the need to remove identification allowing access to the premises or information systems used during the employment period. Timely coordination of activities between the importer and supply chain partners is important because of the interaction between employees at different stages of the trade process. Notification of new or replacement employees must be immediate and certain in order to reduce problems with unauthorized access by employees terminated for any reason.

If an employee is terminated for cause, he or she should be immediately denied access to information in any form, required to turn in all identification, and escorted from the premises, and appropriate trade partners must be informed that the employee is no longer a part of the organization. Disgruntled employees may be targets for terrorist contact as an opportunity for gaining access to the importer or its supply chain. Action must be quick and decisive, all the time remembering that mistakes are likely sources of liability.

Procedural Security

Security measures must be in place to ensure the integrity and security of processes relevant to the transportation, handling, and storage of cargo in the supply chain.[23]

This criterion addresses the movement of cargo along the supply chain and the information necessary to permit that movement. The information includes all documentation for import or export, including manifests, purchase and delivery orders, transshipment agreements, and other forms of documentation. It is important to carefully check actual count, weight, and other measures against purchase or delivery orders and manifests. With additional Homeland Security requirements going into effect regarding submission of manifests and the like prior to entering the United States, the confidentiality and credibility of documentation takes on increased importance.

Access procedures and restrictions upon accessing information or documentation are extremely important. Only authorized persons should be able to have access to transportation documents "at any stage in the transportation process."[24] To allow otherwise would invite tampering, wrongful delivery, theft, and other problems to occur. It is the importer's responsibility to make certain that information and documentation along the entire supply chain is secure, confidential, free of tampering, accurate, and timely. This is a big order, even for one's own operation—let alone an intricate supply chain. Remember that in the University of Virginia survey cited earlier, the average respondent had thirty-seven supply chain partners.

Information/documentation includes items that are stored or transferred electronically (the topic of the last criterion). Thus systems and procedures must be in effect to monitor and, if necessary, investigate any discrepancies found as the transportation process proceeds. In order for this to work, the importer must have great confidence in the security procedures established, and in the supply chain partner, to comply with security criteria. Mistakes along the supply chain are certainly foreseeable and are thus subject to the duty of reasonable care on the part of the importer.

Security Training and Threat Awareness

A threat awareness program should be established and maintained by security personnel to recognize and foster awareness of the threat posed by terrorists at each point in the supply chain. Employees must be made aware of the procedures the company has in place to address a situation and how to report it. Additionally, specific training should be offered to assist employees in maintaining cargo integrity, recognizing internal conspiracies, and protecting access programs. These programs should offer incentives for active employee participation.[25]

This criterion is associated with training security personnel employed by the importer to perform assigned duties with C-TPAT in mind. The appropriate employees must also be aware of new developments in areas that threaten the business and must meet new and changing requirements of Homeland Security and the importer program. Efforts must also be made to instruct all employees (not just those devoted to security efforts) in the importance of controlling cargo and information related to cargo, protecting identification systems and access controls, and a very interesting area referred to as "recognizing internal conspiracies."

With respect to security personnel, the importer may run into difficulties if an overseas supplier hires local security because no other option is available and cannot (or will not) supply verification of the training, credentials, or other certification of the security personnel. This would not normally meet the criterion and could jeopardize the importer's membership in C-TPAT. Security personnel and efforts must address perimeter security of all facilities (plants, warehouses, offices, etc.), separating domestic and international shipments (this is to limit those who deal with domestic shipments from entering international shipment areas), establishing monitored entrances and exits for all facilities, and carefully installing lighting, alarm systems, locks, and other devices related to monitoring and controlling entrance and exit.

As with many of the other criteria, what is standard in the United States with respect to security training and facility security will not be the standard in all other countries. Training may not be readily available for some supply chain partners or may be of a different nature than acceptable by the CBP. This is also true of types of alarm systems, monitoring devices at entrances/exits, and so forth. If there are concerns or problems, the importer must check with the CBP to determine the correct path to meeting the C-TPAT requirements. The importer should under no circumstances substitute its own methods of security for those recommended by the CBP unless approval is given by the CBP. All approvals should be in writing and must be kept indefinitely for the importer's protection if a terrorist event occurs at a later date.

Information Technology Security

Automated systems must use individually assigned accounts that require a periodic change of password. IT security policies, procedures and standards must be in place and provided to employees in the form of training. A system must be in place to identify the abuse of IT including improper access, tampering or the altering of business data. All system violators must be subject to appropriate disciplinary actions for abuse.[26]

The final criterion is one of the most difficult to meet. Protection of records, documentation, manifests, and shipment and delivery records is very important to homeland security, for if a terrorist has access to shipment records, it makes planning for an event using cargo and the like as part of the attack much simpler. There is no way security can stop all terrorist activity, but it can slow it down, reduce the number of attacks, and make it less likely that the importer's supply chain will be used as a part of the attack. It is also a fact that many trade intermediaries in other countries do not use electronic systems. In these circumstances, it is best to check with the CBP for suggestions regarding how to meet this particular criterion.

One of the real problems with information security is that electronic data control and storage is not used throughout the world, and even in places where it is common, not everyone uses it effectively. Of course, passwords and standard password-protection methods (changing periodically, proper construction of passwords, security of the system, etc.) are essential—and required. Systems must also be in place to detect and thwart tampering with information systems, to allow selective access to different types of information, and to audit access to determine proper use and potential problems.

Information technology security is one of the most important areas of growth in international business today. It seems that as soon as methods are developed to hamper intrusion, new ways of unauthorized access begin to counteract security efforts. This area of security is especially in need of expert assistance because of the nature and speed of change. C-TPAT requires continuous updating and monitoring of literally all of its criterion, but this one seems to be the most problematic.

SUMMARY

The ability of international business units and their supply chains to respond to terrorist threats is of utmost importance. The C-TPAT program reviewed in this paper is an example of a set of procedures developed proffered by the Customs and Border Protection unit of the Department of Homeland Security to help private business ventures meet this challenge.

It is clear that no single approach to security will do the job. A thorough, broad-based approach such as that for importers is important and addresses most of the areas usually found to be related to crime or terrorist acts. It must be emphasized that all of the criteria must be met for a true "security program" to be effective. The criteria must also be able to be verified in terms of their effectiveness and must be capable of being monitored and provide sufficient information for the importer to call for changes or adjustments as needed.

The real challenge, of course, is applying all of the criteria in a meaningful way to the importer's supply chain partners. This is required by the C-TPAT program and, if not accomplished, places the importer at risk. All actions of international business interests in relation to trade with the United States should be reviewed in light of the legal concepts of "foreseeable harm" and "duty of reasonable care." Without this last step, an importer or any other international cannot judge its exposure to public liability should the question of negligence reach the U.S. legal system.

NOTES

1. See, for example, "C-TPAT 2008—A Year in Review" for a summary of the Customs and Border Protection discussion of program accomplishments. This is one of many articles and summaries of CBP. See http://www.cbp.gov/linkhandler/cgov/trade/cargo_security/ctpat/what_ctpat/2008_year_review.ctt/2008_year_review.pdf.

2. The introduction of WMD into the terrorism equation expands the potential for loss, as well as making it virtually impossible to adequately respond to attacks of this type. Although WMDs (not necessarily by that name) have been a topic of concern since the use of chemical agents during WWI, their use as a terrorist tool has added to the fear associated with this category of weapons. For a very informative review of WMD, see http://en.wikipedia.org/wiki/Weapons_of_mass_destruction.

3. "Customs-Trade Partnership Against Terrorism—Cost/Benefit Survey; Report of Results," Weldon Cooper Center for Public Service, University of Virginia, August 2007, p. 37.

4. Former CBP Commissioner Robert C. Bonner, in the prologue of "Securing the Global Supply Chain; Customs-Trade Partnership Against Terrorism (C-TPAT) Strategic Plan," U.S. Customs and Border Protection, 2005.

5. "Negligent Security Law in the Commonwealth of Massachusetts in the Post-September 11 Era," Daniel P. Dain and Robert L. Brennan Jr., *New England Law Review* 38, no. 1:88.

6. *Homeland Security Handbook*, Chapter 5, page 5-5; James T. O'Reilly, ed.; LexisNexis, August 2004.

7. For example, see National Association of Manufacturers, "Homeland Security Briefs," http://www.nam.org; International Standards Organization, ISO 17799:2000, "Information Technology—Code of Practice for Information Security Management"; American Petroleum Institute, "Security Vulnerability Assessment Methodology for the Petroleum and Petrochemical Industries," 2nd ed., October 2004; "International Port Security Program," U.S. Coast Guard, http://www.uscg.mil/hq/g-m/mp/ipsp.shtml.

8. The C-TPAT importer program was selected as an example of Homeland Security regulations because of the broad nature of the security criteria applying to import firms. The criteria are sufficiently similar to other programs for other types of firms to allow a broad discussion to take place that can then be applied to other types of international business organizations. Note that each business program has its own specific requirements and criteria. This is just one example—albeit very broad in its application—and should not be used to answer questions about other programs.

9. Tom Ridge, former secretary of Homeland Security, as quoted in a statement by Cresencio Arcos, Director of International Affairs, the Department of Homeland Security, in a June 7, 2004, speech at the Heritage Foundation.

10. U.S. Department of Homeland Security, "C-TPAT Overview," December 13, 2007, http://www.cbp.gov/xp/cgov/trade/cargo_security/ctpat/what_ctpat/ctpat_overview.xml.

11. U.S. Department of Homeland Security, "C-TPAT Overview," December 13, 2007, http://www.cbp.gov/xp/cgov/trade/cargo_security/ctpat/what_ctpat/ctpat_overview.xml, Figure V-24, p. 36.

12. "Customs-Trade Partnership Against Terrorism—Cost/Benefit Survey; Report of Results," Weldon Cooper Center for Public Service, University of Virginia, August 2007.

13. See National Coffee Association, http://ctpat.ncausa.org/SELFASSESSMENT/Pages/User/Home.aspx?name=NCA&content=FAQ; "Boeing Guidelines for International Suppliers/Shippers," http://www.boeing.com/news/frontiers/archive/2005/november/i_ssg.html.

14. The following site provides the current CBP requirements for importers at http://www.customs.gov/xp/cgov/trade/cargo_security/ctpat/security_criteria/criteria_importers/ctpat_importer_criteria.xml.

15. U.S. Department of Homeland Security, "Importer Criteria," February 18, 2008, http://www.customs.gov/xp/cgov/trade/cargo_security/ctpat/security_criteria/criteria_importers/ctpat_importer_criteria.xml.

16. The interesting article, "Homeland Security and Emerging Economies," by James Jay Carafano and Ha Nguyen, the Heritage Foundation's Institute for International Studies, September 14, 2004.

17. U.S. Department of Homeland Security, "Importer Criteria," February 18, 2008, http://www.customs.gov/xp/cgov/trade/cargo_security/ctpat/security_criteria/criteria_importers/ctpat_importer_criteria.xml.

18. See Transportation Security Administration Web site for a more detailed review of container security: http://www.TSA.gov for cargo security grants and other information and http://www.DHS.gov for details on the Maritime Transportation Security Act, one of the broadest-based attempts to secure trade traveling through seaports.

19. U.S. Department of Homeland Security, "Importer Criteria," February 18, 2008, http://www.customs.gov/xp/cgov/trade/cargo_security/ctpat/security_criteria/criteria_importers/ctpat_importer_criteria.xml.

20. U.S. Department of Homeland Security, "Importer Criteria," February 18, 2008, http://www.customs.gov/xp/cgov/trade/cargo_security/ctpat/security_criteria/criteria_importers/ctpat_importer_criteria.xml.

21. U.S. Department of Homeland Security, "Importer Criteria," February 18, 2008, http://www.customs.gov/xp/cgov/trade/cargo_security/ctpat/security_criteria/criteria_importers/ctpat_importer_criteria.xml.

22. U.S. Department of Homeland Security, "Importer Criteria," February 18, 2008, http://www.customs.gov/xp/cgov/trade/cargo_security/ctpat/security_criteria/criteria_importers/ctpat_importer_criteria.xml.

23. U.S. Department of Homeland Security, "Importer Criteria," February 18, 2008, http://www.customs.gov/xp/cgov/trade/cargo_security/ctpat/security_criteria/criteria_importers/ctpat_importer_criteria.xml.

24. U.S. Department of Homeland Security, "Importer Criteria," February 18, 2008, http://www.customs.gov/xp/cgov/trade/cargo_security/ctpat/security_criteria/criteria_importers/ctpat_importer_criteria.xml.

25. U.S. Department of Homeland Security, "Importer Criteria," February 18, 2008, http://www.customs.gov/xp/cgov/trade/cargo_security/ctpat/security_criteria/criteria_importers/ctpat_importer_criteria.xml.

26. U.S. Department of Homeland Security, "Importer Criteria," February 18, 2008, http://www.customs.gov/xp/cgov/trade/cargo_security/ctpat/security_criteria/criteria_importers/ctpat_importer_criteria.xml.

Index

Abacus, 2–3
Access control and land transportation targets, 60
Air cargo. *See* Aviation transportation
Air courier businesses, generic boxes and, 34
Air transportation. *See* Aviation transportation
al-Qaeda, Bleed Business strategy, 52
American Trucking Association (ATA), 10
Asian markets, scrap metals and, 35
Aviation security. *See* Aviation transportation
Aviation transportation, 53–54
   accounting for security expenditures and, 65
   air cargo and, 195–197
   attacks isolate sections of populations, 66
   catering operations and, 194–195
   effectiveness of terrorist targeting, 59
   explosives use against, 63–64
   ground facilities and, 65–67
   growing economies and air cargo, 189
   hijacking, 62
   ICAO standards, 190–195
   isolation of section of the population and, 66
   liquid explosives and, 63–64
   Man-Portable Air Defense System (MANPADS) used against, 64–65
   military systems for protection of aircraft, 65
   need for a joint security and intelligence center, 69
   passenger air craft and air cargo, 197
   private acts of terrorism, 125–126
   state responsibility for acts of private individuals, 130–131
   terrorist desire to embarrass opponents and, 57–58
   terrorist tactics against, 62–67
   terrorist targeting of, 56–57
   Transportation Security Administration of the U.S. and air cargo security, 195–197
   See also Piracy
Aviation Transportation Security Act of 2001 (ATSA; U.S.), 86

Bangladesh, piracy and, 150
"Better Security Drives Business Values" (Gallai), 47

Black market
  cross-dock operation, 7–8
  defined, 7
  economics of, 7
  fixed costs in, 40
  and illegal immigrants and gang members, 7
  international, 42–43
  and legitimate businesses, 8
  money laundering and, 40–42
  parallel businesses and, 46–47
  petty thieves and, 6
  sales of, 14
  supply and demand in, 39–40
  temperature-sensitive commodities, 8
  See also Underground economy; Underground supply chain
Blackstone, Sir William, 126
Bonner, Robert C., 199
Boosting (shoplifting). *See* Shoplifting
Brass, Paul, 162
Brazil, piracy and, 149–150

Cargo protection
  lack of, 19–20
  local law enforcement and, 20
Cargo theft and thieves
  cultural change needed, 49
  economic cost of, 46–48
  impact on the economy, 44–48
  insurance companies and, 45
  not a local problem, 43
  security procedures, 44
  sophistication of, 26–27
  targeted cargo, 43
  terrorism and, 48–49
  worldwide problem, 49
Carmack Amendment, 13, 20
Chicago Convention, 129
Commodity theft, 33–34
Comprehensive Environmental Response, Compensation and Liability Act of 1980 (CERC), 80
Computers, theft costs built-in, 46
Conrail Boyz, 20–21
Containerized shipments, 42
Convention of the High Seas (1958, U.N.), 124

Corporate risk awareness, and criminal behavior, 5
Corporations
  need for esprit de corps, 50
  supply chain theft and, 10
Counterfeiting and counterfeits
  blending and, 24
  defined, 2
  distribution networks and, 25–26
  ingestible products, 26
  shipping, 8
  typical products for, 25
  world supply chain and, 24–25
Construction equipment, 22–23, 34
Consumers, unsuspecting, 33
Creative accounting. *See* Money laundering
Criminal motivation
  criminal enterprises and, 5–6
  factors in, 4–5
  focus of, 6
  simple greed and, 5
Criminal organizations, supply chain theft and, 30
Critical Infrastructure Information Act of 2002 (U.S.), 85
Culture of theft and theft-related events, 1
Customs Trade Partnership Against Terrorism (C-TPAT), 44, 48, 198–199
  business partner and, 204–205, 211–212
  container inspection, 206–207
  container security, 206
  cost-benefit survey of, 202–203
  importer program requirements, 203–204
  information security problems, 211
  information technology security, 210–211
  overview, 201–202
  personnel security, 208–209
  physical access controls, 207–208
  potential benefits, 202
  procedural security, 209
  security training, 210
  selection of business partners under, 205
  supply chain partners and, 205
  threat awareness, 210

DelBianco, Steve, on new legislation, 15–16
Department of Defense. *See* United States Department of Defense (DOD)
Department of Homeland Security. *See* United States Department of Homeland Security
Diversion and diverters, 23–24

eBay and stolen goods reports, 9
Embezzlement, 5
Employee infidelity clause in carrier insurance, 13
Environment
　arable land, 140–141
　climate change, 138–140
　extreme weather events, 137–138
　hazmat response, 80–81
　modeling effects of change, 141
　overview, 135
　packing materials and the, 139
　precipitation patterns and groundwater levels, 140
　sea level rise, 136–137
Exercises and drills for emergency response, 179–181

511 systems, 186
Failure Modes and Effects Analysis (FMEA), 116
Federal Bureau of Investigation (FBI), 10
　dissolution of cargo theft task forces, 12
Federal Emergency Management Agency (FEMA), 83
Federal Highway Administration (FHWA), 84
Federal Railroad Administration (FRA), 84
Fences and fencing
　as cognitive and reactive marketers, 28
　connections required for, 26–27
　defined, 13
　gold buyers and, 36
　job of, 31
　and legitimate businesses, 27
　theft-to-order, 29
　thieves and, 28, 30
　time and, 28
　as way of life, 27–28
Fingar, Thomas, 140
Food and alcohol, stolen, 32
Ford, Thomas, 45

Gillai, Dr. Barchi, 47
Global Fraud Report (2007/2008; Kroll Associates), 18–19
Globalization
　climate change and, 138
　and supply chain security, vii–viii
Gold buyers, 36
Gray market, defined, 23
Great Britain, reactions to piracy, 147–148
Gross national product, effect of property crime on, 11–12
Grotius, Hugo, 126

Hazardous materials, stolen, 36
Hijacking, 22. *See also* Piracy
　aviation targets, 62–64
Homeland Security Act of 2002 (U.S.), 85
Huber, Max, 129

Imbedded components, 37
Immediate-use data, 32–33
Immigration and Customs Enforcement (ICE), 83
India
　caste-based agitations, 162–163
　communal riots, 162
　Naxalite movement, 163
　supply chain in, 161–162
　threat of communalism, 162
Industrial espionage, 32
Industrial thefts
　criminal behavior and, 5
　cumulative effect of, 7
　factors in, 4–5
　nontraceable pilferage, 6
Inland Marine Underwriters Association (IMUA), 11
"Innovators in Supply Chair Security" study, 161

Insurance
  cargo theft and, 20
  carrier employee infidelity clauses, 13, 38
  carriers and, 38
  loss prevention and, 45–46
  need for adjustable rates for carriers and airports, 68–69
  piracy and, 149
  theft reporting and, 45
Intellectual property, theft of, 32–33
International Civil Aviation Organization, air transportation standards, 190–195
International Convention for the Suppression of the Financing of Terrorism, 127–128
International Court of Justice (ICJ), *Corfu Channel* case, 129–130
International Criminal Court
  Rome Statute, 128–129
  war crime definition, 129
International delivery of goods, legal complexities in, 81
International Law Association, 124
International Law Commission, 128
International Standards Organization (ISO), ISO 28000:2007, 169–170
Internet, and supply chains, 159
Island of Palmas case, 129
ISO 28000:2007 standards, 169–170

Just-in-time delivery system, 52
  supply chain risks and, 89–90
  vulnerability of, 160
Just-Stolen.net, 17

Keller, Kenneth, 140
Kroll Associates, 18

Law enforcement
  local, and cargo protection, 20
  stolen goods and, 15
Legal systems
  complex network of interlocking agencies and laws, 85
  developing transportation security law (U.S.), 87
  federal preemption (U.S.), 86–87
  liability and, 75
  supply chain ownership and, 75
  variations around the world, 81
Legislation
  e-Fencing Enforcement Act of 2008, 15
  and movement of stolen goods, 15
  Organized Retail Crime Act, 16
Legitimate businesses and money laundering, 40–42
Logistics industry, 54

Malacca Straits, piracy and, 149
Man-Portable Air Defense System (MANPADS) used against airplanes, 64–65
Maritime Administration (MARAD; U.S.), 84
Maritime security policy (U.S.), 79–80
Maritime transportation
  high risk sea areas, 145–146
  security plans, 80
  United Nations Convention on Maritime Law and piracy, 150–151
  See also Piracy
Maritime Transportation Security Act of 2002 (U.S.), 86
Metals, stolen, 34–36
Misuse of equipment, 34
Money laundering, 40–43

National carriers, terrorist targeting of, 56
National economy, property crime and, 18. *See also* World economy
National Intelligence Assessment on the National Security Implications of Global Climate Change to 2030, 140
Nationalism, piracy and, 152
National Retail Federation (NRF), 6, 10, 49
  on Internet sale of stolen goods, 9
National Strategy for Homeland Security (NASHS), 75
Naxalites, 163
Net Choice, 15
New York and New Jersey, Port of, 136

New York City Office of Emergency
    Management (NYC OEM) Corp
    Net program, 186
Nicaragua, piracy and, 150

Office of Pipeline Safety (OPS), 85
Organized crime, cargo theft and, 44.
    See also Criminal organizations
Organized Retail Crime Act, 16
Ownership and empowerment, 50

Partners in Protection (PIP, Canada), 48
Pharmaceuticals, stolen, 31–32
    black markets and, 39–40
    level of, 45
Philippines, piracy and, 149
Piracy
    actions to control, 147
    ancient origins, 144
    antipiracy force requirements,
        156–157
    causes of rise in modern, 145–146
    coalition response to, 155–157
    common areas for, 145–146
    defined, 124–125
    and definition of "pirate ship," 151
    history of, 144–145
    impact of international, 148–150
    international agreements and cooperation essential, 154–156
    international law and, 124
    international nature of, 125
    modern, 144–146
    nationalism and, 152
    need for pursuit and punishment of
        pirate organizations, 147
    options for minimizing the effect of
        blockade of ports that harbor
            pirates, 152
        convoy operations, 153
        execution of pirates "En Scene,"
            154
        pursuit/capture of pirates, 153
        ransom or tribute payments,
            153–154
    "pirate ship," defined, 151
    political will and control of, 157
    protection of vessels and, 146
    ransom payments and, 147

    recent trends in, 62
    rules of engagement (ROE) and, 155
    Somalia and, 145
    state responsibility and, 125–130
    success of modern, 146
    terrorism and, 122, 123
    United Nations actions against, 147
    United Nations Convention on Maritime Law and, 150–151
Pirate ship, defined, 151
Planning and partnerships following
    emergencies, 177–179
Property crime
    growth of, 18
    lax prosecutorial remedies for, in
        U.S., 1
PropertyRoom.com, 17
Purchases, perception of value in, 3–4
Purtell, Dan, 43, 44

Rail transportation
    history of attacks on, 61–62
    threats to, 60–61
Red Sea shipping route, use of, 148
Retail businesses
    data on shoplifting and other retail
        fraud, 10–11
    deterrent technologies, 37
Robert T. Stafford Disaster Relief and
    Emergency Act, 86

Safe and Secure Tradelanes (SST), 167
SAFETY Act (2002, U.S.), 86
St. Lawrence Seaway Development
    Corporation (SLSDC), 84
Sea level, rise in, 136–137
Security education, reactive, 54
Service fraud, 34
Sheffi, Yossi, 90
Shoplifting (boosting), 37
Somalia
    government in, 146
    overview of piracy and, 121 (*see also*
        Piracy)
    pirates operating from, 145
    Transitional Federal Government
        (TFG), 121
    the United Nations and, 146
Somali Republic. *See* Somalia

220 Index

Stafford Act, 86
States (nations)
    complicity in a private act, 126
    condonation theory, 126–129
    international conduct by, 130
    liability for failure to act, 127
    responsibility for private acts of individuals, 130–131
    theory of complicity, 126
Stolen goods
    best left unrecovered, 9
    blending, 24
    collateral losses, 2
    collected data, 11
    commodity theft, 33–34
    containerized shipments and, 42
    counterfeiting and, 24
    demand and, 22
    distribution of, 13–15
    dumpsters, 34
    food and alcohol, 32
    gangs and, 21
    gateway cities and, 21–22
    hard-to-steal, 36
    hazardous materials, 36
    imbedded components, 37
    individual users and, 33
    industrial pilferage, 23
    infrastructure for moving, 15
    intellectual property, 32–33
    international distribution of, 32, 38–39
    the Internet and, 9, 38
    jewelry, 36
    known shippers, 22
    and law enforcement, 9–10
    low prosecution for thieves, 11
    marketing of, 30–31
    metals, 34–36
    motivations and, 4–6 (*see also* Criminal motivation)
    movement of, 2–3, 13–15
    nontraceable pilferage, 6
    and online sales, 17
    purchasing, 1
    range of, 2, 31
    recovery of, 17
    resale of, 31–32 (*see also individual types of goods*)
    risks in property crime theft, 6
    sale prior to theft, 14
    unattended cargo and, 19–20
    unattended theft, 22–23
    unsuspecting consumers and, 33
"Street" vendors, 14
Suez Canal, use of, 148
Supply chain
    all-of-staff approach to protecting, 71
    amount of theft in, 37
    analysis of terrorism operations, 68
    arable land and, 140–141
    aviation transportation, 53–54
    benefits of investments in security initiatives, 161
    best way to protect, 60
    carbon dioxide emissions controls and, 139
    challenges for, 160–161
    counterfeiting and, 24–25
    defined, vii
    elements of, 52–53
    free on board (f.o.b.) destination and theft, 37–38
    gateway cities and theft levels, 21–22
    global environment and, 135 (*see also* Environment)
    high growth in, viii
    ideas and risk control, 67–68
    importance of security in, vii–viii
    in India, 161–162
    international distribution and security, 48
    international system and global security, 140–141
    Internet and, 159
    land transportation, 53
    maritime transportation, 53
    as multinational stage for terrorists, 56
    nontraceable pilferage, 6
    ownership and liability (*see* Supply chain security)
    piracy, impact of, 148–150
    radical changes and the political landscape, 141
    rail transportation and, 60–62 (*see also* Rail transportation)
    resiliency in, 141

Index   221

ripple effects of disruptions to, 160–161
risks (*see* Supply chain risks)
security benefits, 47–48
security costs, 47
staff and training to protect, 69–71
standards and information sharing, risk control and, 68
tactical level analysis need, 69
terrorist targeting of, 55–59
theft and corporate losses and profits, 10, 39
threat versus risk in, 54–55 (*see also* Threat[s])
threats and risks to, 67
total quality management (TQM) and, 161
types of theft in, 20–23
vulnerability during crises or disasters, 161
See also Supply chain risks; Supply chain security
Supply chain risks
acts imputed to a state, 130
analytical modeling approach conclusions, 111
assessing with simulation, 111–112
assessment of, 89–92
carbon dioxide emissions controls and, 139
complexity of modeling
aggregation of events, 100–103
concurrent disruptions, likelihood of, 103–106
number of possible disruptive events, 97–100
current state of the supply chain and, 105–106
data, availability and accuracy of, 108–110
data, historic, 109
disruptive events, dependence of, 106–109
disruptive events, exhaustive specification of, 107–108
duration of disruption, 109
dynamics of disruptions, 91
global versus local, 89–90
GM network analysis, 92–94

knowledge, role of, 129–130
mitigation tactics, 94, 115–116
model of, 92–94
model scope and fidelity, 110–111
modes and effects of disruptions, 116
non-criminal disruptions, 89–90
probabilistic risk analysis and, 93–94
probability distributions for disruptions, 95–97
rare events and, 112–114
sea level rise, 136–137
simplifying assumptions, 114–115
smaller companies and, 105
states (nations) and, 126–129
Supply chain security
aviation security. *See* Aviation transportation
blurring of geographical boundaries and, 159–160
carbon dioxide emissions controls and, 139
climate change and, 138–140
complexity of laws and, 81
developing economies and, 173
enablers
analysis opf interactions among, 171–172
contractual agreements, 168
knowledge and process backup, 168–169
resilience, 166
Safe and Secure Tradelanes (SST), 167
security-dedicated communications and technology, 166–167
security strategy, 165
sharing risks and rewards with partners, 168
supplier relationships, 163–164
third-party logistics (3PLs), 165–166
extreme weather events and, 137–138
global environment and, 135 (*see also* Environment)
Homeland Security Advisory System (U.S.), 79–80
Internet and, 159
investments and cost savings, 171

Supply chain security (*continued*)
  legal environment of, 77t
  legal systems and, 75
  maritime security policy (U.S.), 79–80
  mobilization of workforce after emergencies, 176–177
  national security plan (U.S.), 78t
  planning for business as usual following emergency, 187
  protection of public and, 200–201
  public-private partnerships and, 170–171
  risks and (*see* Supply chain risks)
  security certifications (ISO 28000:2007), 169–170
  and September 11, 2001, 160
  sharing information, 169
  terrorist attacks and, 159–160
  U.S. national strategy for, 80
  varying international regulations and, 81
  vulnerabilities during crises or disasters, 161
  See also Workforce mobilization

Technology Asset Protection Association (TAPA), 44
Terrorism
  defined, 122–123
  earliest form of, 123
  International Convention for the Suppression of the Financing of Terrorism, 127–128
  origin of term, 122
  private acts of, 125–126
  as a *sui generis* offense, 123–124
Terrorists
  attacks as retaliatory measures, 58
  and cargo thieves, 12, 48–49
  desire for economic impact on the target, 57
  economic, 12
  land transportation targets, 60
  missile threats, 65
  passengers as targets, 62
  political protests and retaliation as attack motives, 63
  target selection, 55–59
  and thieves, 24

Theft
  cost to retailers, 16
  document manipulation, 19
  employee, 16–17
  impact beyond tangible monetary losses, 10
  to order, 29
  unreported, 10
Theory of complicity, 126
Theory of condonation, 126–129
Thieves
  and terrorists, 24
  typical, 30
Threat(s)
  defined, 54
  versus risk, 54–55
Training industry, need to move beyond government reliance, 70
Transportation industry
  air transportation. *See* Aviation transportation
  aviation security. *See* Aviation transportation
  cargo theft growth, 22
  cargo theft losses, 11
  Carmack Amendment and, 13
  covert security devices and, 29
  cross-dock operations, 7–8
  distribution of stolen goods, 13–15
  effectiveness of terrorist targeting, 59
  land transportation, 53
  maritime transportation, 53
  and movement of stolen goods, 2–3
  need for speed in illicit logistics, 3
  piracy and (*see* Piracy)
  and theft-based transportation, 7–8
  theft procedures, 12–13
  Transportation Security Administration of the U.S. and air cargo security, 195–197
  types of theft, 20–23
  See also Air courier businesses; Supply Chain
Transportation Security Administration (TSA), 83

Underground economy. *See also* Black market; Underground supply chain

defined, 4
participants in, 30
United Kingdom, reactions to piracy, 147–148
United Nations
  actions against piracy, 147
  Charter, Article 51, 128
  Convention of the High Seas (1958), 124
  General Assembly Resolution No. 1105 (XI) of 1957, 124
  International Convention for the Suppression of the Financing of Terrorism, 127–128
  Somalia and, 146
United States
  history of border protection, 198–200
  view of terrorism after 9/11, 200–201
  view of terrorism before 9/11, 199–200
United States Coast Guard, 83
United States Customs Service, 10
  and Border Protection, 83
United States Department of Defense (DOD), 83–84
United States Department of Energy (DOE), 85
United States Department of Homeland Security
  complexity of organization of, 81, 82t
  Homeland Security Advisory System, 79
  Homeland Security Presidential Directive 3, 79
  Homeland Security Presidential Directive 5, 79
  Homeland Security Presidential Directive 7, 79
  Homeland Security Presidential Directive 41/Homeland Security Presidential Directive 13 (NSPD-41/HSPD-13), 79
  maritime security policy, 79–80
  National Incident Management System (NIMS), 79
  National Strategy for Homeland Security (NASHS), 75
  and non-U.S. businesses, 201–202
  strategic objectives, 76t
  supply chain issues and, 75
United States Department of Justice (DOJ), 85
United States Department of Transportation, 84
  Highway Watch program, 3
United States Drug Enforcement Agency (DEA), 10
United States Government Accounting Office (GAO), 11
United States Transportation Security Administration and air cargo security, 195–197
United States v. Locke, 529 U.S. 89 (2002), 86–87
USA PATRIOT Act of 2001, 86

Vattel, Emerich de, 126
Votes and Violence (Wikinson), 162

Wikinson, Steve I., 162
Workforce mobilization following emergency
  best practices for, 176–177
  corporate emergency access, 186
  emergency notification systems, 185–186
  exercises and drills, 179–181
  geographic information systems and, 186–187
  institutional communications, 181
  internal communications, 181–182
  memorandums of understanding and, 178–179
  planning and partnerships, 177
  planning for business as usual, 187
  regional communications, 183
  resource sharing, 177–179
  telecommuting systems and, 183–185
World economy, cargo and supply chain theft and, 19

Zebra mussels, 138

About the Editor and Contributors

ANDREW R. THOMAS is Assistant Professor of International Business at the University of Akron. A bestselling business writer, he is author, coauthor, or editor of more than a dozen books, including *Direct Marketing in Action*, which was a finalist for the American Marketing Association's Berry Award for the Best Marketing Book of 2008.

Professor Thomas writes, consults, and speaks extensively on building the sustainable global enterprise, from supply chain security, production, and operations to marketing, sales, and distribution. His research has appeared in *The Wall Street Journal*, the *MIT Sloan Management Review*, and *Business Horizons*.

A successful entrepreneur, Dr. Thomas has traveled to and conducted business in more than 120 countries on every continent. He also serves on the visiting faculties of the International School of Management and Emmanuel University in Oradea, Romania. Andrew is founding editor-in-chief of the *Journal of Transportation Security* and a regularly featured media analyst for MSNBC, CNN, BBC, and FOX NEWS.

RUWANTISSA ABEYRATNE has worked in the field of aviation law and management for over twenty-five years. He is currently acting deputy director of the Air Transport Bureau of the International Civil Aviation Organization. He also teaches aero politics, law, and policy at the John Molson School of Business, Concordia University, Montreal, in the Global Aviation M.B.A. program. Dr. Abeyratne is a fellow of both the Royal Aeronautical Society and the Chartered Institute of Logistics and Transport. He is also a member of the International Law Association, in which he serves as member of both the association's International Trade Law Committee and Space Law Committee. He is a founder member of the Montreal Branch of the Royal Aeronautical Society. Dr. Abeyratne has published numerous books and over 300 leading journal articles on international law and air law, in addition to many papers presented to conferences.

MOSES A. "MOE" ALEMÁN has over fifty-six years of professional experience in the investigations and security field, with over 36 of those years in civil aviation security. His professional experience consists of eight years as a special agent, OSI (IG) USAF (1952–1960); four years, three months as a special agent, FBI, U.S. Dept. of Justice (1960–1964); seven years, six months as chief investigator, General Dynamics Corp. (1965–1972); twenty-two years, three months as aviation security specialist, FAA, U.S. Dept. of Transportation (1972–1995); and fourteen years as owner and president of AVSEC, Inc., an aviation security consulting firm (1995–present). During his FAA career, Alemán was detailed on numerous occasions to the International Civil Aviation Organization (ICAO), during which time he directed or provided aviation security technical assistance expertise to member States of ICAO, serving as an aviation security advisor to the governments of over 50 countries in English or in Spanish. Since his retirement from the U.S. government, Mr. Alemán has served as a consultant or training instructor in 30 countries, most recently for ICAO, IATA, U.S. embassies in Mexico and the Dominican Republic, the Boeing Service Co., and projects funded by the Inter-American Development Bank (IDB) and by the Japan International Cooperation Agency (JICA). He also has provided AVSEC Quality Control Training sponsored by the U.S. TSA and TDA under contract to Aerospace Services International (ASI), and in Colombia under contract to the International Aviation Services Group (IASG). From 2000 to 2007, Mr. Alemán conducted sixty-three aviation security training courses and seminars (thirty-seven in Spanish and twenty-six in English) in nineteen member nations of ICAO.

JAMES R. BRADLEY is an associate professor in the Mason School of Business at the College of William and Mary in Williamsburg, Virginia, where he teaches manufacturing, operations management, supply chain management, and information technology at the graduate and undergraduate levels. He was previously on the faculty at the S. C. Johnson Graduate School of Management at Cornell University. He has published academic research on supply chain management, supply chain risk management, life cycle management, inventory management, lean manufacturing, performance measurement, the management of manufacturing capacity, and the joint optimization of manufacturing capacity, inventory, and subcontracting policies. His research makes extensive use of applied probability, optimization, and computer simulation. Prior to earning his Ph.D., Professor Bradley worked for fifteen years in manufacturing with General Motors. His consulting clients have included 3M, Digital Equipment Corporation, the Virginia Port Authority, and the Commonwealth of Virginia Employment Commission.

CHARLES BUMSTEAD has been involved in aviation affairs for sixty years, having spent a career as a fighter pilot in the U.S. military (USAF), twenty-seven years with the FAA, and seven years with ICAO (Bangkok) and IATA (Bangkok). He has specialized in international relations and international terrorism. Charles has served as a regional air defense liaison officer at Roosevelt Roads, Puerto Rico, military affairs officer in the San Juan ARTCC, and crew chief in the San Juan ARTCC. He served as an assistant to the airports division chief in the Central Region, as deputy branch chief of the Operations Branch, Air Traffic Division, Central Region, and as deputy chief of the Kansas City ARTCC at Olathe, Kansas. He is currently retired and is still deeply involved with international affairs. He is a charter member of the Alpha Phi Chapter of Alpha Sigma Lambda (National Honor Society), a graduate the USAF Air Command and Staff College, Fighter Weapons Commanders Course, and a distinguished graduate of the USAF Air War College. He has served in the Korean Conflict, the Viet Nam Conflict, the Cuban Crisis, and several other military actions. His last military assignment was from 1965 until 1971 with the Puerto Rico Air National Guard as a fighter pilot flying the F-104C Starfighter.

SEAN S. COSTIGAN is director of the Lower Manhattan Project and assistant professor at the Graduate Program in International Affairs. Previously he was Director for Strategic Initiatives, Center for Security Studies, ETH Zurich, and a visiting scholar at the New School. He is cochair of the Economics of Security Study Group and a member of the Council on Foreign Relations Homeland Security Working Group. He is also chair of the editorial board, Partnership for Peace Consortium of Defense Academies and Security Studies Institutes. He previously served as executive editor of *Columbia International Affairs Online*, Research Associate for Science, Technology and Defense Industrial Policy at the Council on Foreign Relations, and as a member of the staff of the Weatherhead Center for International Affairs, Harvard University. His research interests include technology and international security, terrorism and the Internet, environment and energy issues, and the history of science. He is the author or editor of a number of works, including *Arming the Future*, *Terrornomics*, and the forthcoming *Encyclopedia of International Security* (CQ Press, 2010).

MOHD. NISHAT FAISAL (nishat786@yahoo.com) is currently assistant professor at the Institute of Management Technology Dubai, Dubai International Academic City, United Arab Emirates. He is on sabbatical from the Department of Business Administration, Aligarh Muslim University, India, where he is a senior faculty member in the area of decision sciences and operations management. Formerly, he was a national doctoral fellow at the

Department of Management Studies, Indian Institute of Technology Delhi (India). His research interests are in the areas of supply chain management, small business management, decision sciences, operations management, and information technology. He has published articles in journals such as *Industrial Management and Data Systems, International Journal of Services and Operations Management, International Journal of Industrial and Systems Engineering, European Journal of Industrial Engineering, Journal of Enterprise Information Management, International Journal of Management and Enterprise Development, E-Government: An International Journal, Supply Chain Forum: An International Journal,* and *Waste Management.* He is also the recipient of Emerald Highly Commended Award 2008.

JOHN HARRISON is an assistant professor at the S. Rajaratnam School of International Studies and Head of Terrorism Research at the International Center for Political Violence and Terrorism Research. He was also the coordinator for the transportation security program at the Center for Excellence in National Security. He is one of the leading specialists on aviation security and is the associate editor of the *Journal of Transportation Security*. He is the author of *International Aviation and Terrorism*, published in 2009 by Routledge, and his chapter "Aviation Security Practice and Education: 1968 and Onward" appeared in *Aviation Security Management*, published by Praeger Security International. He has briefed a wide range of government and private sector bodies and is technical advisor to Borderpol, the international association for border police. He has also embedded with U.S. forces in Iraq. Dr. Harrison holds a Ph.D. in International Relations from St Andrews University and an M.Litt. in international security studies from St Andrews, as well as an M.A. in political science from the American University in Washington, D.C. and a B.A. in political science from Wheeling Jesuit University. He has also worked for and on various political campaigns in the United States and Scotland.

ERIK HOFFER is an inventor, entrepreneur, recognized expert, and thought leader in the field of transportation and cargo security. He began his career in cargo security while serving in the U.S. military, receiving training and experience while conducting port and logistic operations in Viet Nam. Today, he remains active in the field of military logistics security as a member of the U.S. Navy's Lock and Seal engineering group, developing new approaches and technologies to enhance cargo security devices and handling operations. In this role, he maintains an active security clearance with the U.S. Department of Defense and consults regularly with the Department of Homeland Security's Transportation Security Administration, the U.S. Department of State, and private sector clients on a variety of air, sea, and truck transportation security issues.

As an educator, and while chairman of the International Cargo Security Council's seminar committee, Erik developed the master's program in cargo security for the Merchant Marine Academy's Global Maritime and Transportation School. Hoffer is a frequent presenter on cargo security at seminars, conferences, and other events and is a former chairman of educational events for the International Cargo Security Council. Hoffer has authored many white papers on the topic of cargo security and best logistical practices and is a contributor to industry groups and trade publications including *Air Cargo World*, the American Trucking Association, *Transport Topics*, and *Logistics Management*. Most recently he wrote a chapter on air cargo security for *Aviation Security Management*, a book published in 2008 by Praeger Security International.

Hoffer recently started a new company based in Florida to develop and manufacture newly patented antitheft devices for trucks and trailers, including the category-leading TS4A Air Brake Security Lock.

LISA MORAIYA MCNALLY is a senior associate at ICF International with more than six years' experience in transportation planning and sustainable development. Ms. McNally is skilled in technical analysis, conducting project assessments, and developing guidance documents to support decision making for program funding and policy development. More recently, Ms. McNally has been applying transportation planning concepts to emergency management. In 2008, Ms. McNally assisted the City of Los Angeles in developing transportation management plans for twenty-five points of dispensing facilities throughout the city. She also conducted a best practices study on emergency management, business continuity, and travel options for the Sacramento Area Council of Governments. Prior to joining ICF, Ms. McNally was a research analyst at Chicago's Center for Neighborhood Technology, a think tank promoting urban sustainability through the more effective use of existing resources and community assets. Ms. McNally is a LEED Accredited Professional and holds two undergraduate degrees from the University of California at Berkeley and an M.Sc. in environmental change and management from Oxford University.

FRANK T. MONGIOI JR. is a manager at ICF International and has more than twelve years' experience in transportation demand management (TDM) with expertise in marketing, community, and employer outreach, as well as operations, incentive program development, and ridesharing. He designed and led a best practices study on emergency management, business continuity, and travel options for the Sacramento Area Council of Governments. Prior to working for ICF International, he worked for Meadowlink, one of the largest and most progressive nonprofit transportation management associations (TMA) in the country. He has managed a six-county TDM program for the New Jersey Department of Transportation and NJ Transit utilizing aggressive employer outreach strategies. Mr. Mongioi is currently part of a team working with the New York State Department of Transportation supporting the Clean Air NY program by developing marketing plans, recruiting partners for the program, and facilitating presentations. Mr. Mongioi has recently completed his M.B.A. from Montclair State University in New Jersey.

JOHN O'CONNELL has been a professor of global business and the C.V. Starr Chair of International Risk Management at Thunderbird School of Global Management since 1984. His professional and academic achievements have earned him international recognition as one of the foremost experts in international risk management, emergency planning, and global insurance issues. Dr. O'Connell has devoted a great deal of his time and efforts in the study of local, national, and international security. In 2006, he was selected by the secretary of the Air Force to participate in the National Security Forum, held at the Air Force War College at Maxwell Air Force Base, and in 2008 attended a similar program at Nellis Air Force Base. He also visited Kabul, Afghanistan, in 2009 to offer assistance in developing an Afghanistan Disaster Plan. Dr. O'Connell is a coeditor and a major contributor to *The Blackwell Encyclopedia of Management* and *The Blackwell Encyclopedia Dictionary of International Management*. He has authored nearly forty articles related to risk management and insurance in a variety of academic journals and trade publications. He was appointed to the executive editorial board of the *Journal of Transportation Security* in 2008. He received his Ph.D. in insurance and organizational behavior from Ohio State University in 1975.

MARY F. SCHIAVO. Throughout her distinguished career in law and public service, Mary Schiavo has held corporations, institutions, and the government accountable for their obligation to protect the safety and security of the traveling public. From 1990 to 1996, Schiavo served as the inspector general of the U.S. Department of Transportation. She is the author of the *New York Times* bestseller *Flying Blind, Flying Safe*, which exposed the poor safety and security practices of airlines and the failures of the federal government to properly police aviation. She also served as a professor of aviation and public administration at the Ohio State University, prosecuted federal cases for the U.S. Department of Justice as an assistant U.S. attorney, and served as a prosecutor in the Organized Crime and Racketeering Strike Force. She is a cum laude graduate of Harvard University and earned a master's degree in public administration from Ohio State University, where she was a university fellow. Schiavo earned a juris doctorate from New York University and was a Root–Tilden Public Interest Law Scholar. After leaving the Transportation Department, Schiavo joined the international plaintiffs' law firm, Motley Rice, where she leads the aviation team. She has represented passenger and crew families in nearly every major U.S. air crash and in many foreign crashes. Recognized by television audiences worldwide, Schiavo was a consultant for NBC and ABC News and frequently appears on NBC, ABC, CBS, CNN, Fox News, the History and Discovery Channels, the BBC, and Canadian Broadcasting. Schiavo was also a White House Fellow, assistant secretary of the U.S. Department of Labor, and Special Assistant to the U.S. Attorney General.

RYAN ELIZABETH THOMPSON is an analyst at ICF International with experience in transportation demand management and transportation planning. For the Sacramento Area Council of Governments, she led interviews and developed the report on Emergency Management, Business Continuity, and Travel Options. In addition to providing research support for best practices studies on transportation, she provides technical support for the New York State Department of Transportation's Clean Air NY program. Ms. Thompson has a B.A. in political science from Davidson College.

Also by Andrew R. Thomas

Aviation Security Management: A Three-Volume Set

The Handbook of Supply Chain Security

Aviation Insecurity: The New Challenges of Air Travel

Air Rage: Crisis in the Skies

The Distribution Trap: Keeping Your Innovations from Becoming Commodities (with Timothy Wilkinson)

Direct Marketing in Action: Proven Strategies for Finding and Keeping the Best Customers (with Dale Lewison, William Hauser, and Linda Foley)

Defining the Really Great Boss (with M. David Dealy)

Global Manifest Destiny: Growing Your Business in a Borderless Economy (with John Caslione)

Managing by Accountability: What Every Leader Needs to Know About Responsibility, Integrity . . . and Results (with M. David Dealy)

The Rise of Women Entrepreneurs: People, Processes, and Global Trends (with Jeanne Halladay-Coughlin)

The New World Marketing, Volume 3 of *Marketing in the 21st Century* (with Timothy Wilkinson)

Growing Your Business in Emerging Markets: Promise and Perils (with John Caslione)

Change or Die! How to Transform Your Organization from the Inside Out (with M. David Dealy)

The Greatest Thing Ever Built: The Saturn V Spaceship (with Paul Thomarios)